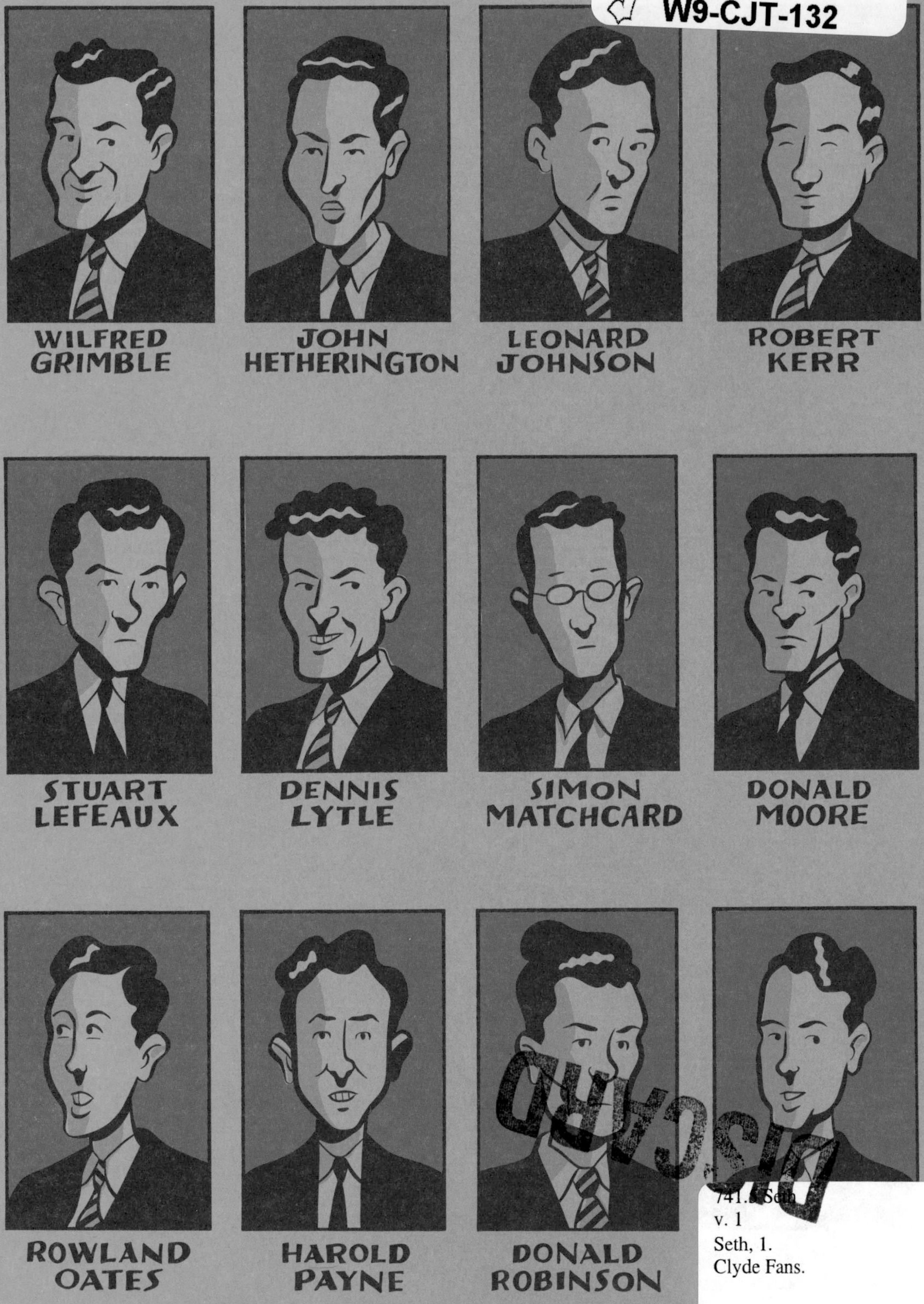
WILFRED GRIMBLE
JOHN HETHERINGTON
LEONARD JOHNSON
ROBERT KERR
STUART LEFEAUX
DENNIS LYTLE
SIMON MATCHCARD
DONALD MOORE
ROWLAND OATES
HAROLD PAYNE
DONALD ROBINSON

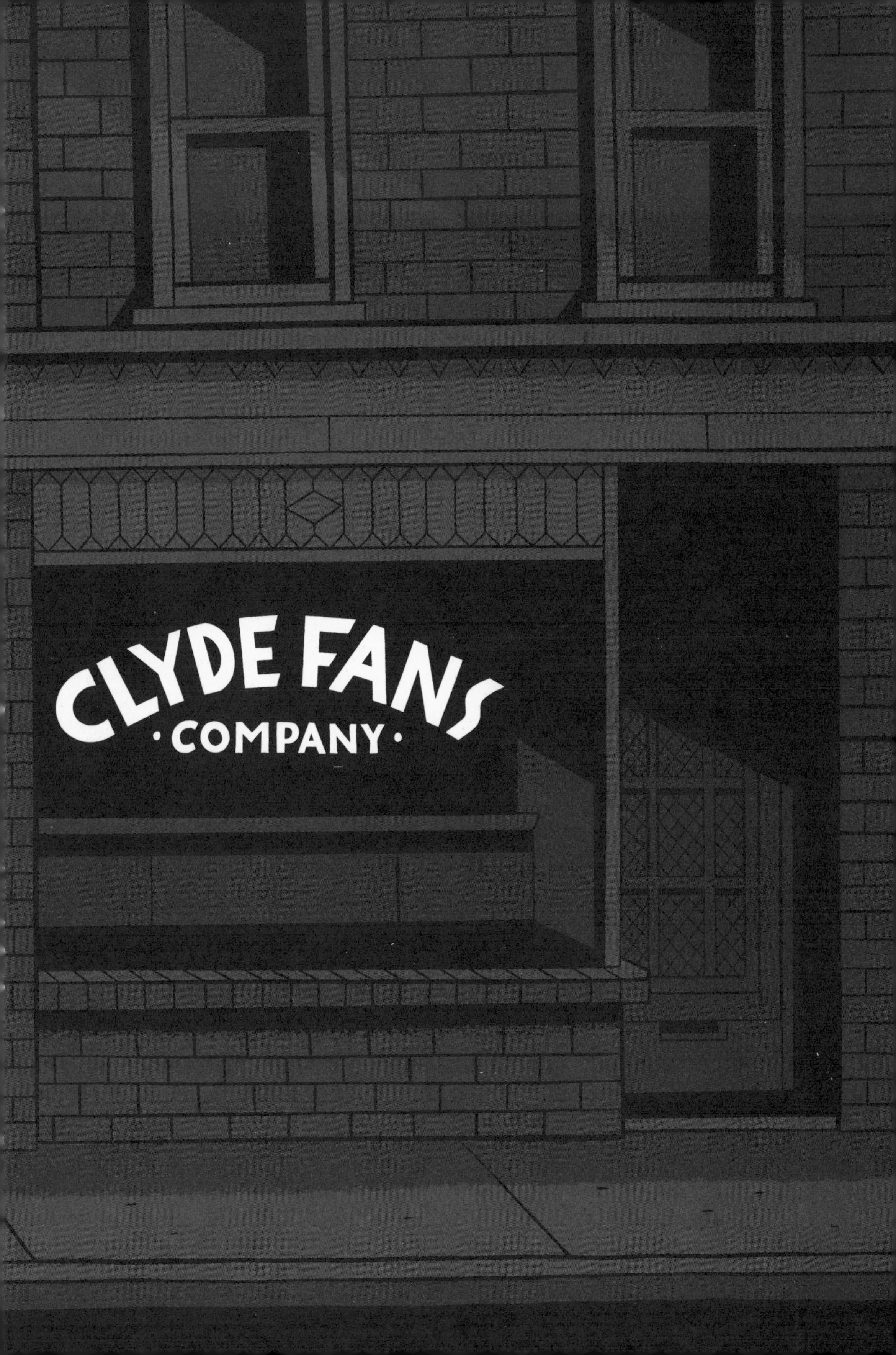
CLYDE FANS
·COMPANY·

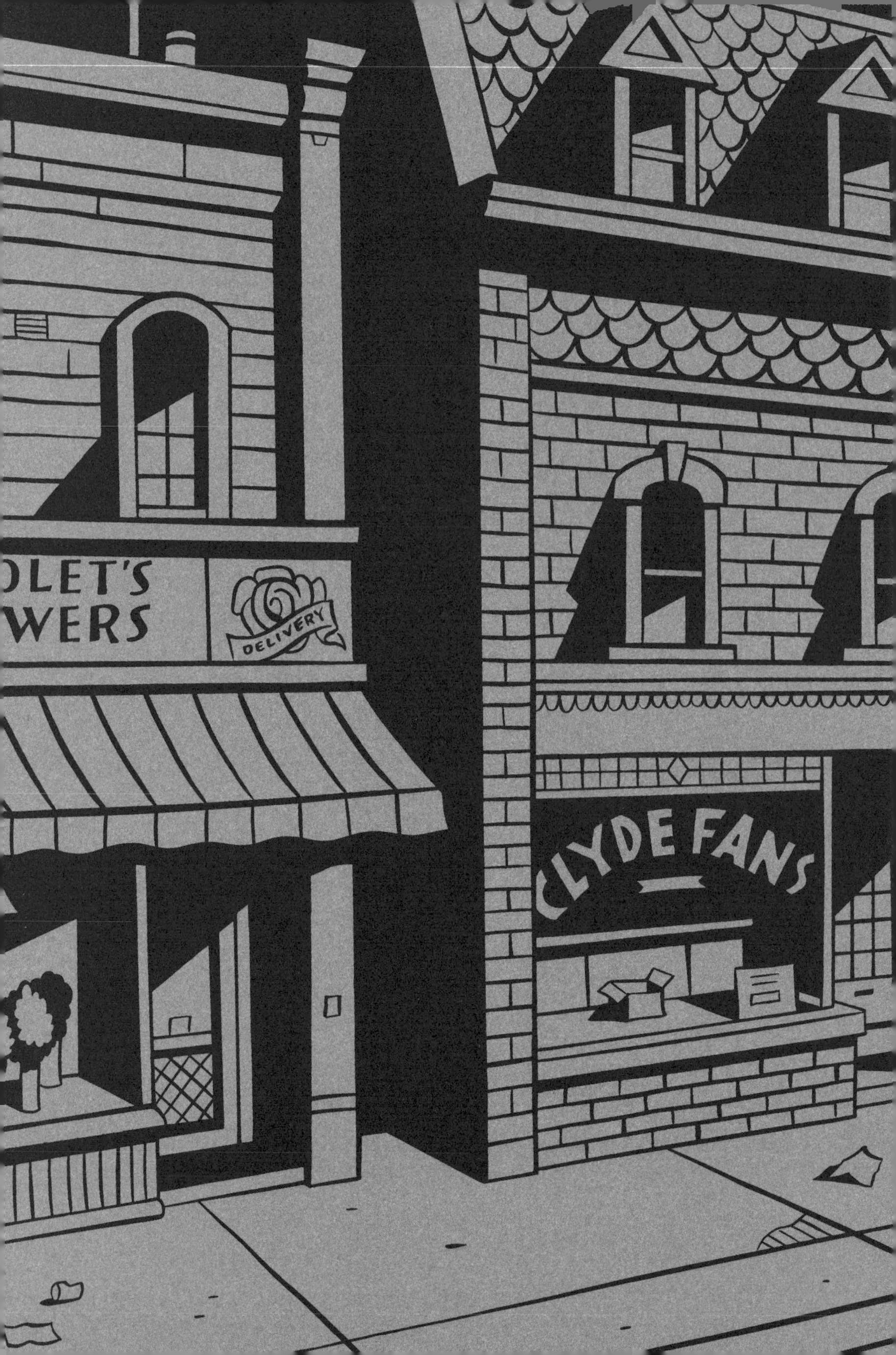
OLET'S
WERS
DELIVERY
CLYDE FANS

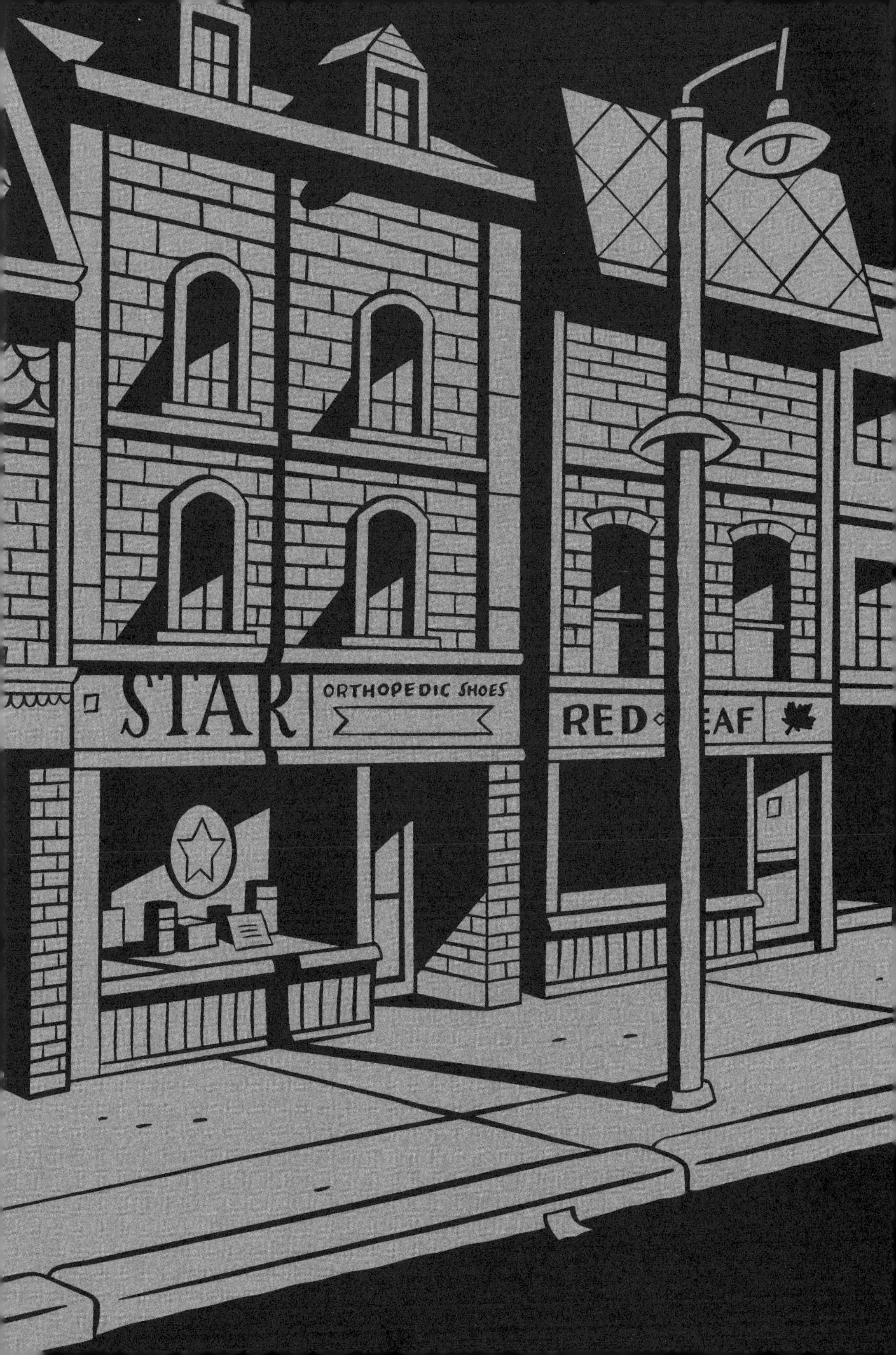
STAR
ORTHOPEDIC SHOES
RED
EAF

DEDICATED, WITH LOVE,
TO MY PRECIOUS WIFE
TANIA

The story presented here was originally serialized in issues ten
through fifteen of the comic book series, PALOOKAVILLE.

Book design: Seth.
Publisher: Chris Oliveros. Publicity: Peggy Burns.

Drawn & Quarterly, Post Office Box 48056, Montreal, Quebec H2V 4S8
www.drawnandquarterly.com

First edition: March 2004. Second printing: September 2004.
10 9 8 7 6 5 4 3 2

National Library of Canada Cataloguing in Publication
Seth, 1962-
Clyde Fans / Seth.
ISBN 1-896597-84-X (bk. 1)
I. Title.
PN6733.S48C59 2004   741.5'971   C2004-900252-X

The publisher gratefully acknowledges the support of
The Canada Council for The Arts for this edition.

Distributed in the USA by:
Farrar, Straus and Giroux, 19 Union Square West, New York, NY 10003
Orders: 888.330.8477

Distributed in Canada by:
Raincoast Books, 9050 Shaughnessy Street, Vancouver, BC V6P 6E5
Orders: 800.663.5714

"Special thanks to Chester Brown, Joe Matt, Chris Ware, and Chris Oliveros."
— SETH

CLYDE FANS

BOOK ONE

A PICTURE NOVELLA
IN TWO BOOKS
BY SETH

DRAWN AND QUARTERLY OF MONTREAL
CANADA

CLYDE FANS CO.

PART ONE

· 1997 ·

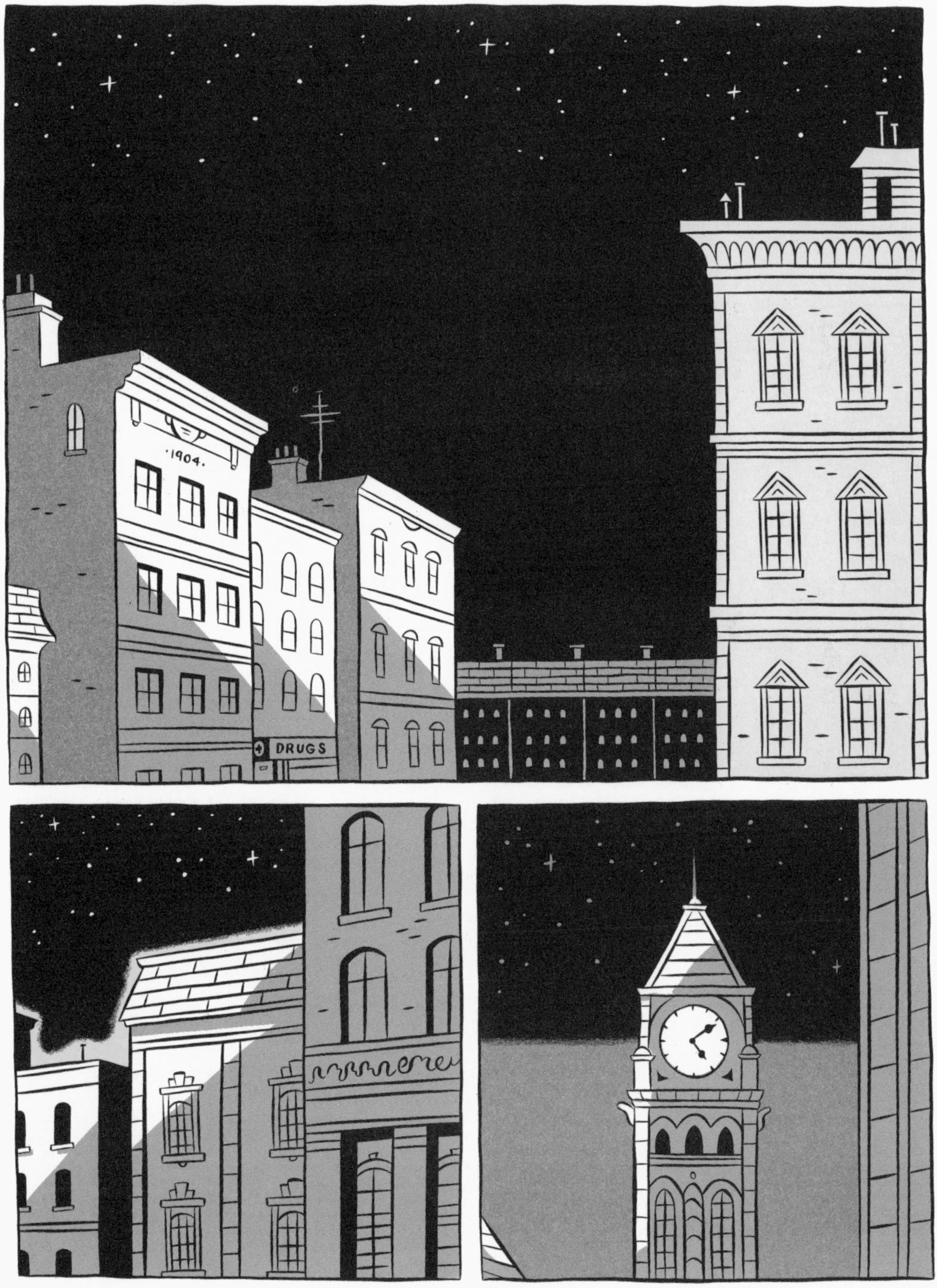

·1904·
DRUGS

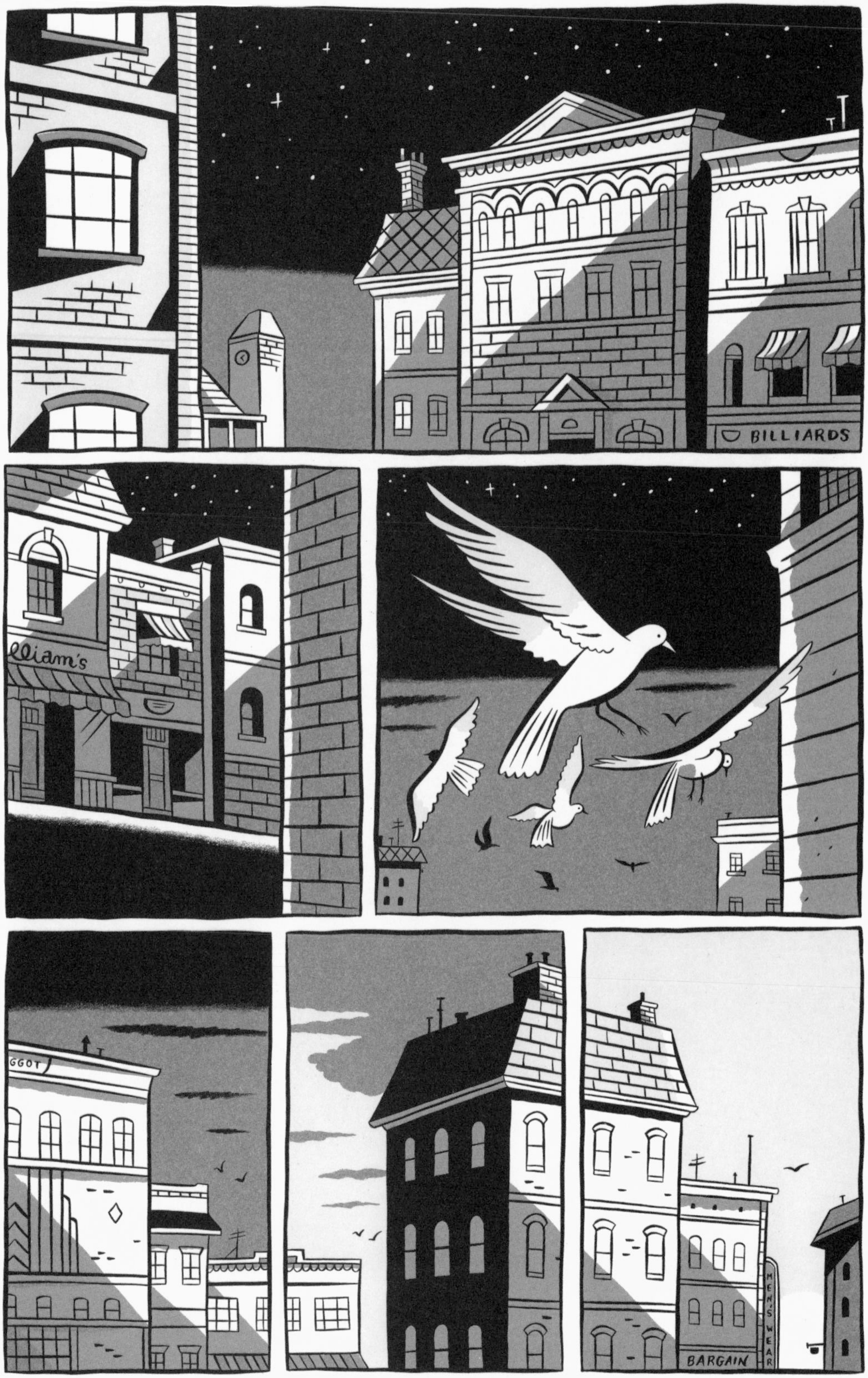
BILLIARDS
lliam's
GGOT
MEN'S WEAR
BARGAIN

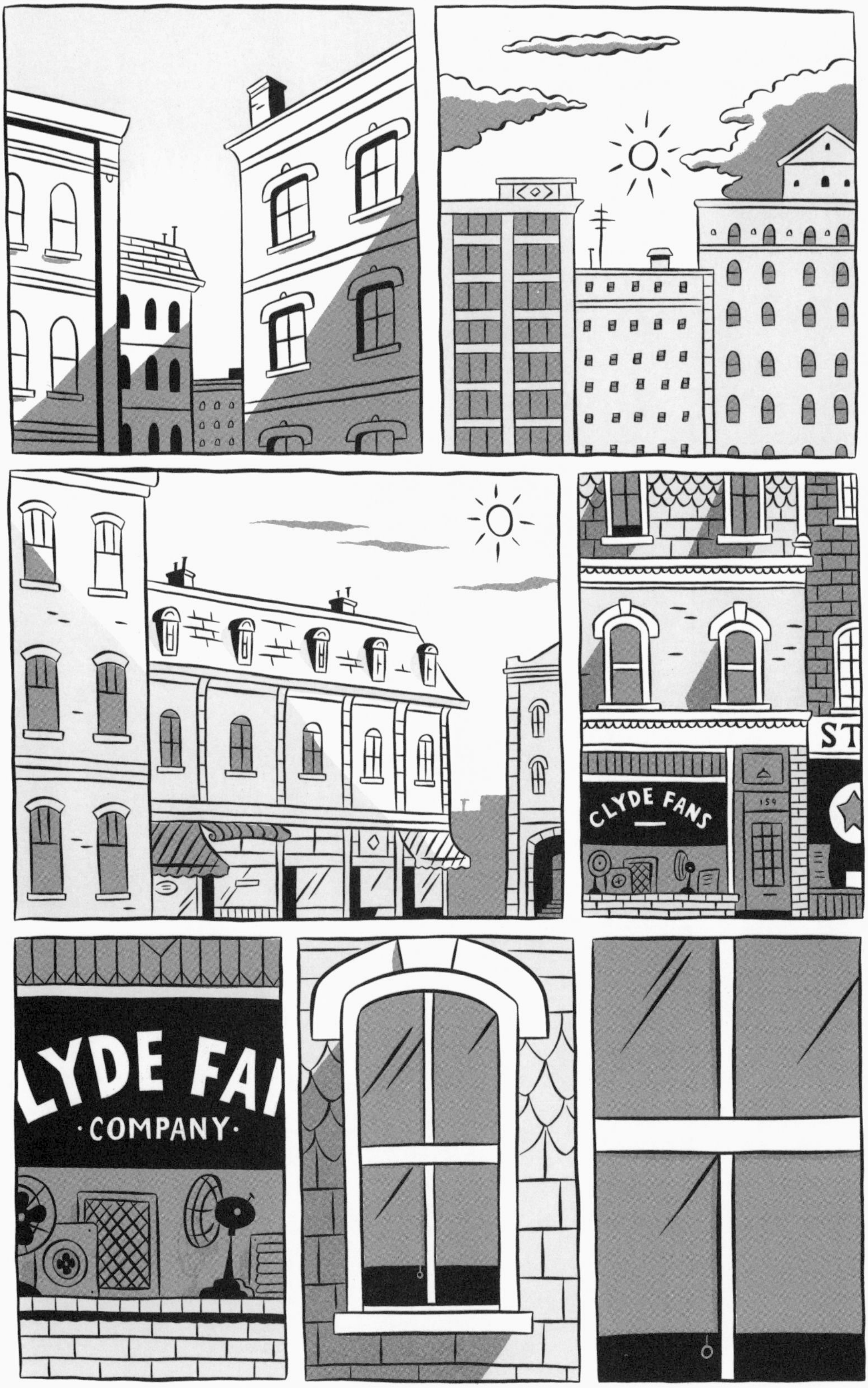
CLYDE FANS
159
ST
LYDE FA
·COMPANY·

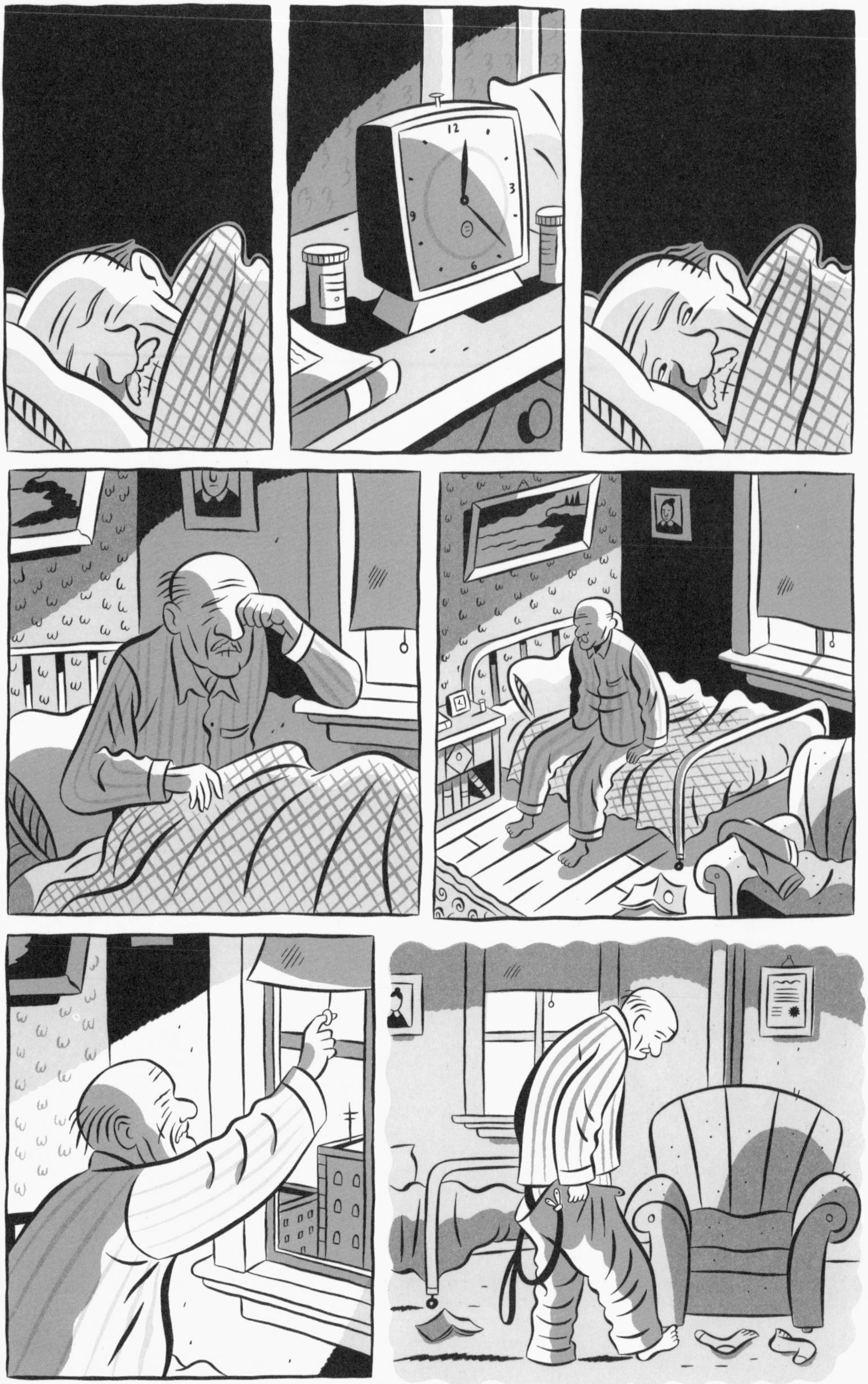

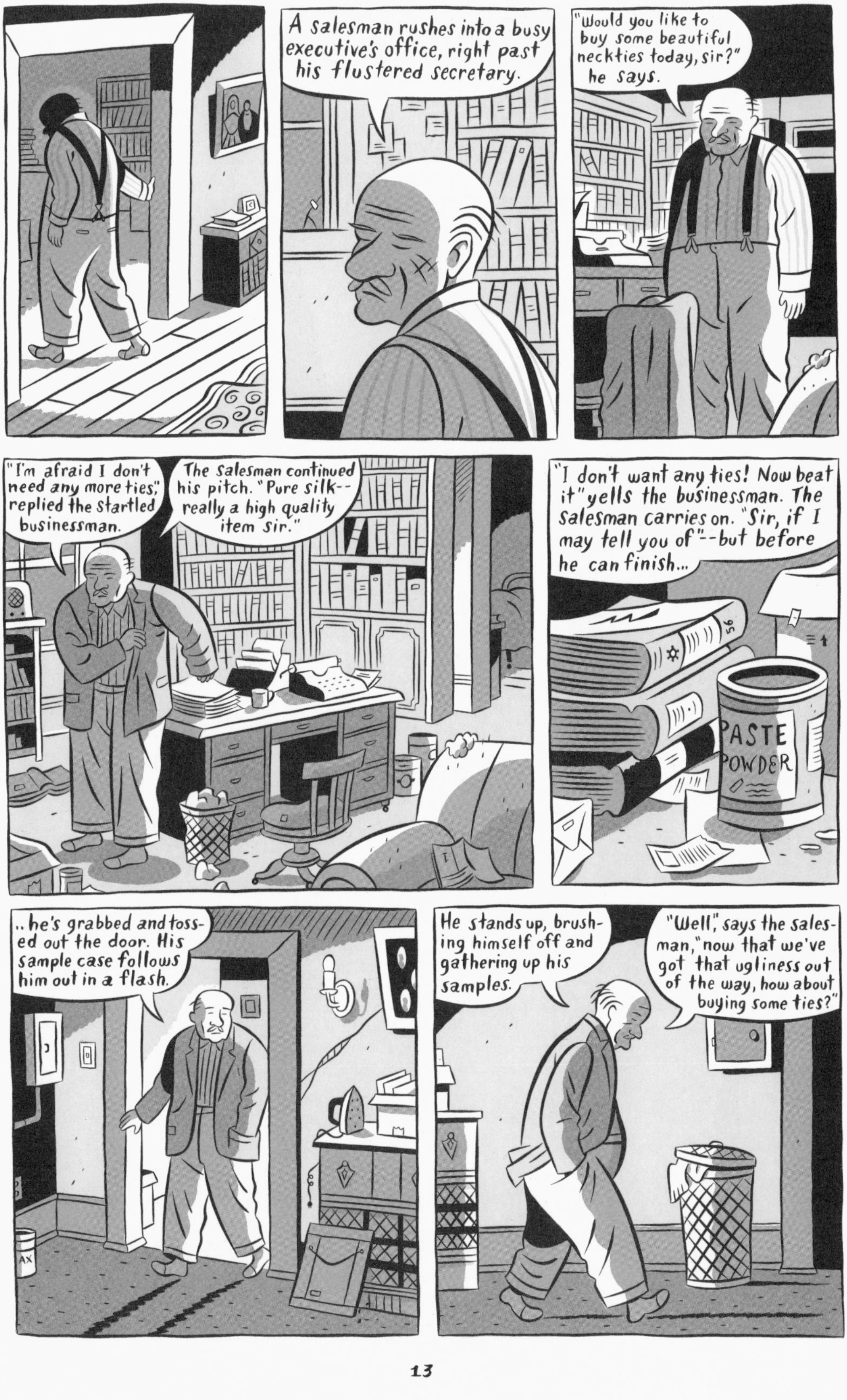
A salesman rushes into a busy executive's office, right past his flustered secretary.
"Would you like to buy some beautiful neckties today, sir?" he says.
"I'm afraid I don't need any more ties," replied the startled businessman.
The salesman continued his pitch. "Pure silk-- really a high quality item sir."
"I don't want any ties! Now beat it" yells the businessman. The salesman carries on. "Sir, if I may tell you of"--but before he can finish...
56
PASTE POWDER
..he's grabbed and tossed out the door. His sample case follows him out in a flash.
He stands up, brushing himself off and gathering up his samples.
"Well," says the salesman, "now that we've got that ugliness out of the way, how about buying some ties?"

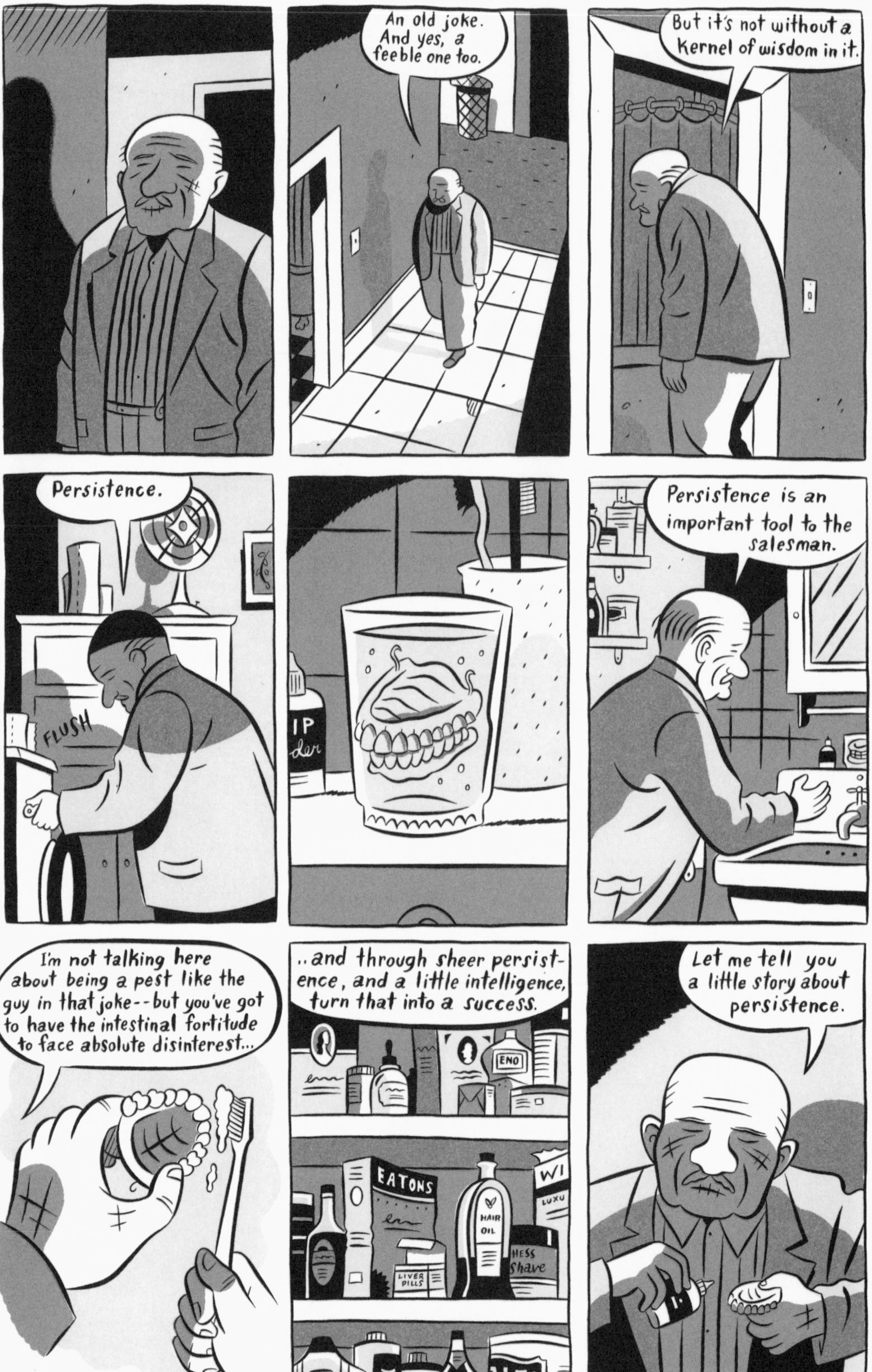

An old joke. And yes, a feeble one too.
But it's not without a kernel of wisdom in it.
Persistence.
FLUSH
Persistence is an important tool to the salesman.
I'm not talking here about being a pest like the guy in that joke--but you've got to have the intestinal fortitude to face absolute disinterest...
..and through sheer persistence, and a little intelligence, turn that into a success.
ENO
EATONS
HAIR OIL
LIVER PILLS
HESS Shave
Let me tell you a little story about persistence.

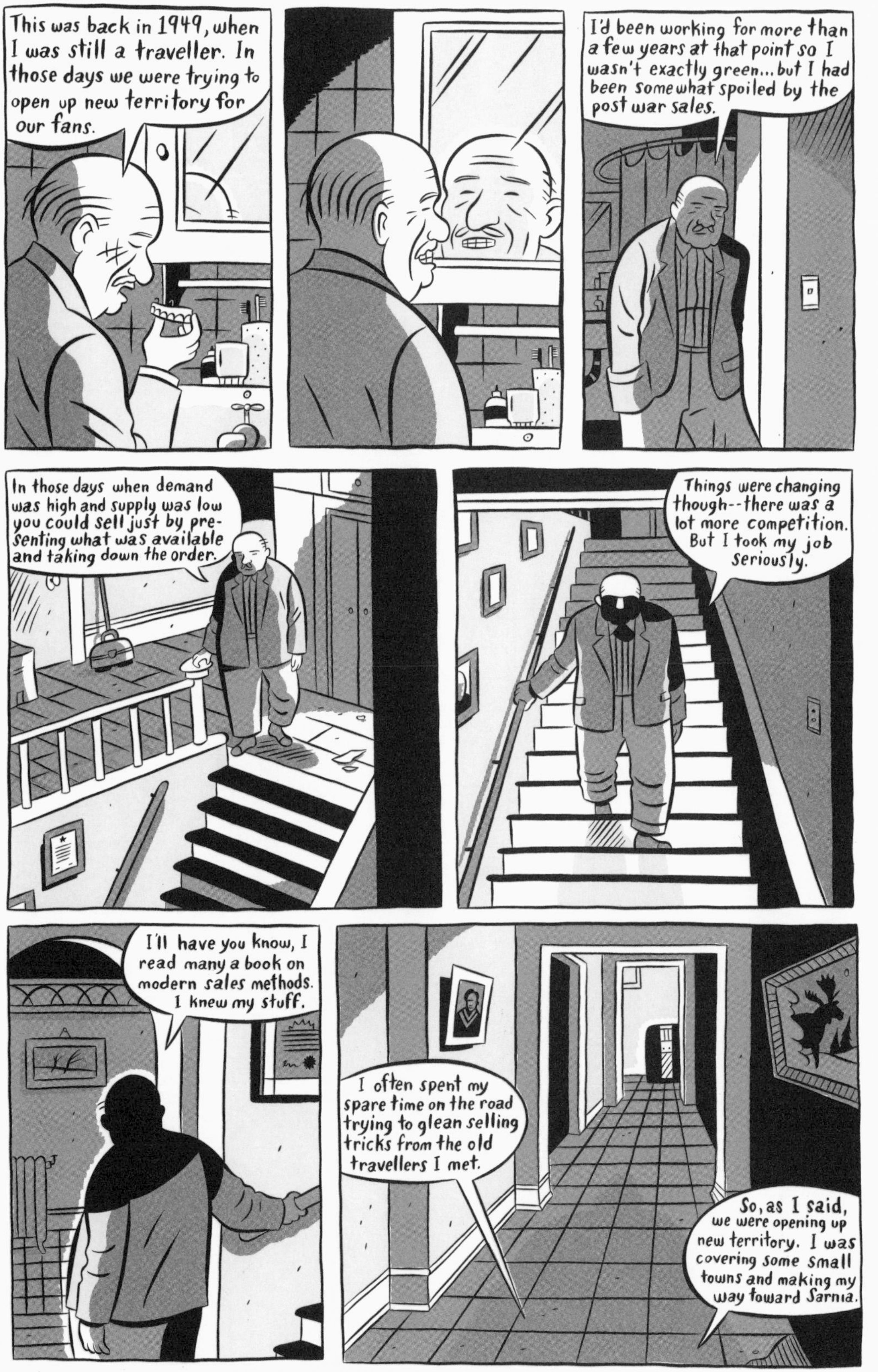
This was back in 1949, when I was still a traveller. In those days we were trying to open up new territory for our fans.
I'd been working for more than a few years at that point so I wasn't exactly green... but I had been somewhat spoiled by the post war sales.
In those days when demand was high and supply was low you could sell just by pre-senting what was available and taking down the order.
Things were changing though--there was a lot more competition. But I took my job seriously.
I'll have you know, I read many a book on modern sales methods. I knew my stuff.
I often spent my spare time on the road trying to glean selling tricks from the old travellers I met.
So, as I said, we were opening up new territory. I was covering some small towns and making my way toward Sarnia.

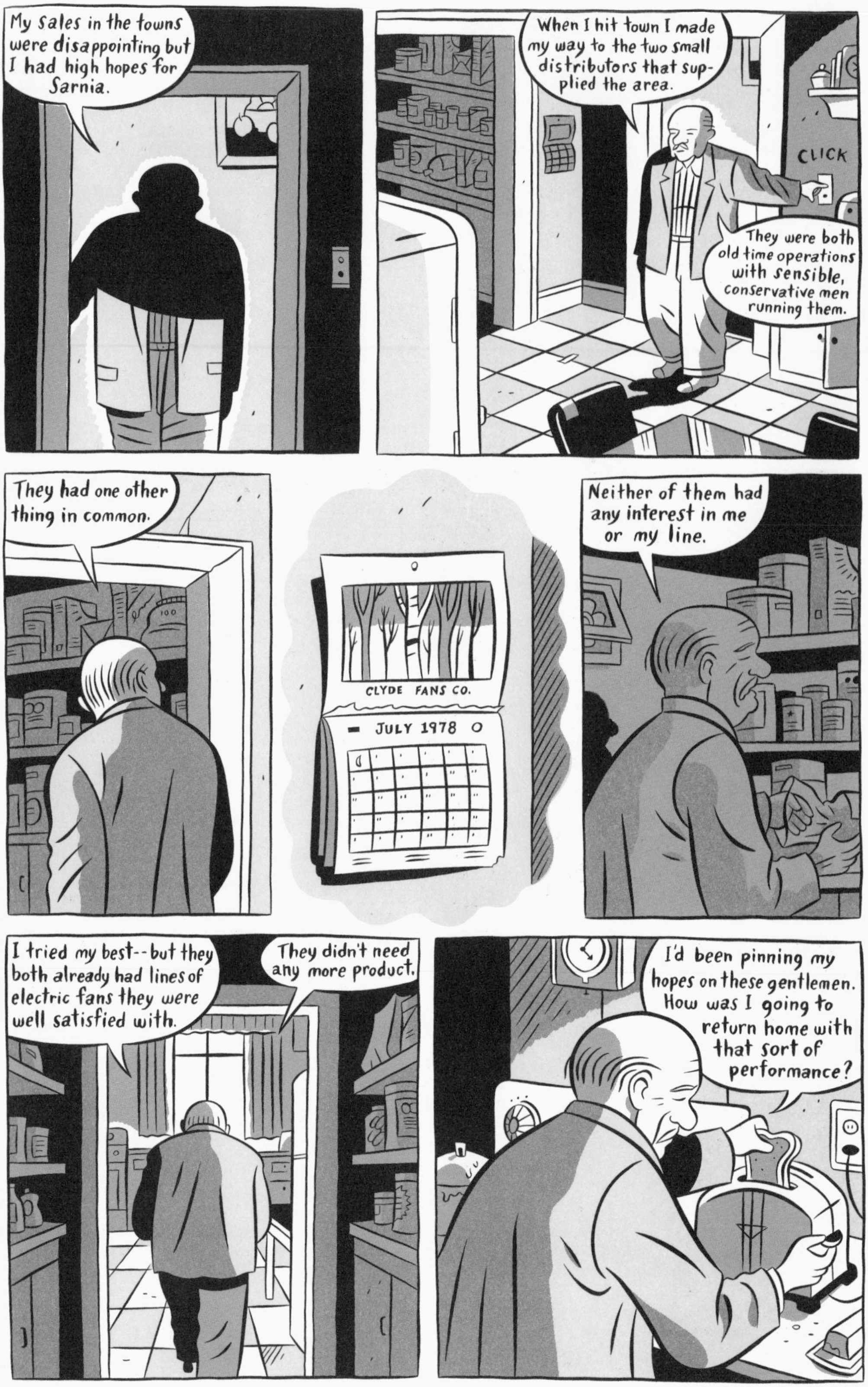
My sales in the towns were disappointing but I had high hopes for Sarnia.
When I hit town I made my way to the two small distributors that supplied the area.
CLICK
They were both old time operations with sensible, conservative men running them.
They had one other thing in common.
CLYDE FANS CO.
JULY 1978
Neither of them had any interest in me or my line.
I tried my best--but they both already had lines of electric fans they were well satisfied with.
They didn't need any more product.
I'd been pinning my hopes on these gentlemen. How was I going to return home with that sort of performance?

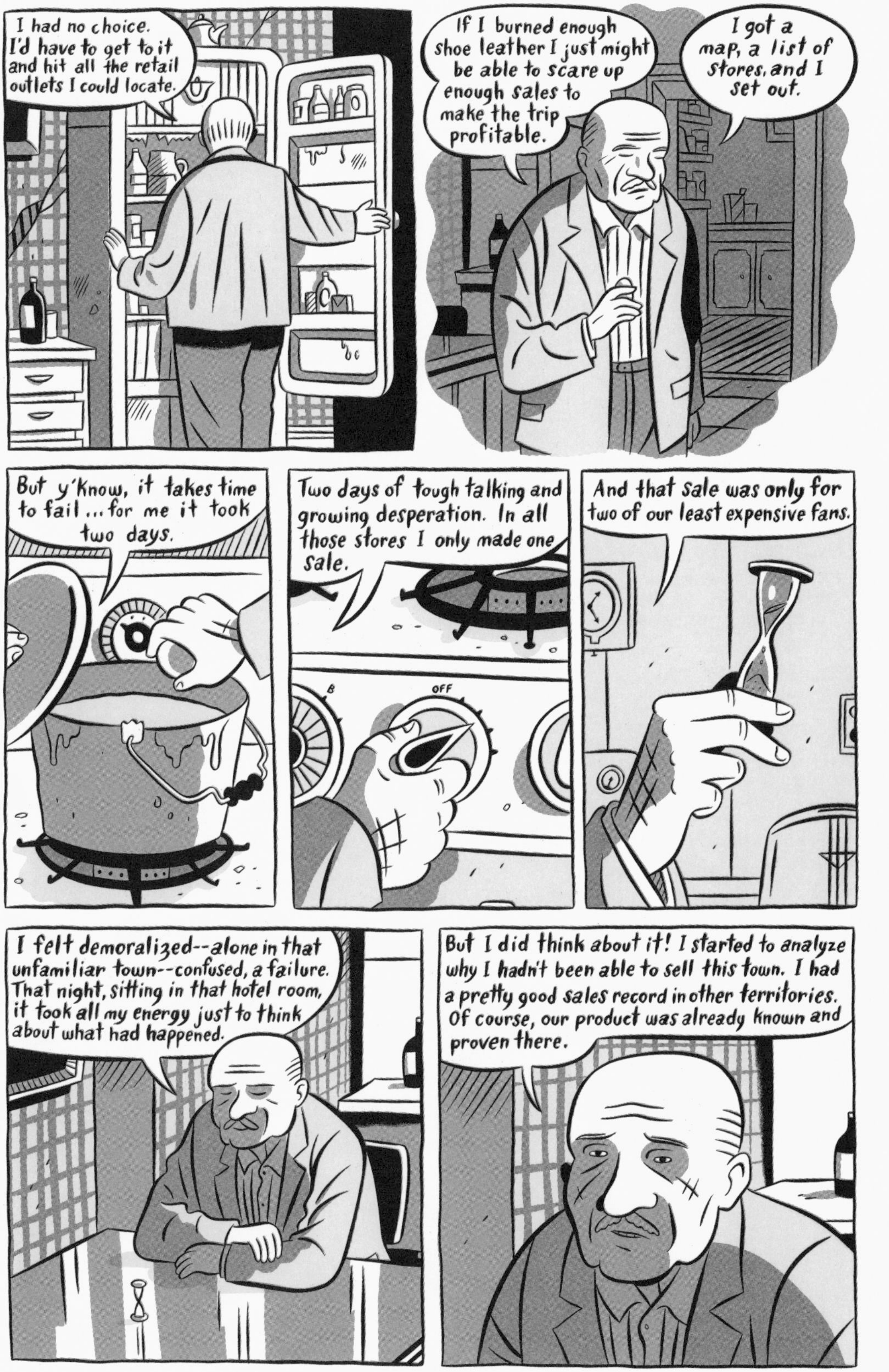
I had no choice. I'd have to get to it and hit all the retail outlets I could locate.
If I burned enough shoe leather I just might be able to scare up enough sales to make the trip profitable.
I got a map, a list of stores, and I set out.
But y'know, it takes time to fail ... for me it took two days.
Two days of tough talking and growing desperation. In all those stores I only made one sale.
B
OFF
And that sale was only for two of our least expensive fans.
I felt demoralized--alone in that unfamiliar town--confused, a failure. That night, sitting in that hotel room, it took all my energy just to think about what had happened.
But I did think about it! I started to analyze why I hadn't been able to sell this town. I had a pretty good sales record in other territories. Of course, our product was already known and proven there.

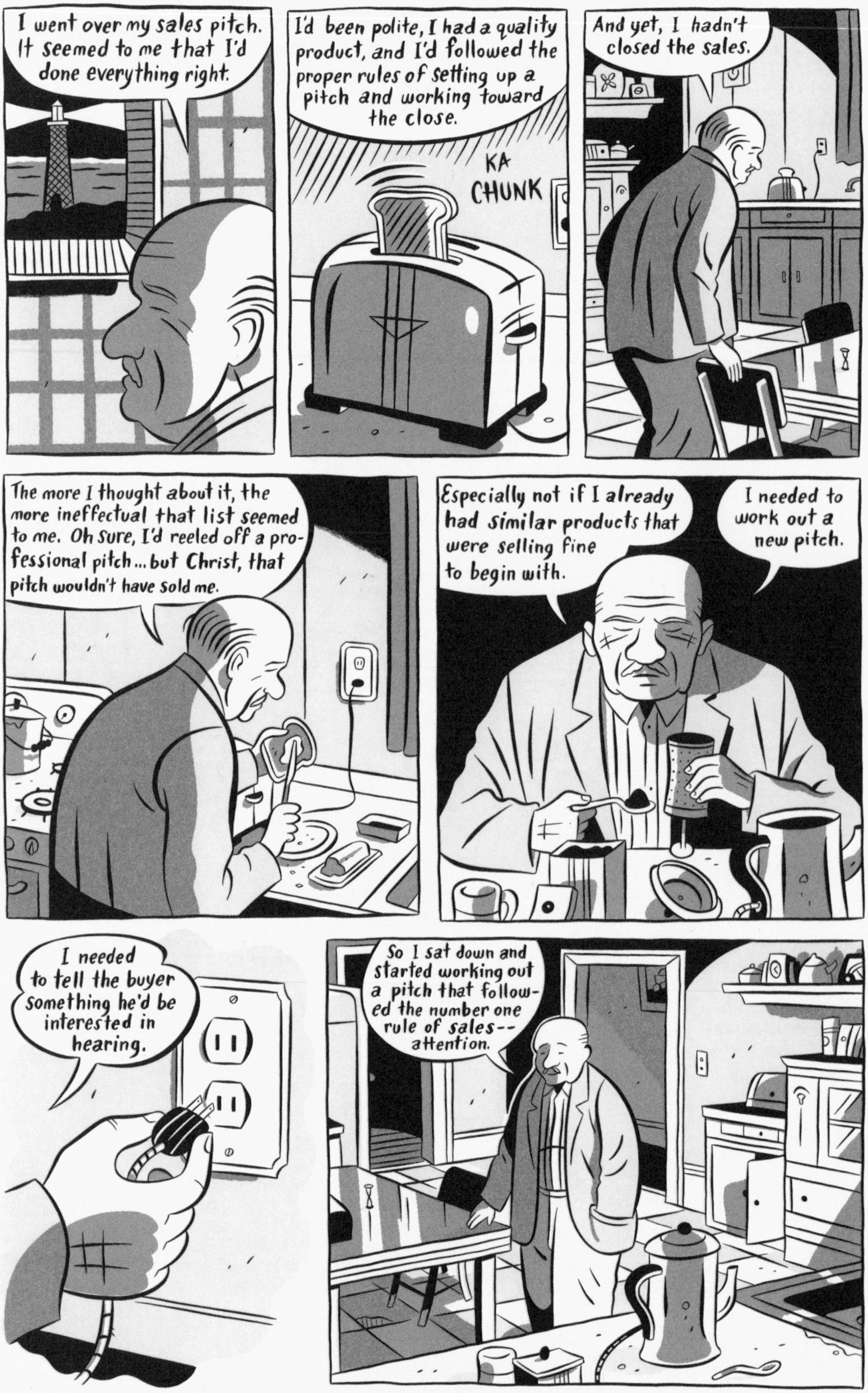
I went over my sales pitch. It seemed to me that I'd done everything right.
I'd been polite, I had a quality product, and I'd followed the proper rules of setting up a pitch and working toward the close.
KA CHUNK
And yet, I hadn't closed the sales.
The more I thought about it, the more ineffectual that list seemed to me. Oh sure, I'd reeled off a professional pitch... but Christ, that pitch wouldn't have sold me.
Especially not if I already had similar products that were selling fine to begin with.
I needed to work out a new pitch.
I needed to tell the buyer something he'd be interested in hearing.
So I sat down and started working out a pitch that followed the number one rule of sales-- attention.

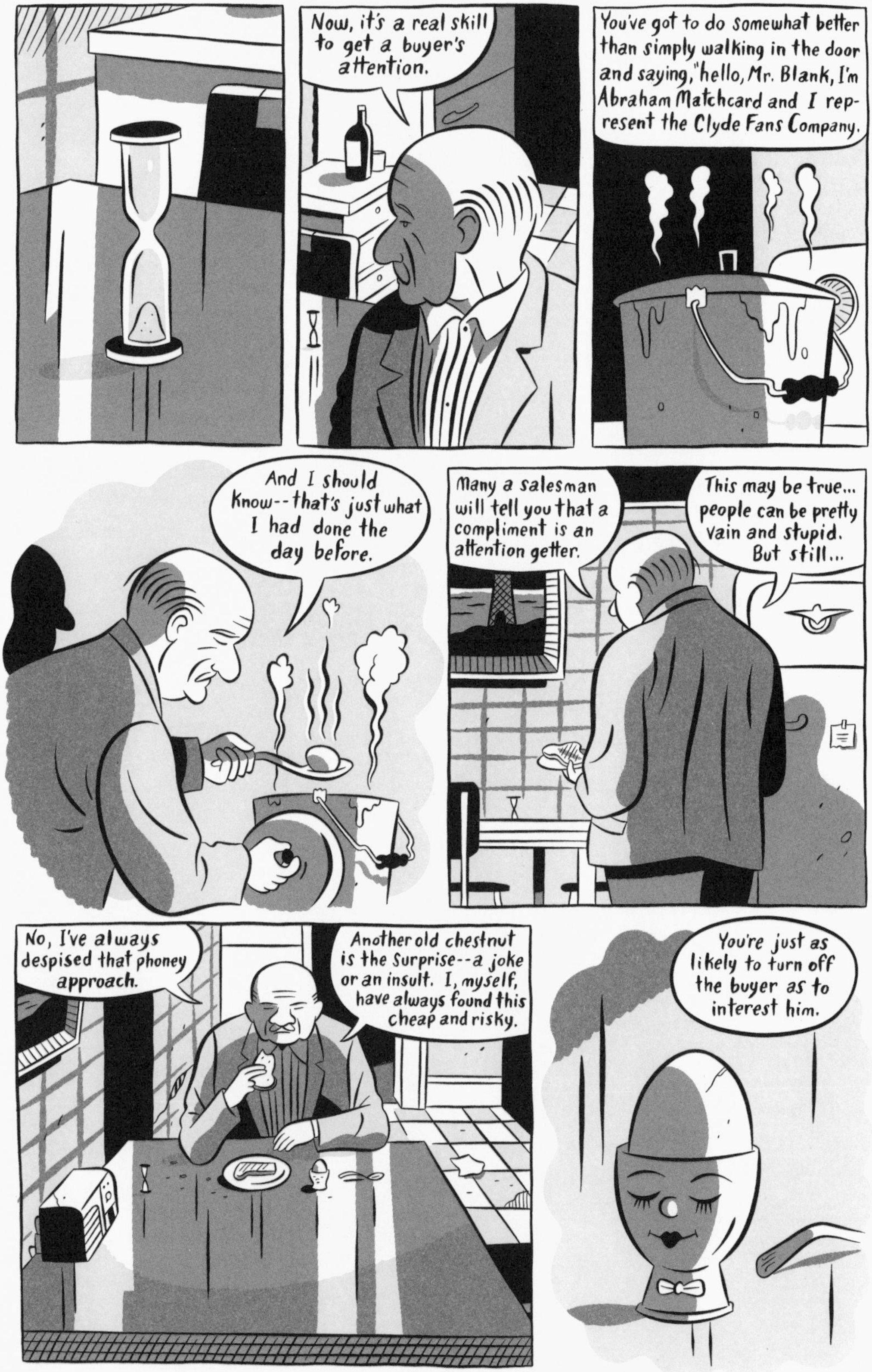
Now, it's a real skill to get a buyer's attention.
You've got to do somewhat better than simply walking in the door and saying, "hello, Mr. Blank, I'm Abraham Matchcard and I represent the Clyde Fans Company.
And I should know--that's just what I had done the day before.
Many a salesman will tell you that a compliment is an attention getter.
This may be true... people can be pretty vain and stupid. But still...
No, I've always despised that phoney approach.
Another old chestnut is the Surprise--a joke or an insult. I, myself, have always found this cheap and risky.
You're just as likely to turn off the buyer as to interest him.

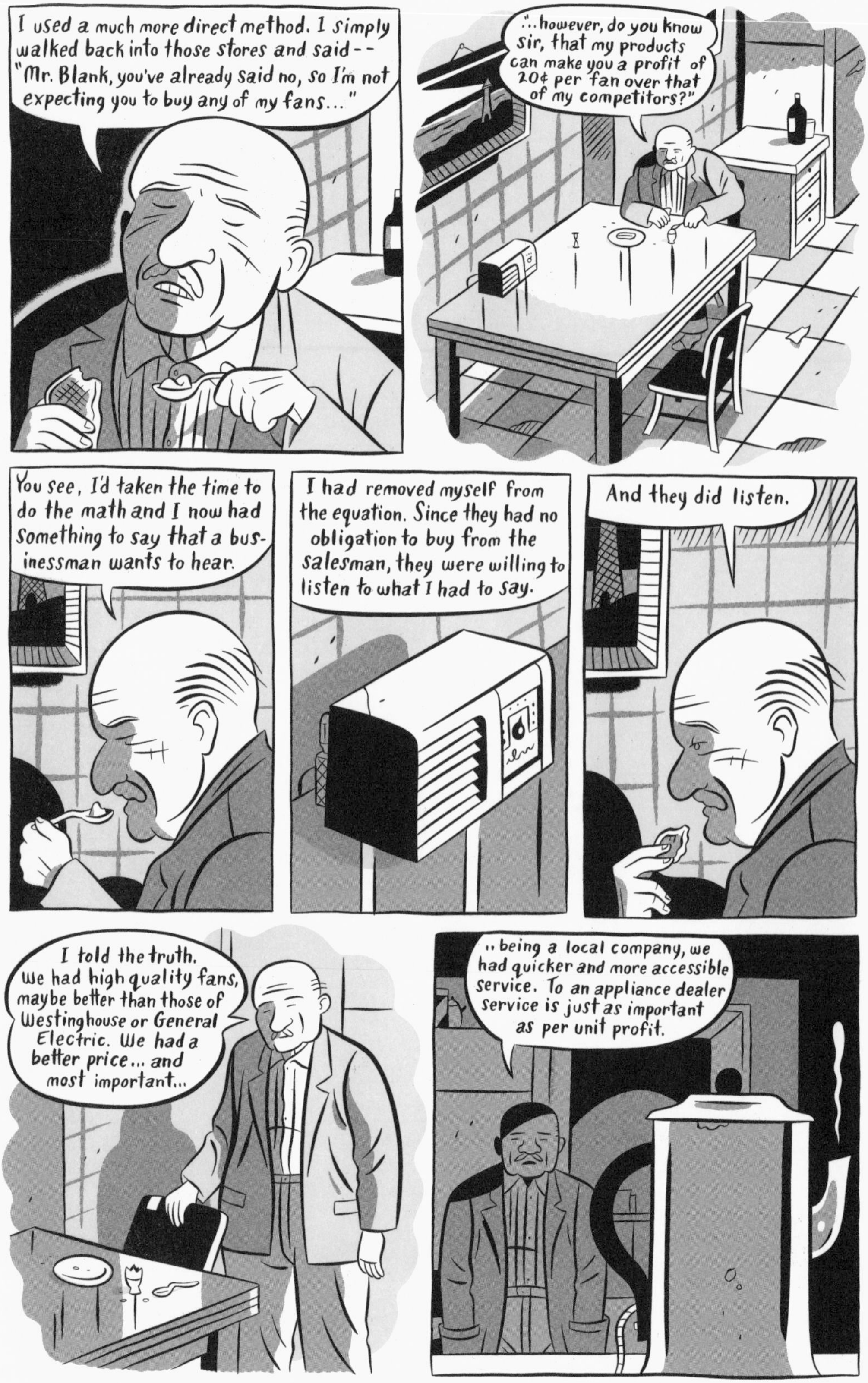
I used a much more direct method. I simply walked back into those stores and said-- "Mr. Blank, you've already said no, so I'm not expecting you to buy any of my fans..."
"...however, do you know sir, that my products can make you a profit of 20¢ per fan over that of my competitors?"
You see, I'd taken the time to do the math and I now had something to say that a businessman wants to hear.
I had removed myself from the equation. Since they had no obligation to buy from the salesman, they were willing to listen to what I had to say.
And they did listen.
I told the truth. We had high quality fans, maybe better than those of Westinghouse or General Electric. We had a better price... and most important...
..being a local company, we had quicker and more accessible service. To an appliance dealer service is just as important as per unit profit.

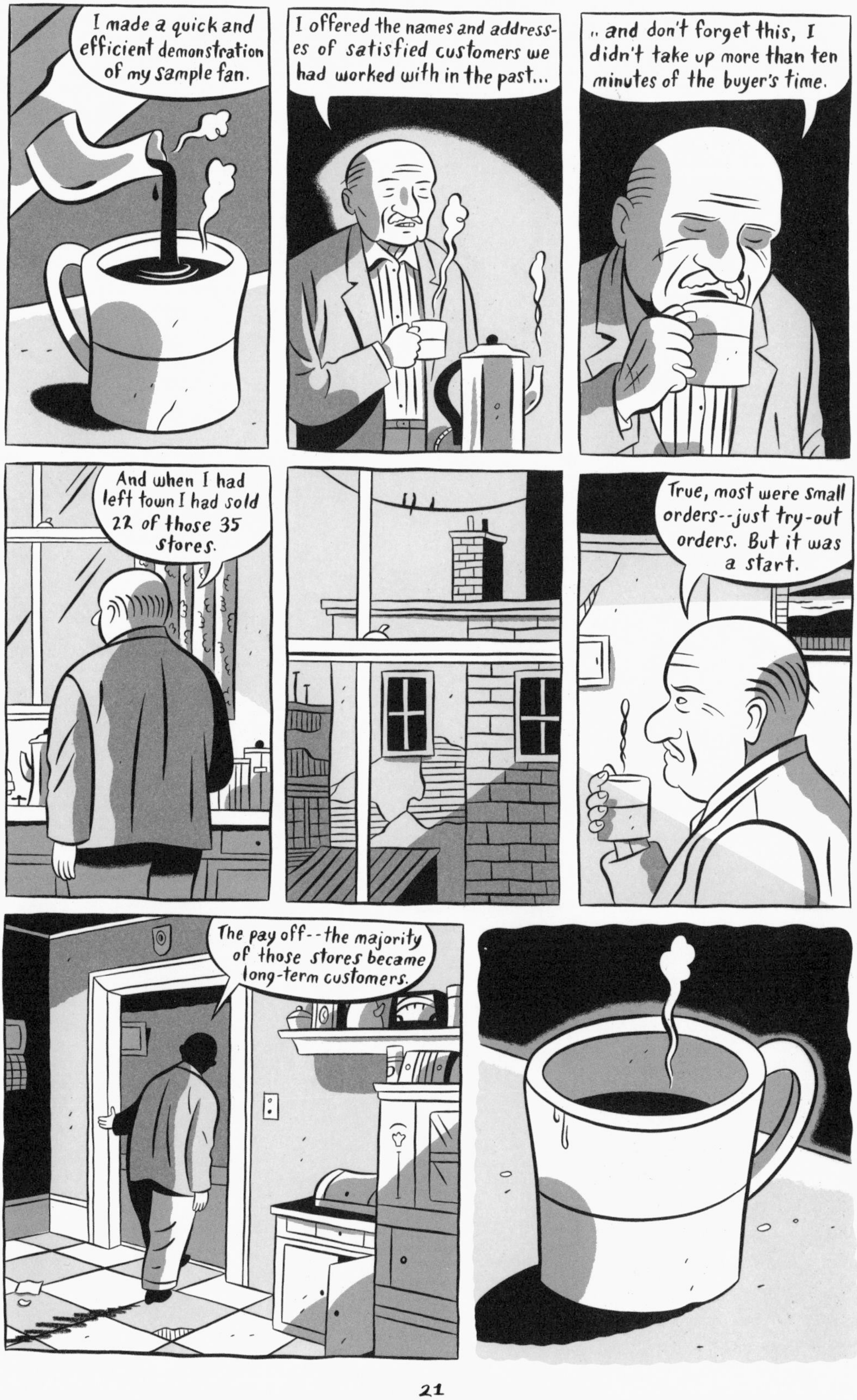
I made a quick and efficient demonstration of my sample fan.
I offered the names and addresses of satisfied customers we had worked with in the past...
.. and don't forget this, I didn't take up more than ten minutes of the buyer's time.
And when I had left town I had sold 22 of those 35 stores.
True, most were small orders--just try-out orders. But it was a start.
The pay off--the majority of those stores became long-term customers.

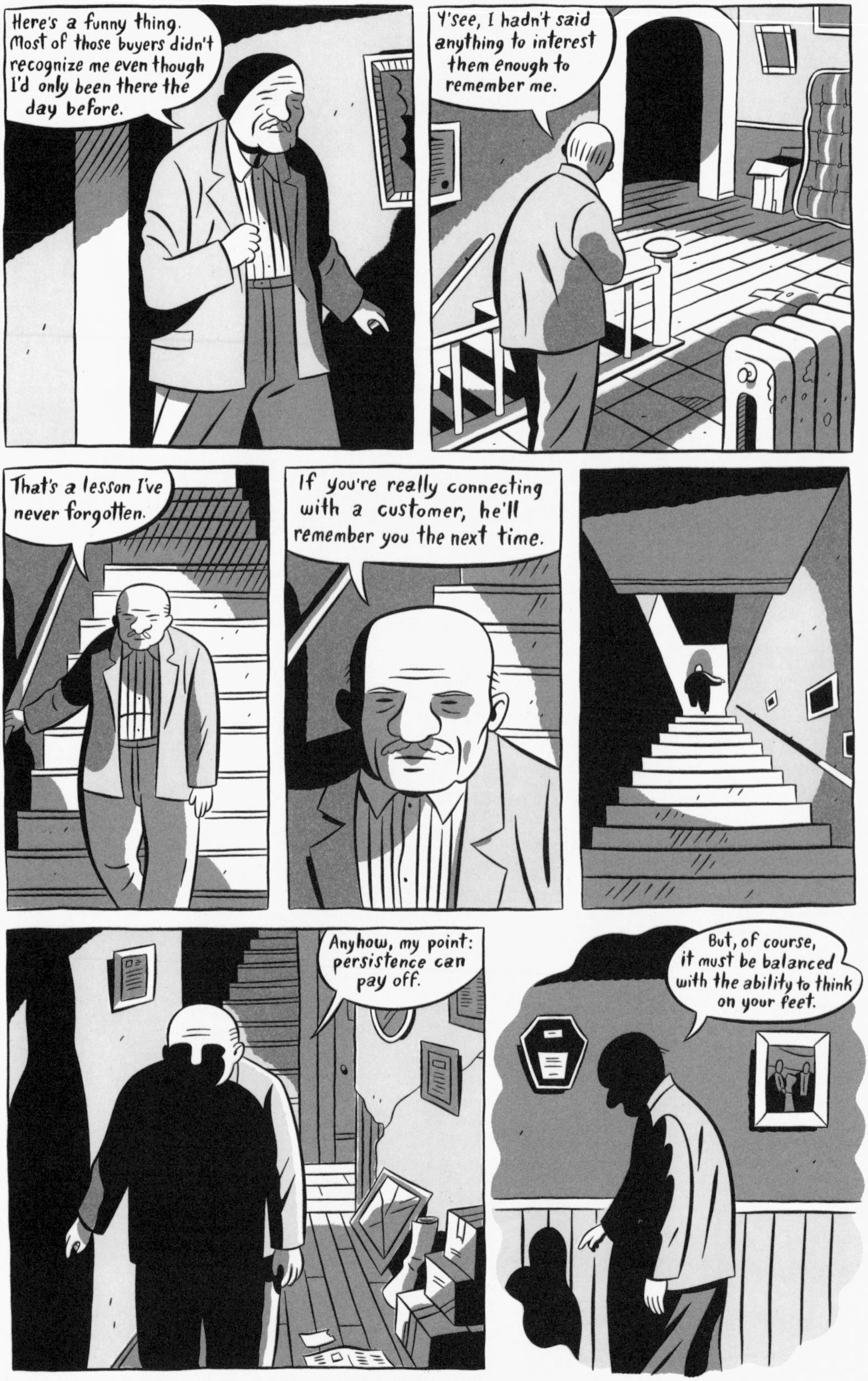
Here's a funny thing. Most of those buyers didn't recognize me even though I'd only been there the day before.
Y'see, I hadn't said anything to interest them enough to remember me.
That's a lesson I've never forgotten.
If you're really connecting with a customer, he'll remember you the next time.
Anyhow, my point: persistence can pay off.
But, of course, it must be balanced with the ability to think on your feet.

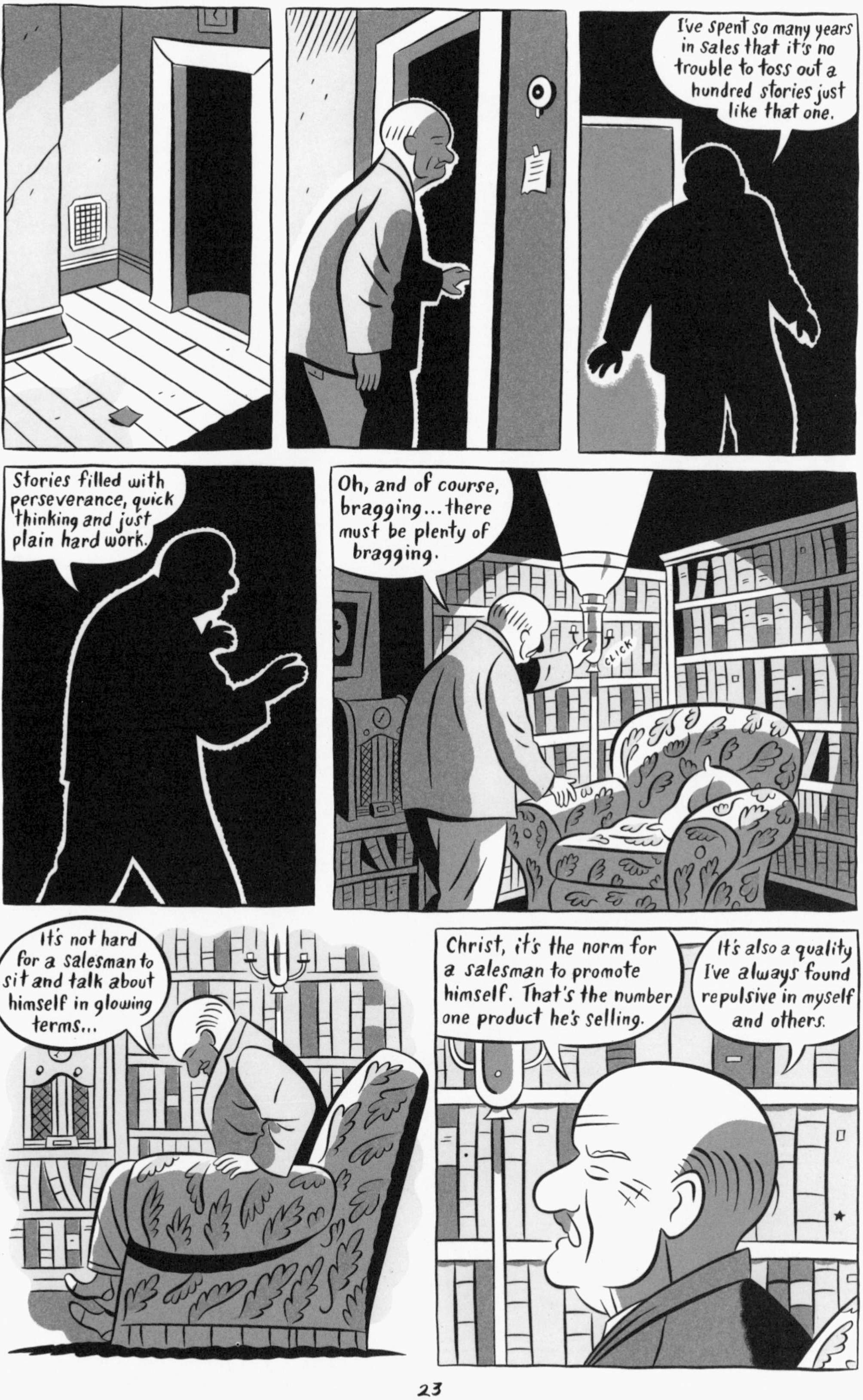

I've spent so many years in sales that it's no trouble to toss out a hundred stories just like that one.
Stories filled with perseverance, quick thinking and just plain hard work.
Oh, and of course, bragging... there must be plenty of bragging.
CLICK
It's not hard for a salesman to sit and talk about himself in glowing terms...
Christ, it's the norm for a salesman to promote himself. That's the number one product he's selling.
It's also a quality I've always found repulsive in myself and others.

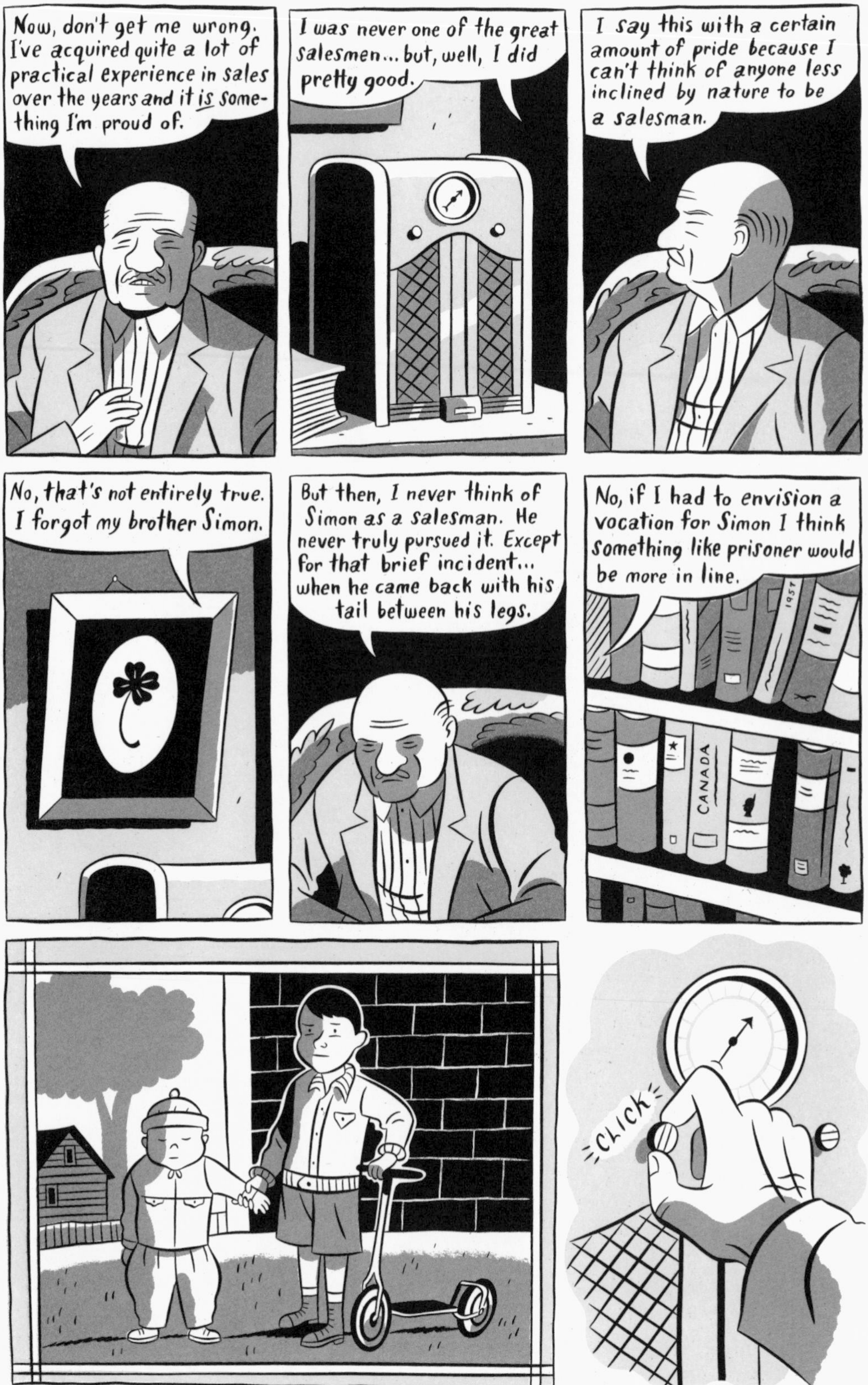

Now, don't get me wrong. I've acquired quite a lot of practical experience in sales over the years and it is something I'm proud of.
I was never one of the great salesmen... but, well, I did pretty good.
I say this with a certain amount of pride because I can't think of anyone less inclined by nature to be a salesman.
No, that's not entirely true. I forgot my brother Simon.
But then, I never think of Simon as a salesman. He never truly pursued it. Except for that brief incident... when he came back with his tail between his legs.
No, if I had to envision a vocation for Simon I think something like prisoner would be more in line.
1957
CANADA
CLICK

..marauding bear. Eaton's tries to fend off bankruptcy. Five more closings were announced today including Guelph...

..ten to fifteen centimetres of snow is expected today with a possibility of freezing rain. Winds may reach up to...

..♪♪♪ Welcome to Morningside, hour one. In our first hour we'll be talking to a curling champ from Regina about...

This was Simon's reading room. I could always find him here at lunch time and in the evenings.

He kept it very tidy then.

He had a real passion for reading. One I didn't share in those days.

Myself, I always liked the radio. In fact, if memory serves, I'm the one who put a radio in here.

THE POPULAR BOOK of STARS

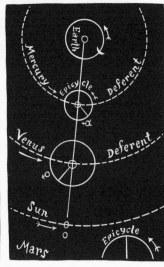

Earth

Mercury

Epicycle

Deferent

α

Venus

Deferent

Sun

Mars

Epicycle

25

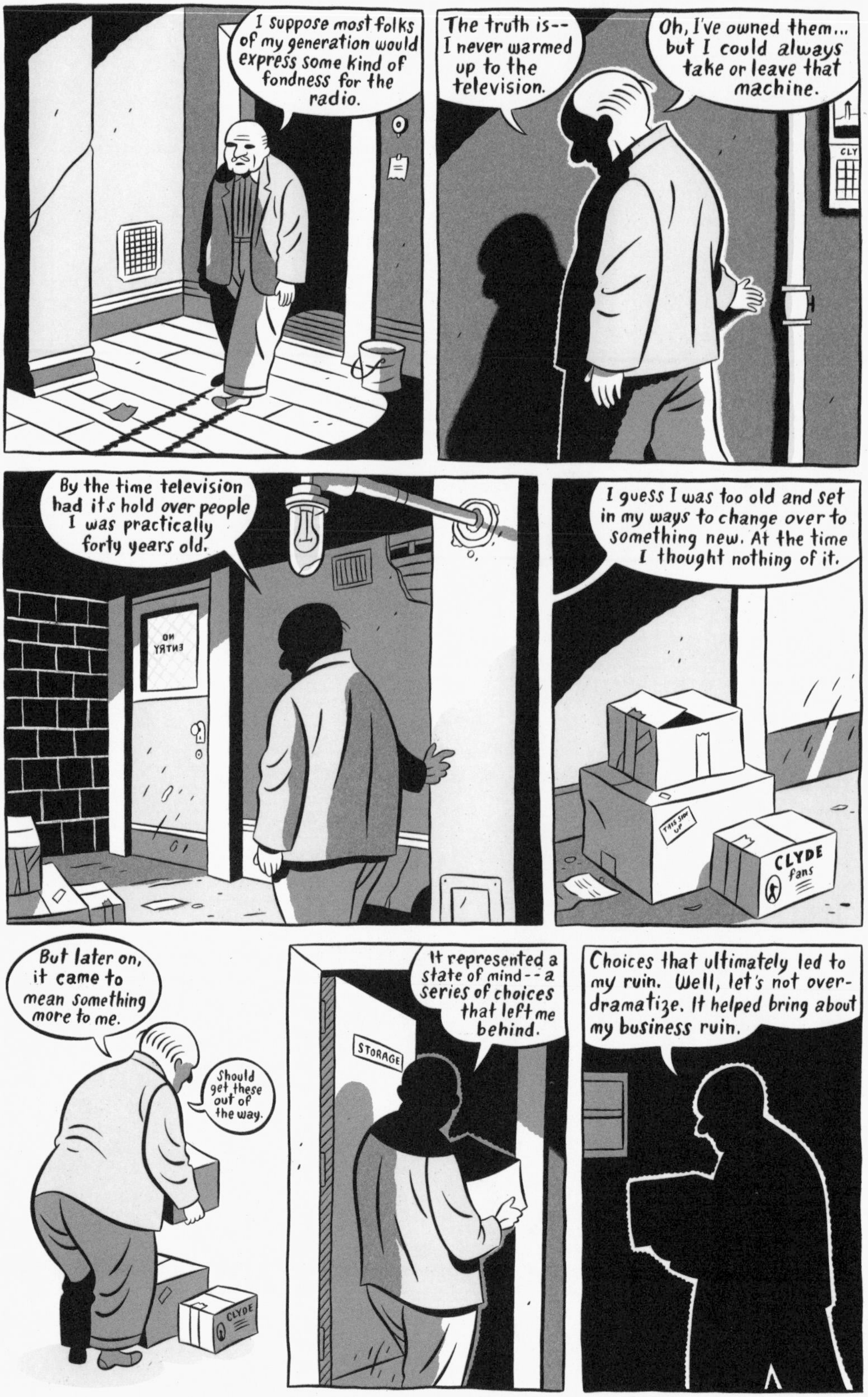
I suppose most folks of my generation would express some kind of fondness for the radio.
The truth is-- I never warmed up to the television.
Oh, I've owned them... but I could always take or leave that machine.
CLY
By the time television had its hold over people I was practically forty years old.
NO ENTRY
I guess I was too old and set in my ways to change over to something new. At the time I thought nothing of it.
THIS SIDE UP
CLYDE fans
But later on, it came to mean something more to me.
Should get these out of the way.
CLYDE
STORAGE
It represented a state of mind-- a series of choices that left me behind.
Choices that ultimately led to my ruin. Well, let's not over-dramatize. It helped bring about my business ruin.

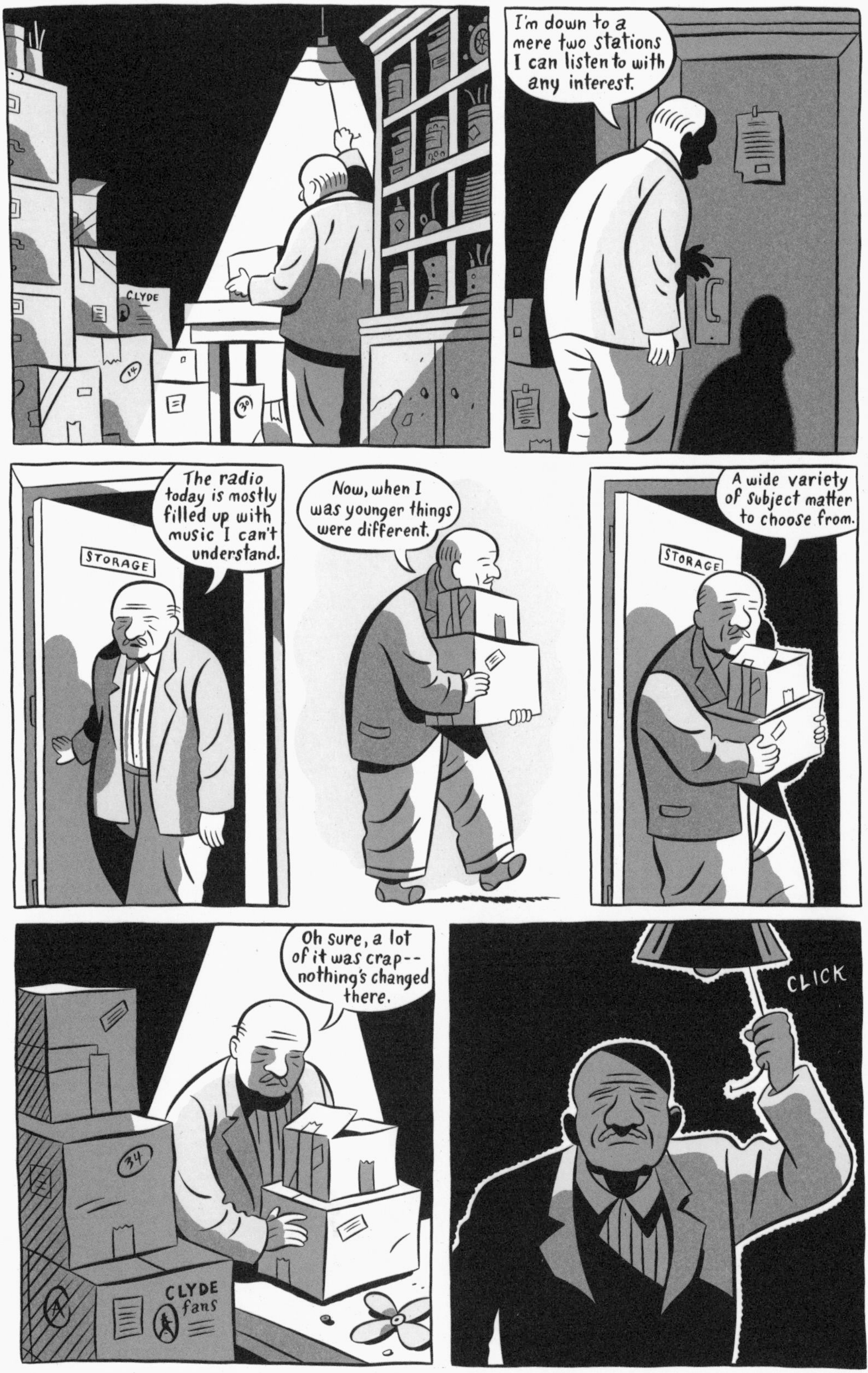
CLYDE
I'm down to a mere two stations I can listen to with any interest.
STORAGE
The radio today is mostly filled up with music I can't understand.
Now, when I was younger things were different.
STORAGE
A wide variety of subject matter to choose from.
Oh sure, a lot of it was crap-- nothing's changed there.
34
CLYDE fans
CLICK

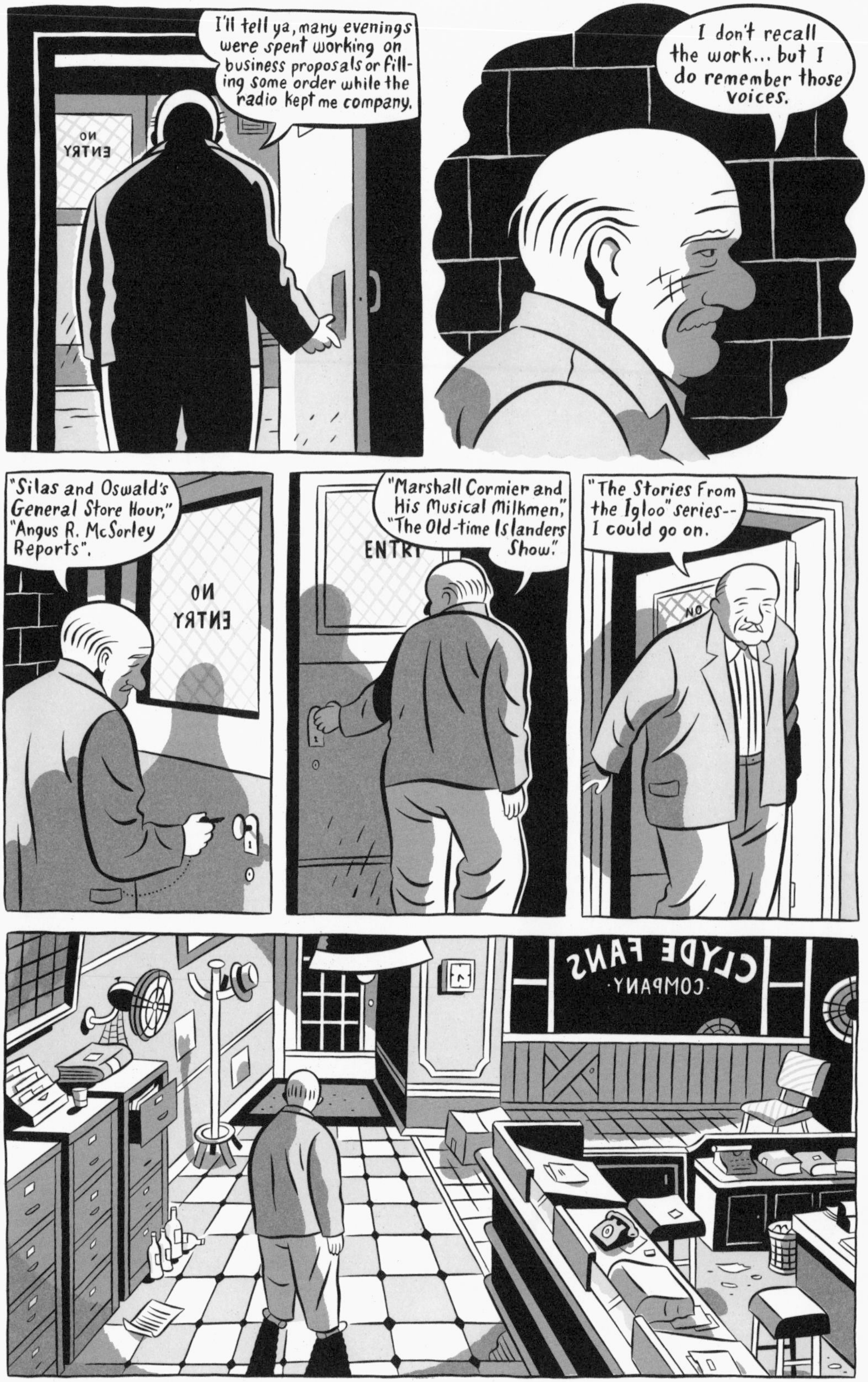
I'll tell ya, many evenings were spent working on business proposals or filling some order while the radio kept me company.
NO ENTRY
I don't recall the work... but I do remember those voices.
"Silas and Oswald's General Store Hour," "Angus R. McSorley Reports".
NO ENTRY
"Marshall Cormier and His Musical Milkmen," "The Old-time Islanders Show."
"The Stories From the Igloo" series-- I could go on.
CLYDE FANS
·COMPANY·

Something of the flavour of those times and those people... has been lost.

I say this with a kind of sadness-- and that is my great failing.

You see, for a man working in a forward-looking business, a business based on progress...

..for that man to turn a blind eye to the future-- well, that man has lost the battle without even knowing it.

And I didn't know it.

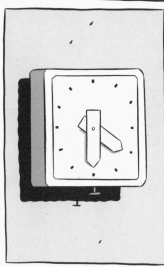

I thought I was a man in step with my times. I didn't realize I was looking backward.

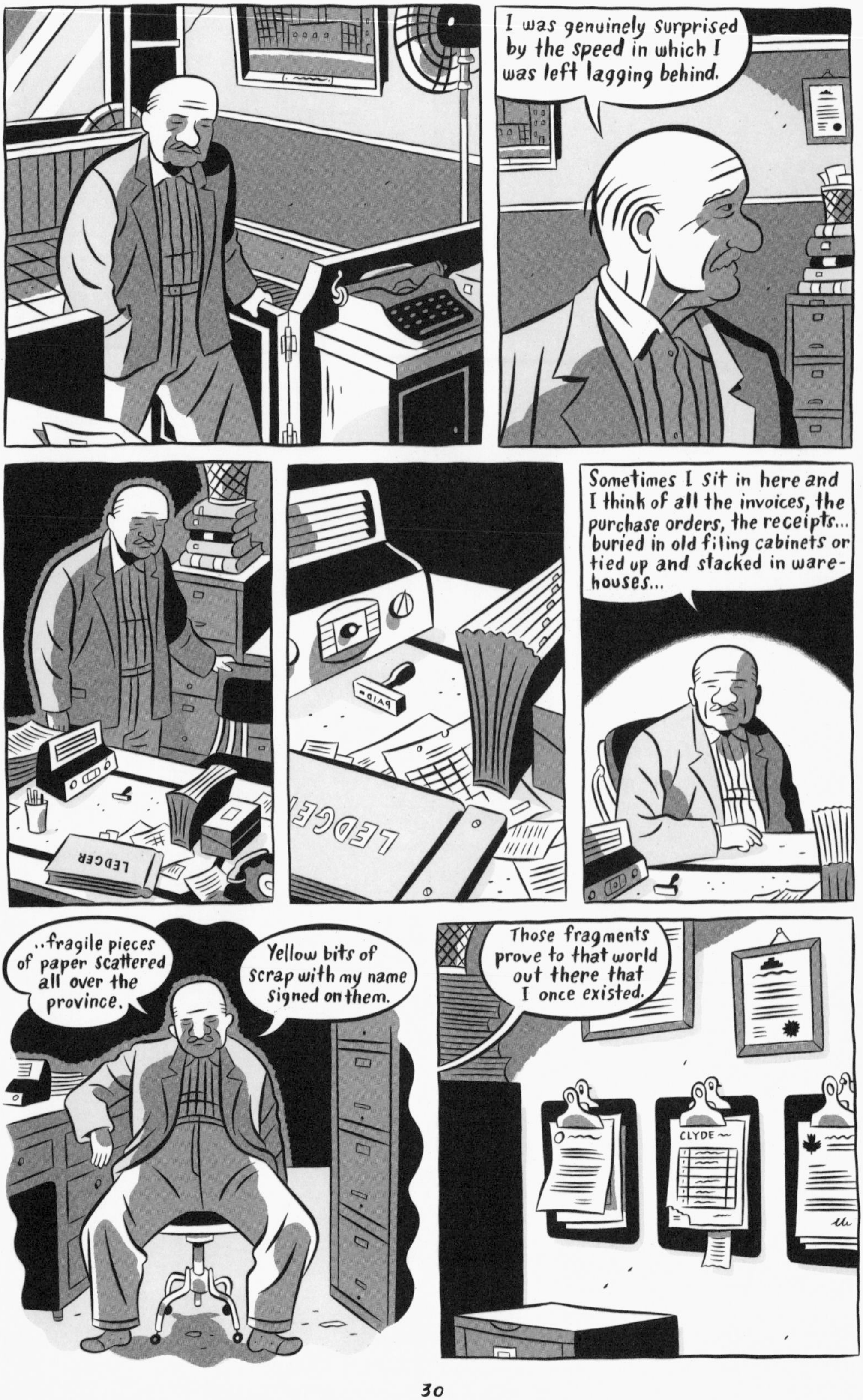
I was genuinely surprised by the speed in which I was left lagging behind.
PAID
LEDGER
LEDGER
Sometimes I sit in here and I think of all the invoices, the purchase orders, the receipts... buried in old filing cabinets or tied up and stacked in warehouses...
..fragile pieces of paper scattered all over the province.
Yellow bits of scrap with my name signed on them.
Those fragments prove to that world out there that I once existed.
CLYDE

It occurs to me that those papers probably have a more meaningful relationship with the outside world than I do.

I doubt I'd be any more isolated in a snow bound cabin in the Yukon.

CLYDE F... COMPANY.

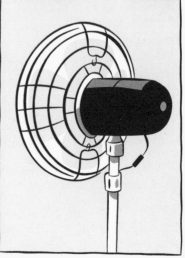

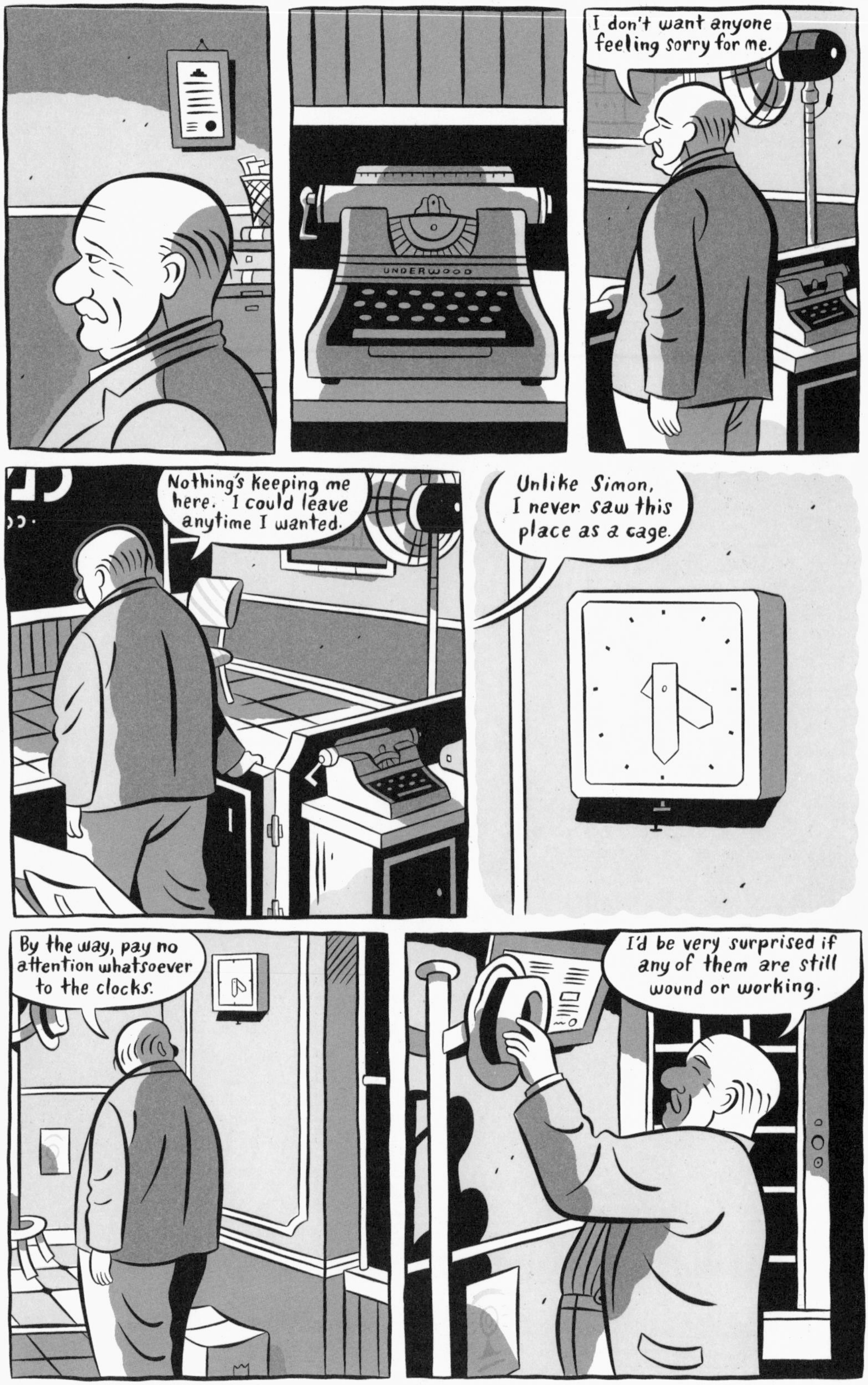
UNDERWOOD
I don't want anyone feeling sorry for me.
Nothing's keeping me here. I could leave anytime I wanted.
Unlike Simon, I never saw this place as a cage.
By the way, pay no attention whatsoever to the clocks.
I'd be very surprised if any of them are still wound or working.

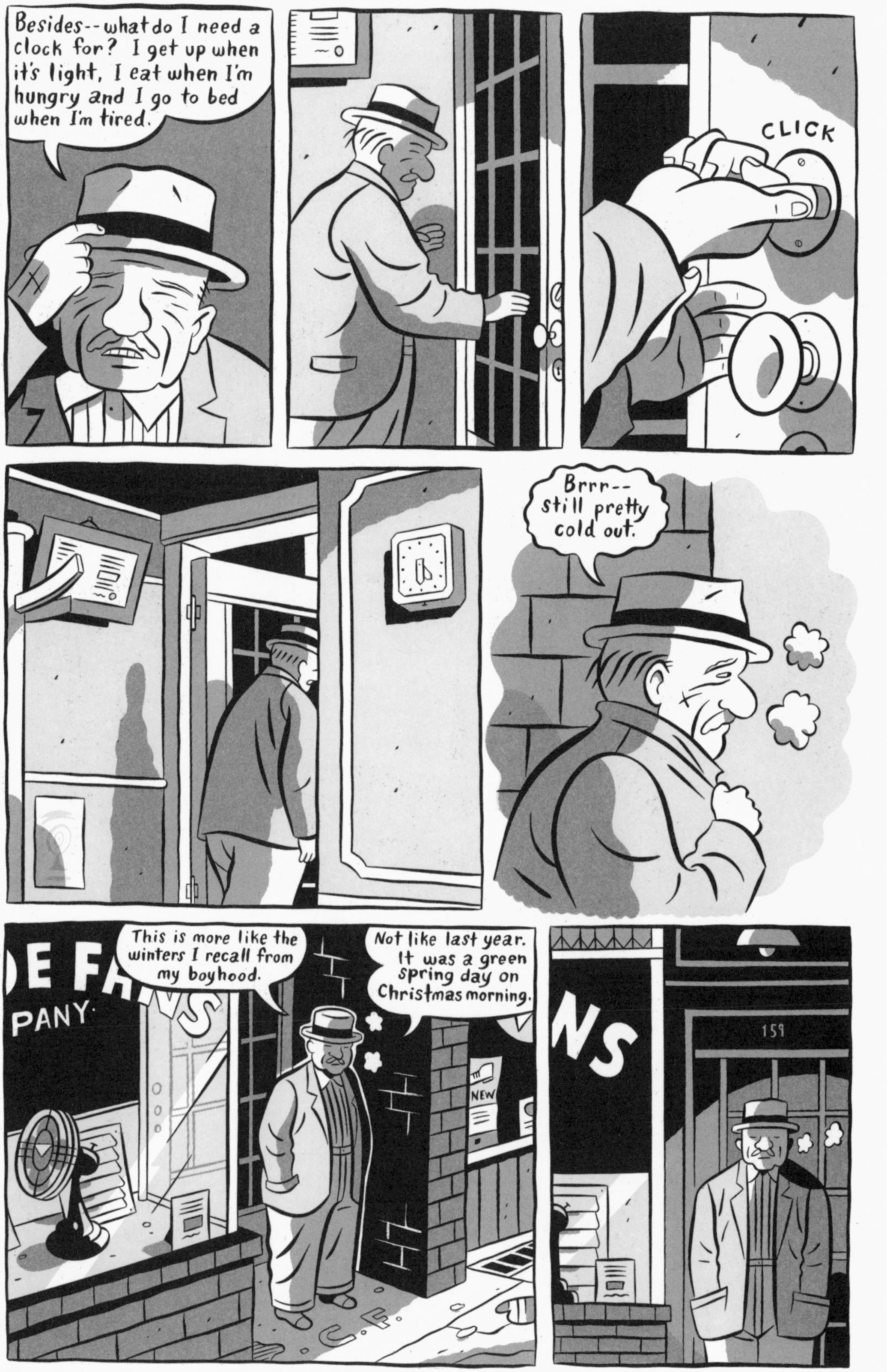
Besides--what do I need a clock for? I get up when it's light, I eat when I'm hungry and I go to bed when I'm tired.
CLICK
Brrr--still pretty cold out.
This is more like the winters I recall from my boyhood.
Not like last year. It was a green spring day on Christmas morning.
PANY
NEW
159

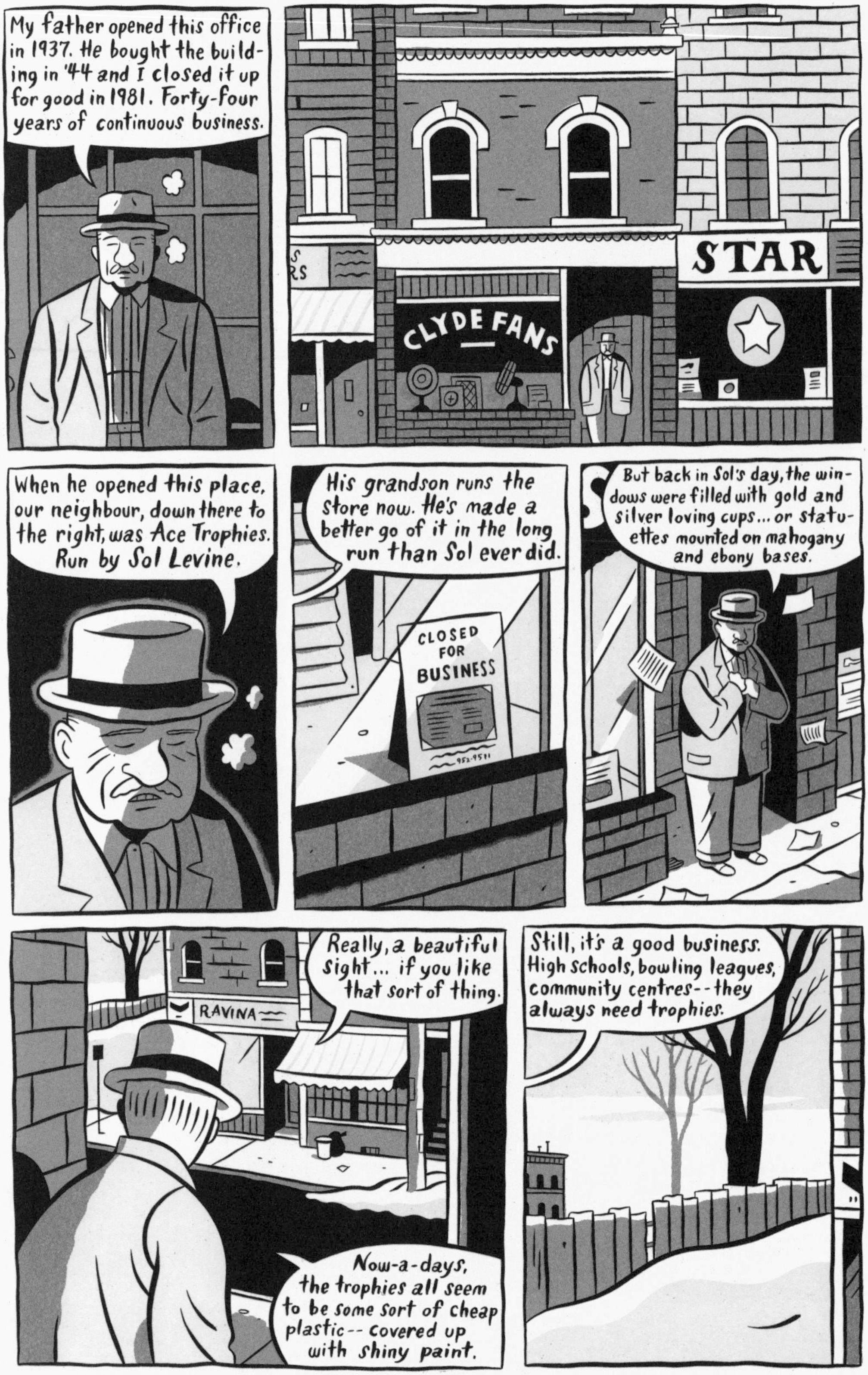
My father opened this office in 1937. He bought the building in '44 and I closed it up for good in 1981. Forty-four years of continuous business.
CLYDE FANS
STAR
When he opened this place, our neighbour, down there to the right, was Ace Trophies. Run by Sol Levine.
His grandson runs the store now. He's made a better go of it in the long run than Sol ever did.
CLOSED FOR BUSINESS
But back in Sol's day, the windows were filled with gold and silver loving cups... or statuettes mounted on mahogany and ebony bases.
RAVINA
Really, a beautiful sight... if you like that sort of thing.
Now-a-days, the trophies all seem to be some sort of cheap plastic-- covered up with shiny paint.
Still, it's a good business. High schools, bowling leagues, community centres--they always need trophies.

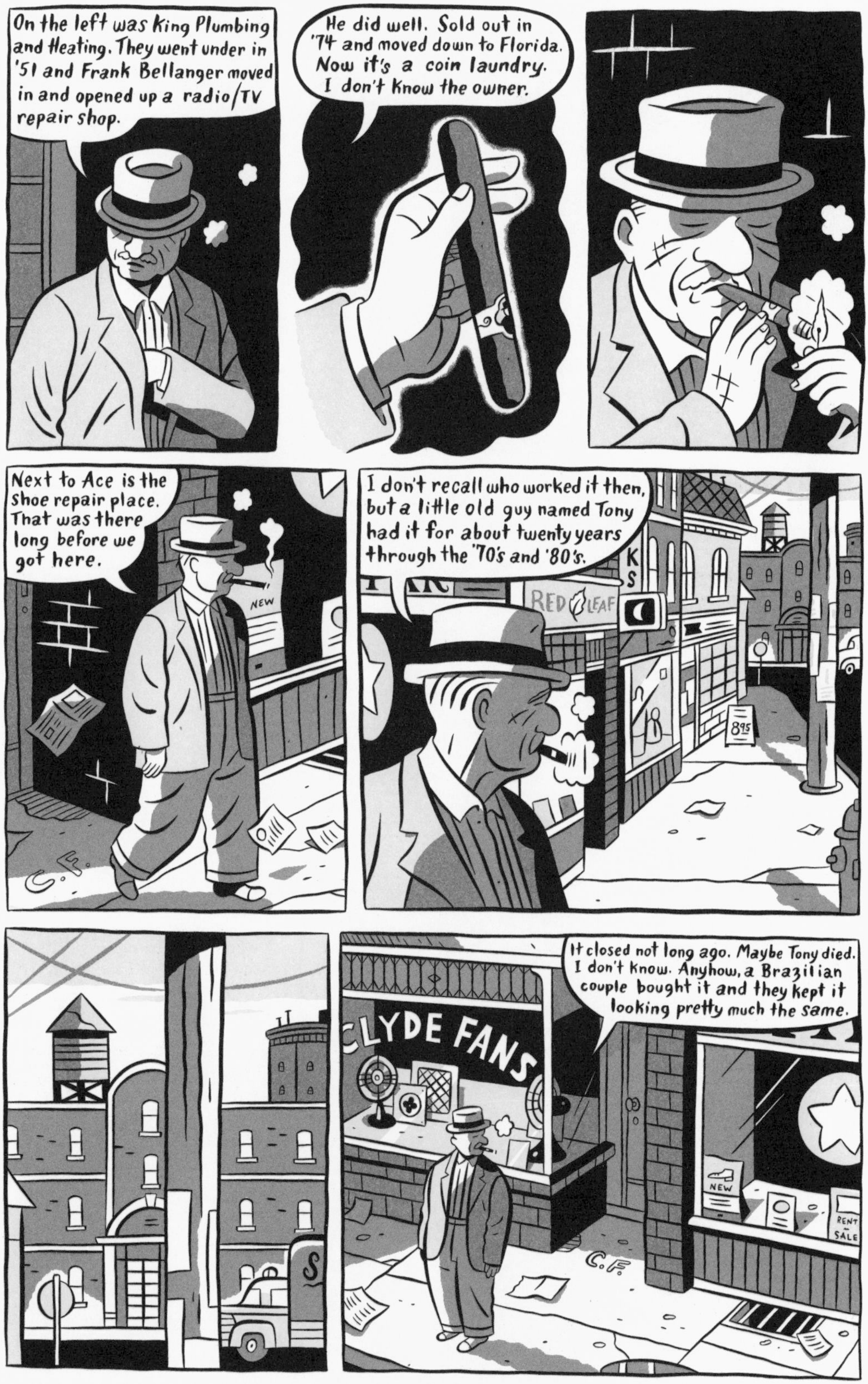
On the left was King Plumbing and Heating. They went under in '51 and Frank Bellanger moved in and opened up a radio/TV repair shop.
He did well. Sold out in '74 and moved down to Florida. Now it's a coin laundry. I don't know the owner.
Next to Ace is the shoe repair place. That was there long before we got here.
NEW
I don't recall who worked it then, but a little old guy named Tony had it for about twenty years through the '70's and '80's.
RED LEAF
8.95
CLYDE FANS
It closed not long ago. Maybe Tony died. I don't know. Anyhow, a Brazilian couple bought it and they kept it looking pretty much the same.
NEW
RENT
SALE

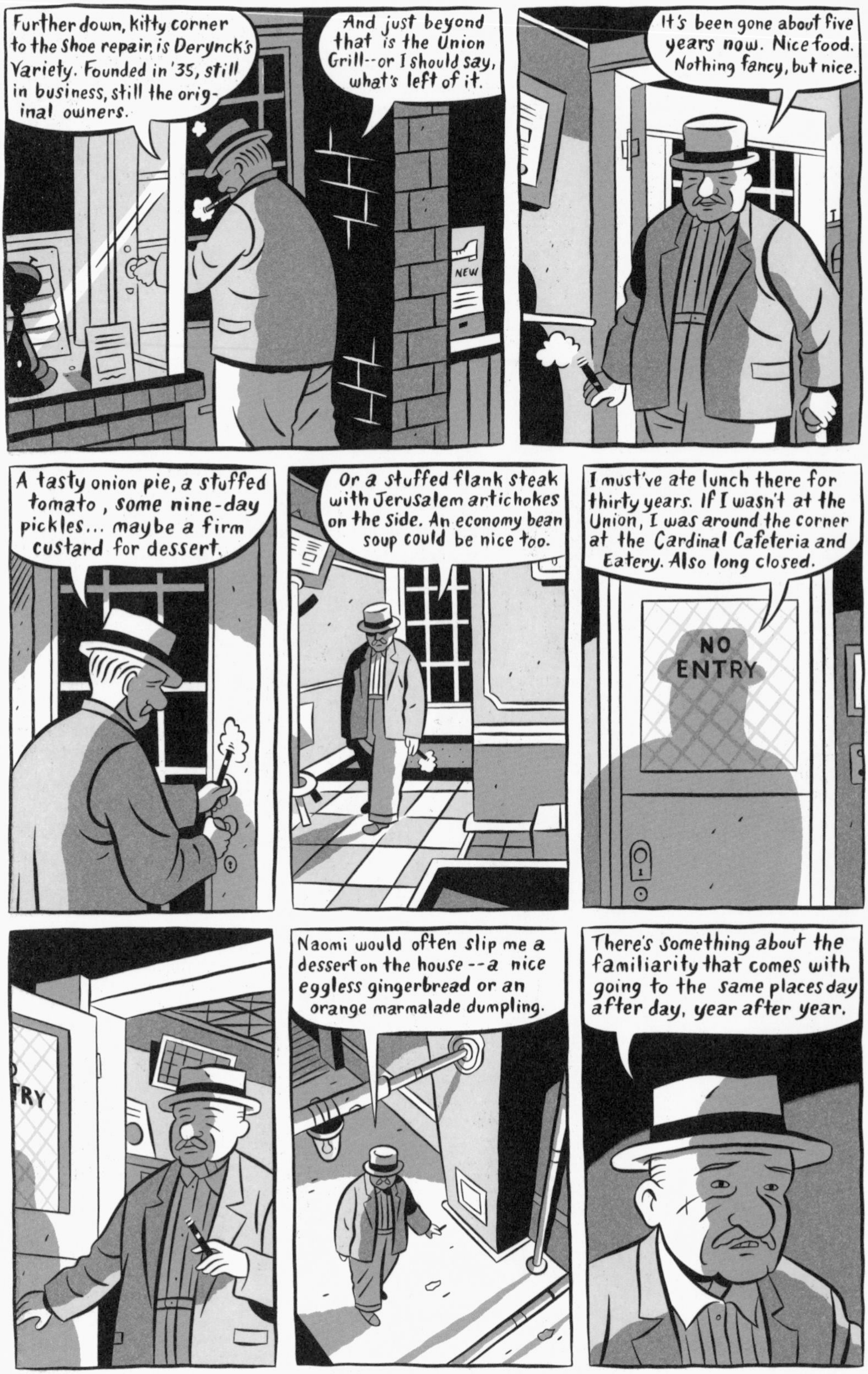
Further down, kitty corner to the shoe repair, is Derynck's Variety. Founded in '35, still in business, still the original owners.
And just beyond that is the Union Grill--or I should say, what's left of it.
NEW
It's been gone about five years now. Nice food. Nothing fancy, but nice.
A tasty onion pie, a stuffed tomato, some nine-day pickles... maybe a firm custard for dessert.
Or a stuffed flank steak with Jerusalem artichokes on the side. An economy bean soup could be nice too.
I must've ate lunch there for thirty years. If I wasn't at the Union, I was around the corner at the Cardinal Cafeteria and Eatery. Also long closed.
NO ENTRY
TRY
Naomi would often slip me a dessert on the house--a nice eggless gingerbread or an orange marmalade dumpling.
There's something about the familiarity that comes with going to the same places day after day, year after year.

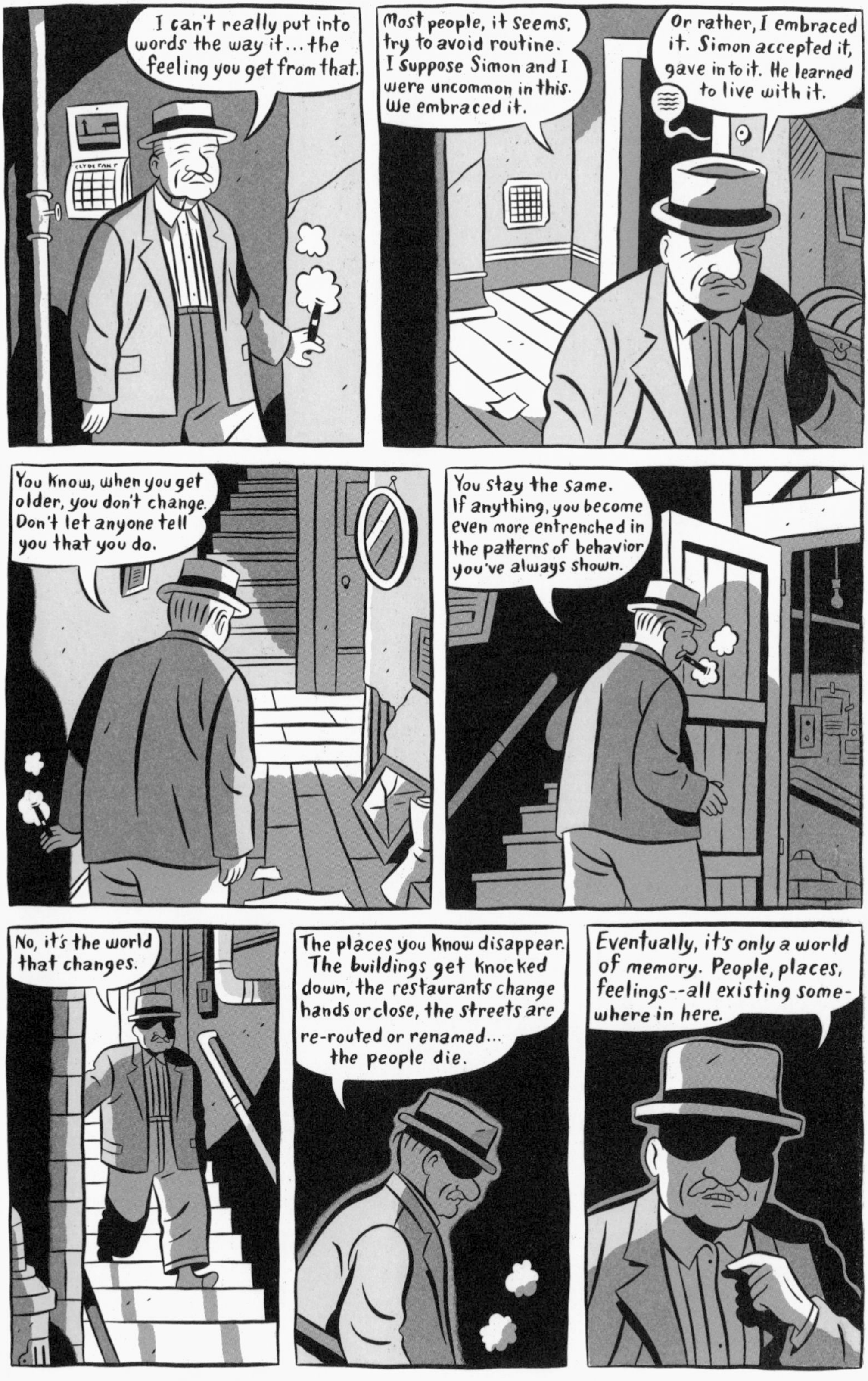
I can't really put into words the way it... the feeling you get from that.
Most people, it seems, try to avoid routine. I suppose Simon and I were uncommon in this. We embraced it.
Or rather, I embraced it. Simon accepted it, gave in to it. He learned to live with it.
You know, when you get older, you don't change. Don't let anyone tell you that you do.
You stay the same. If anything, you become even more entrenched in the patterns of behavior you've always shown.
No, it's the world that changes.
The places you know disappear. The buildings get knocked down, the restaurants change hands or close, the streets are re-routed or renamed... the people die.
Eventually, it's only a world of memory. People, places, feelings--all existing somewhere in here.

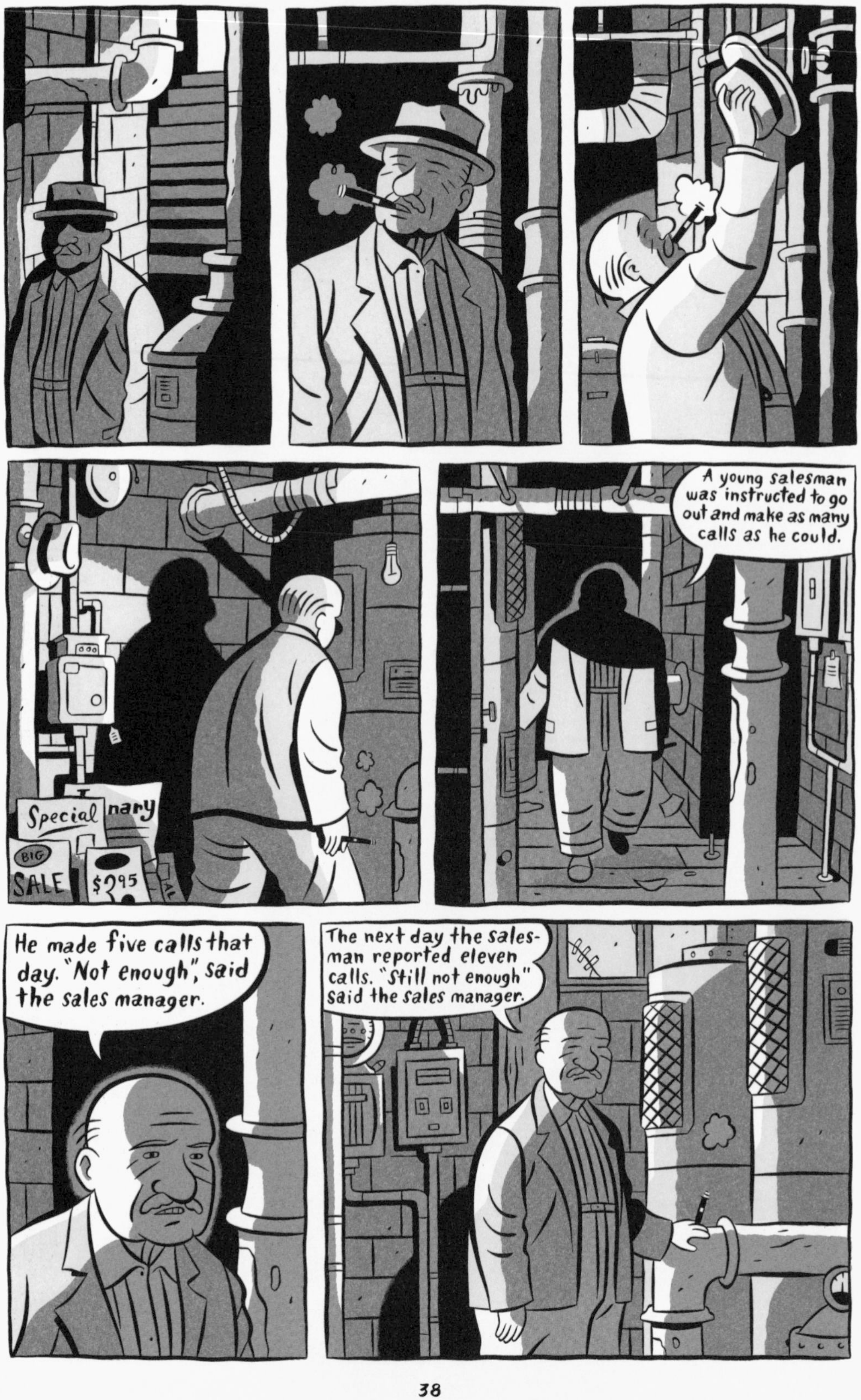
A young salesman was instructed to go out and make as many calls as he could.
Special
nary
BIG
SALE
$2.95
He made five calls that day. "Not enough", said the sales manager.
The next day the salesman reported eleven calls. "Still not enough" said the sales manager.

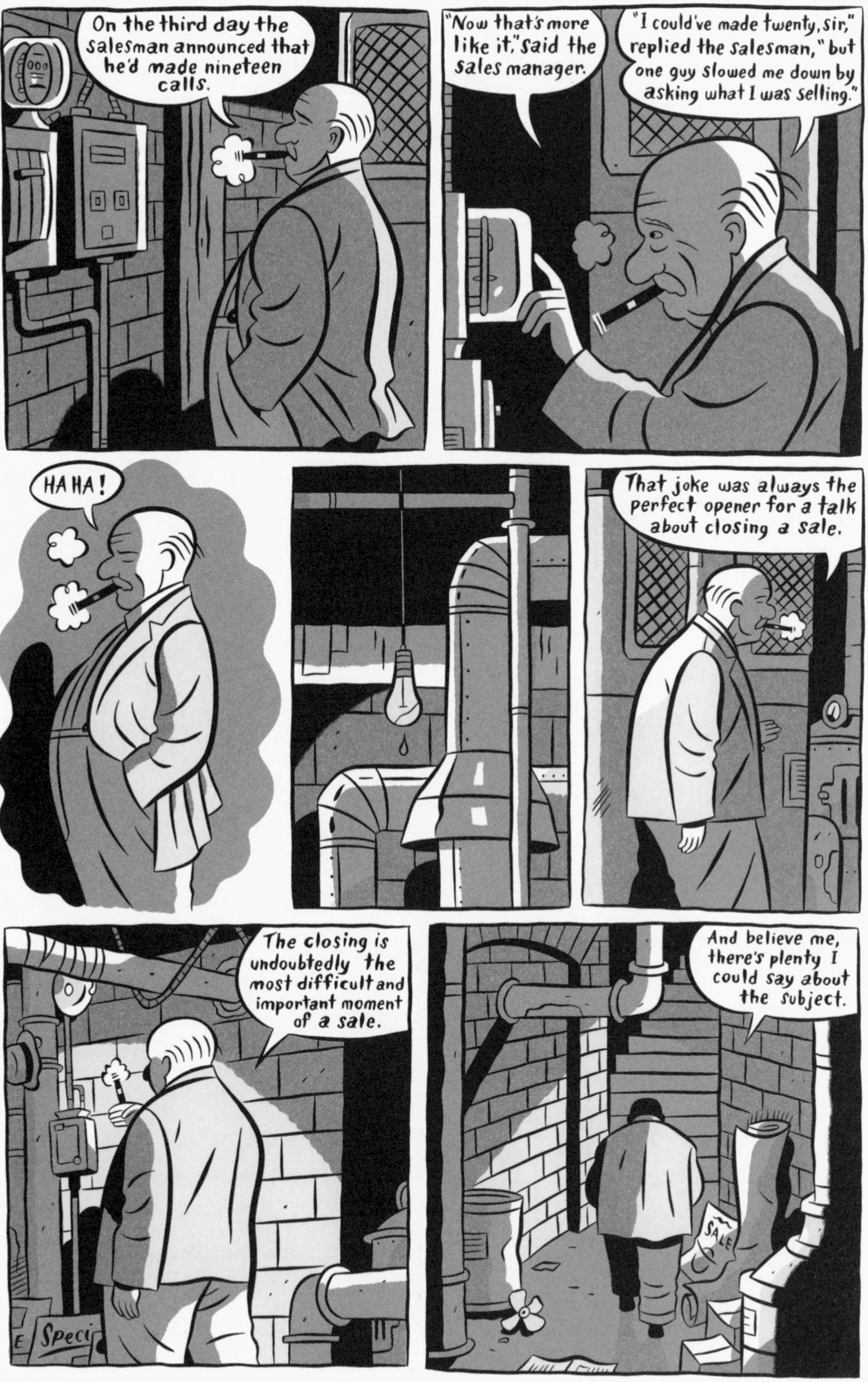
On the third day the salesman announced that he'd made nineteen calls.
"Now that's more like it," said the sales manager.
"I could've made twenty, sir," replied the salesman, "but one guy slowed me down by asking what I was selling."
HA HA!
That joke was always the perfect opener for a talk about closing a sale.
The closing is undoubtedly the most difficult and important moment of a sale.
E
Speci
And believe me, there's plenty I could say about the subject.
SALE

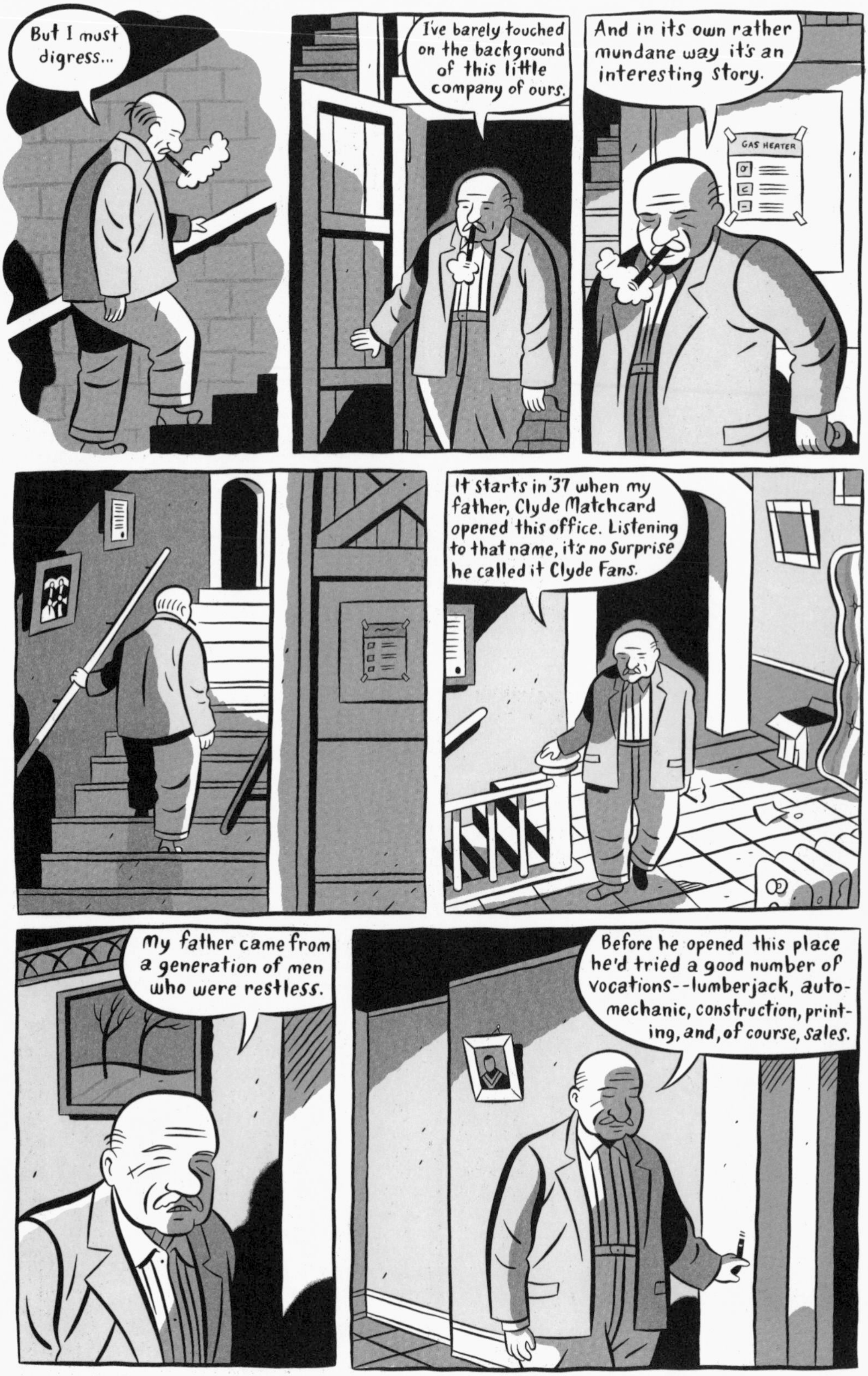
But I must digress...
I've barely touched on the background of this little company of ours.
And in its own rather mundane way it's an interesting story.
GAS HEATER
It starts in '37 when my father, Clyde Matchcard opened this office. Listening to that name, it's no surprise he called it Clyde Fans.
My father came from a generation of men who were restless.
Before he opened this place he'd tried a good number of vocations--lumberjack, auto-mechanic, construction, printing, and, of course, sales.

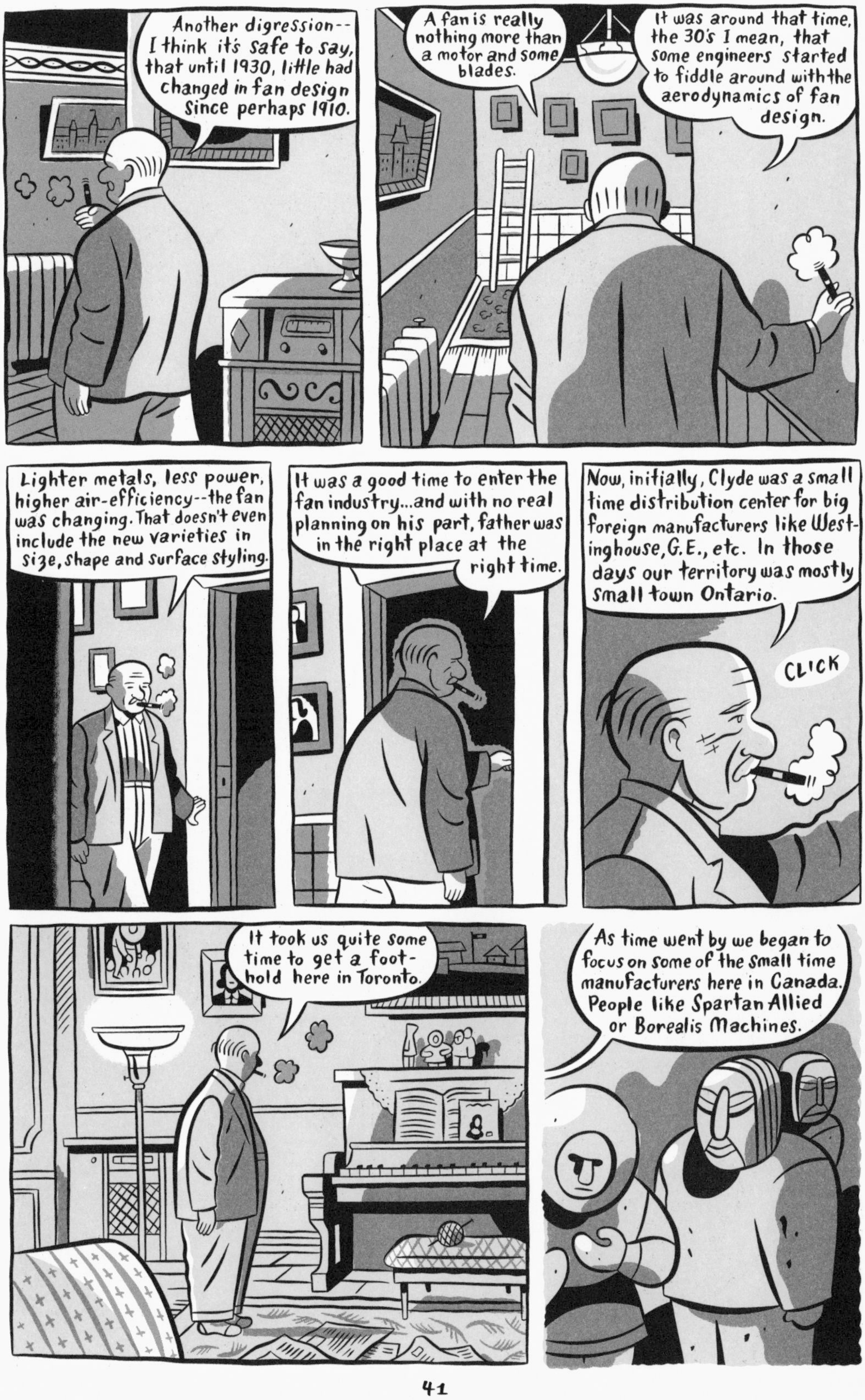
Another digression-- I think it's safe to say, that until 1930, little had changed in fan design since perhaps 1910.
A fan is really nothing more than a motor and some blades.
It was around that time, the 30's I mean, that some engineers started to fiddle around with the aerodynamics of fan design.
Lighter metals, less power, higher air-efficiency--the fan was changing. That doesn't even include the new varieties in size, shape and surface styling.
It was a good time to enter the fan industry...and with no real planning on his part, father was in the right place at the right time.
Now, initially, Clyde was a small time distribution center for big foreign manufacturers like Westinghouse, G.E., etc. In those days our territory was mostly small town Ontario.
CLICK
It took us quite some time to get a foothold here in Toronto.
As time went by we began to focus on some of the small time manufacturers here in Canada. People like Spartan Allied or Borealis Machines.

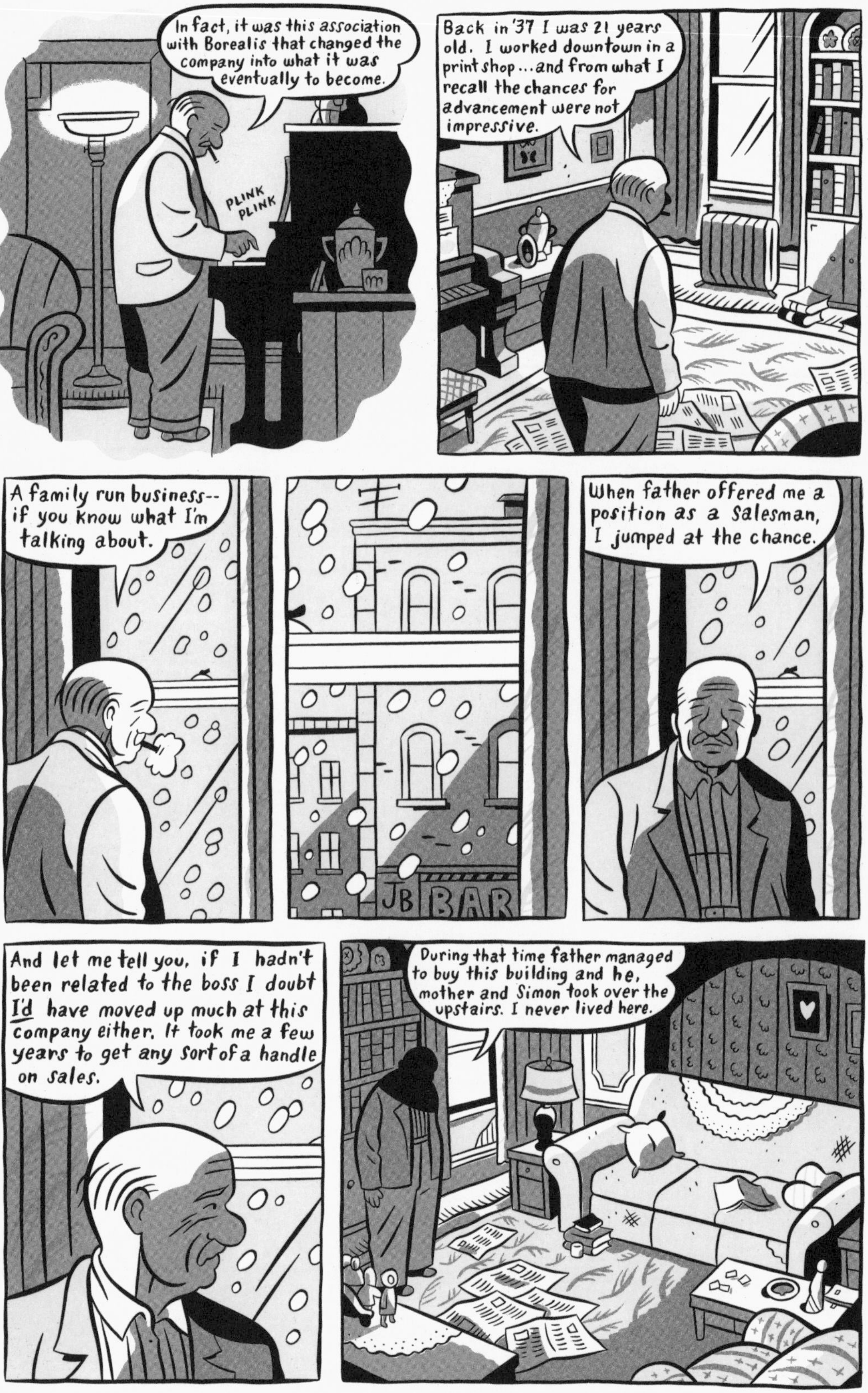
In fact, it was this association with Borealis that changed the company into what it was eventually to become.
PLINK PLINK
Back in '37 I was 21 years old. I worked downtown in a print shop... and from what I recall the chances for advancement were not impressive.
A family run business-- if you know what I'm talking about.
JB BAR
When father offered me a position as a salesman, I jumped at the chance.
And let me tell you, if I hadn't been related to the boss I doubt I'd have moved up much at this company either. It took me a few years to get any sort of a handle on sales.
During that time father managed to buy this building and he, mother and Simon took over the upstairs. I never lived here.

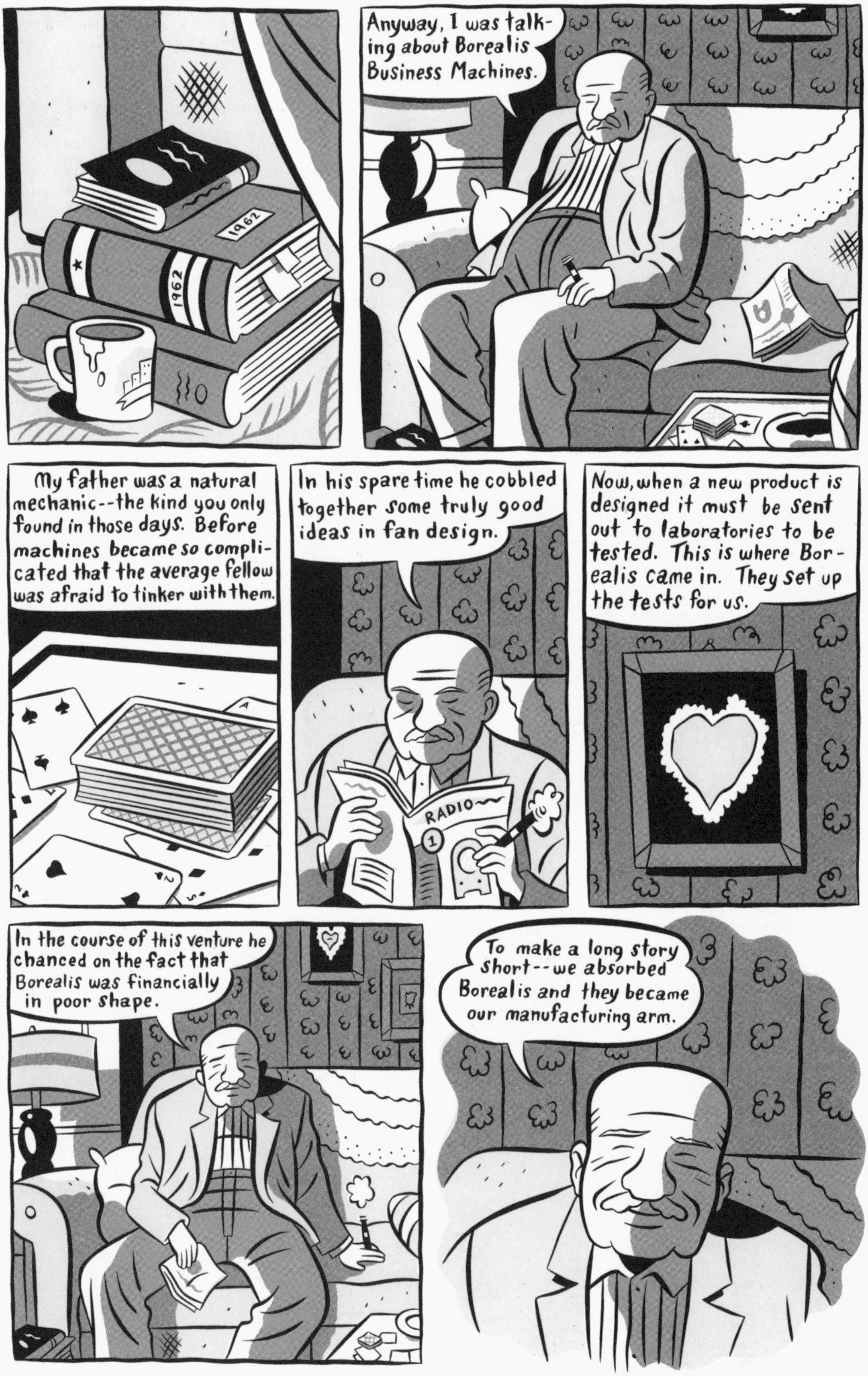
1962
1962
Anyway, I was talking about Borealis Business Machines.
My father was a natural mechanic--the kind you only found in those days. Before machines became so complicated that the average fellow was afraid to tinker with them.
In his spare time he cobbled together some truly good ideas in fan design.
RADIO
Now, when a new product is designed it must be sent out to laboratories to be tested. This is where Borealis came in. They set up the tests for us.
In the course of this venture he chanced on the fact that Borealis was financially in poor shape.
To make a long story short--we absorbed Borealis and they became our manufacturing arm.

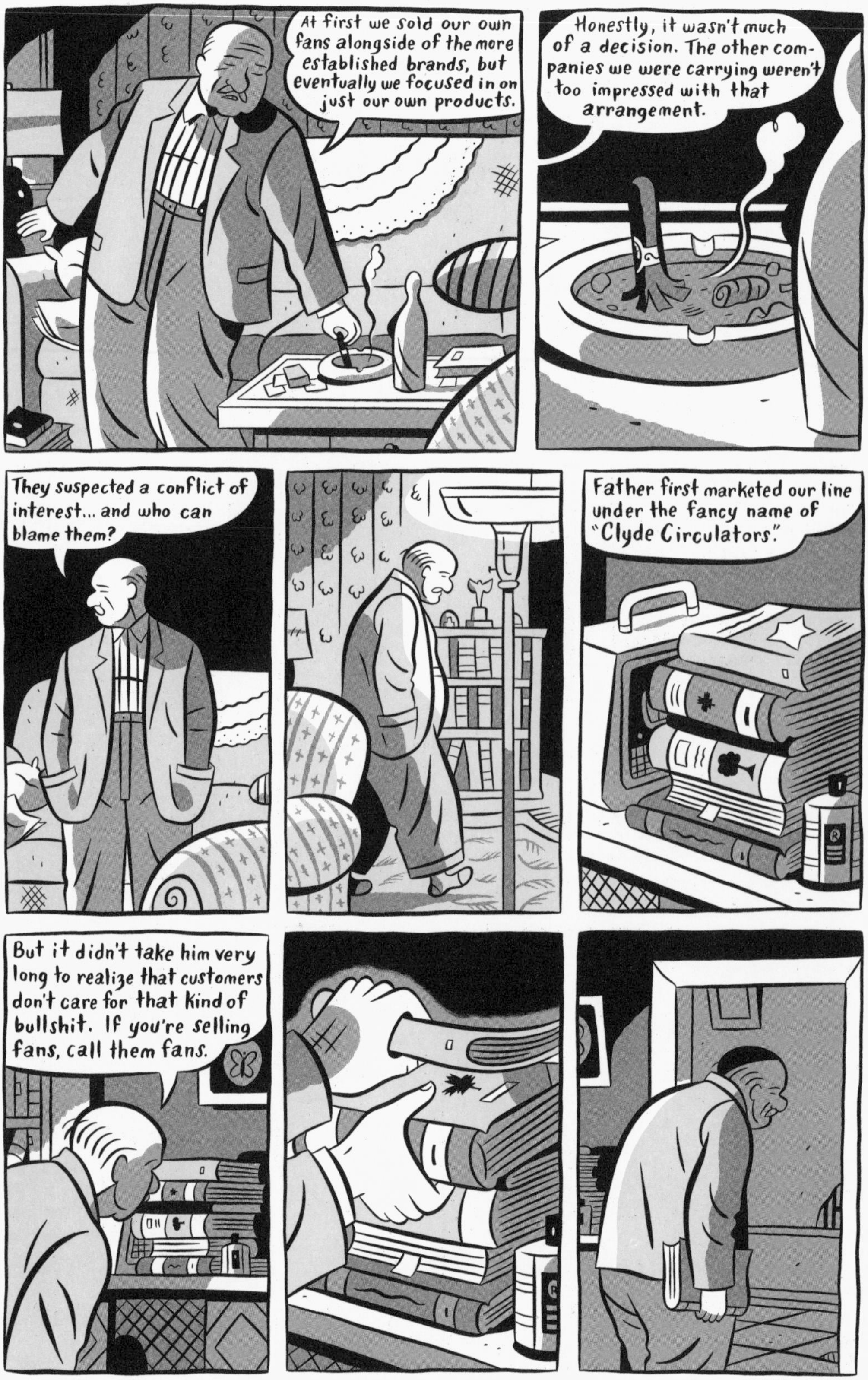
At first we sold our own fans alongside of the more established brands, but eventually we focused in on just our own products.
Honestly, it wasn't much of a decision. The other companies we were carrying weren't too impressed with that arrangement.
They suspected a conflict of interest... and who can blame them?
Father first marketed our line under the fancy name of "Clyde Circulators."
But it didn't take him very long to realize that customers don't care for that kind of bullshit. If you're selling fans, call them fans.

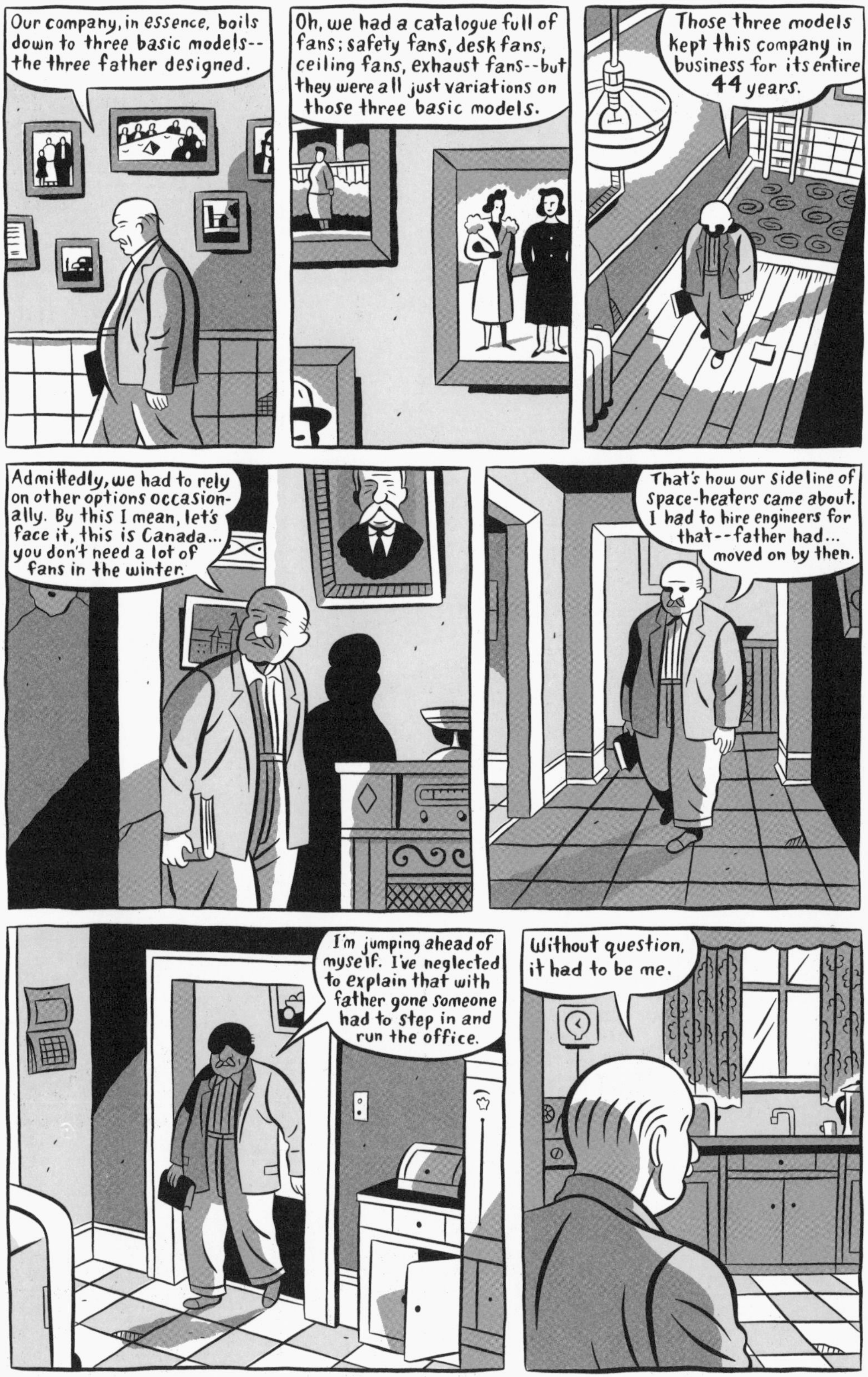
Our company, in essence, boils down to three basic models--the three father designed.
Oh, we had a catalogue full of fans; safety fans, desk fans, ceiling fans, exhaust fans--but they were all just variations on those three basic models.
Those three models kept this company in business for its entire 44 years.
Admittedly, we had to rely on other options occasionally. By this I mean, let's face it, this is Canada... you don't need a lot of fans in the winter.
That's how our sideline of space-heaters came about. I had to hire engineers for that--father had... moved on by then.
I'm jumping ahead of myself. I've neglected to explain that with father gone someone had to step in and run the office.
Without question, it had to be me.

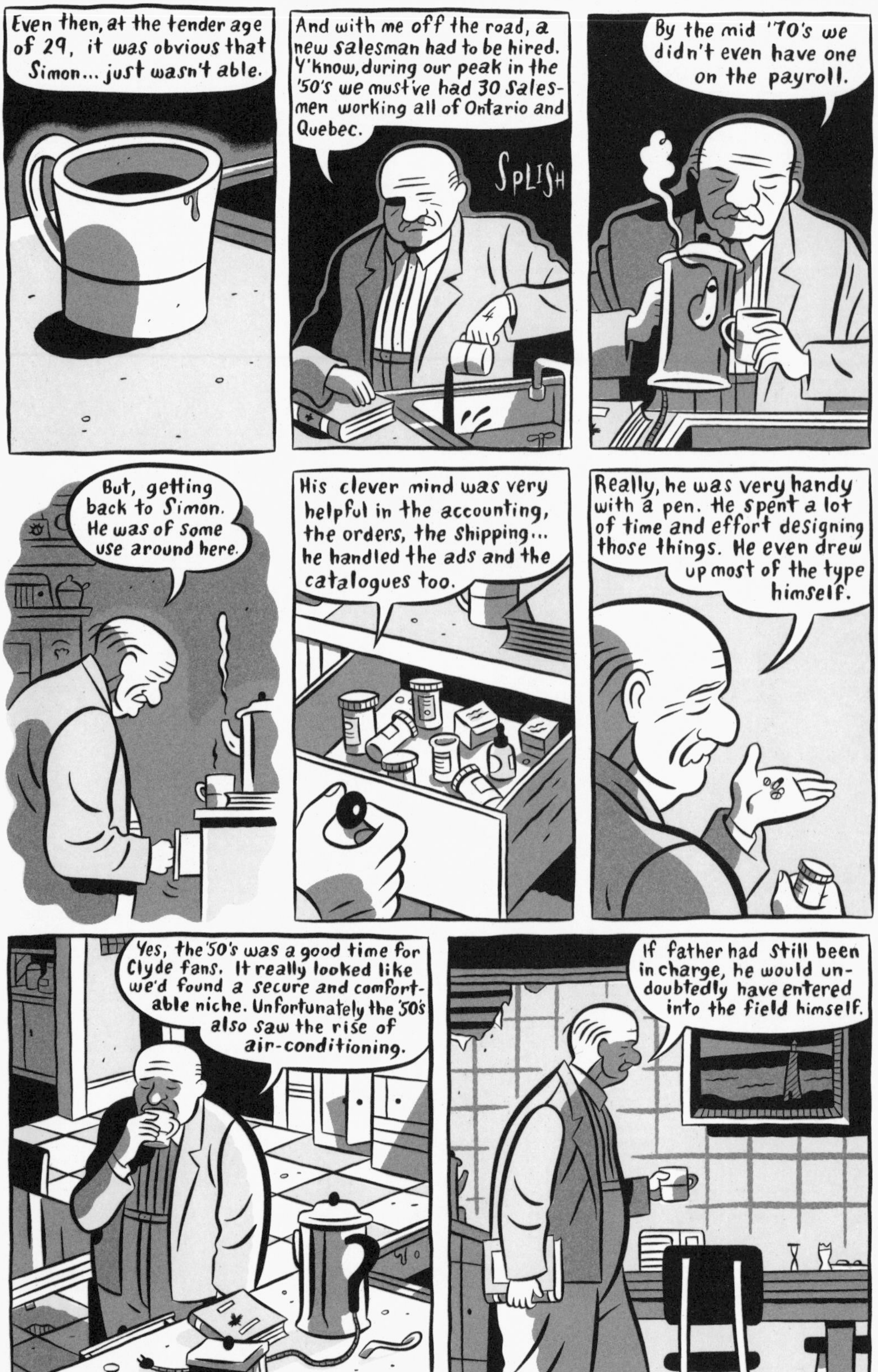
Even then, at the tender age of 29, it was obvious that Simon... just wasn't able.
And with me off the road, a new salesman had to be hired. Y'know, during our peak in the '50's we must've had 30 Salesmen working all of Ontario and Quebec.
SPLISH
By the mid '70's we didn't even have one on the payroll.
But, getting back to Simon. He was of some use around here.
His clever mind was very helpful in the accounting, the orders, the shipping... he handled the ads and the catalogues too.
Really, he was very handy with a pen. He spent a lot of time and effort designing those things. He even drew up most of the type himself.
Yes, the '50's was a good time for Clyde fans. It really looked like we'd found a secure and comfortable niche. Unfortunately the '50's also saw the rise of air-conditioning.
If father had still been in charge, he would undoubtedly have entered into the field himself.

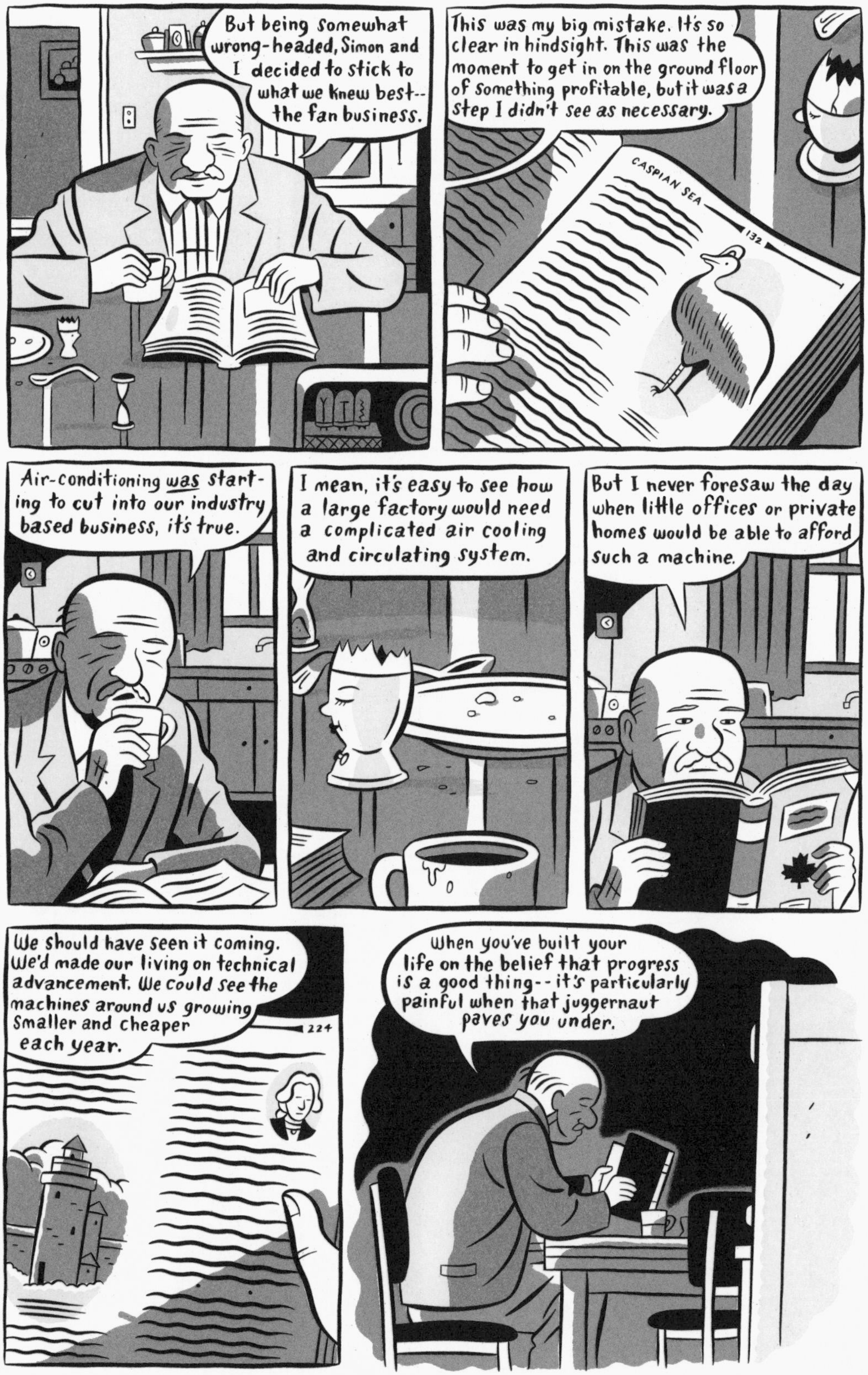
But being somewhat wrong-headed, Simon and I decided to stick to what we knew best-- the fan business.
This was my big mistake. It's so clear in hindsight. This was the moment to get in on the ground floor of something profitable, but it was a step I didn't see as necessary.
CASPIAN SEA
132
Air-conditioning was starting to cut into our industry based business, it's true.
I mean, it's easy to see how a large factory would need a complicated air cooling and circulating system.
But I never foresaw the day when little offices or private homes would be able to afford such a machine.
We should have seen it coming. We'd made our living on technical advancement. We could see the machines around us growing smaller and cheaper each year.
224
When you've built your life on the belief that progress is a good thing-- it's particularly painful when that juggernaut paves you under.

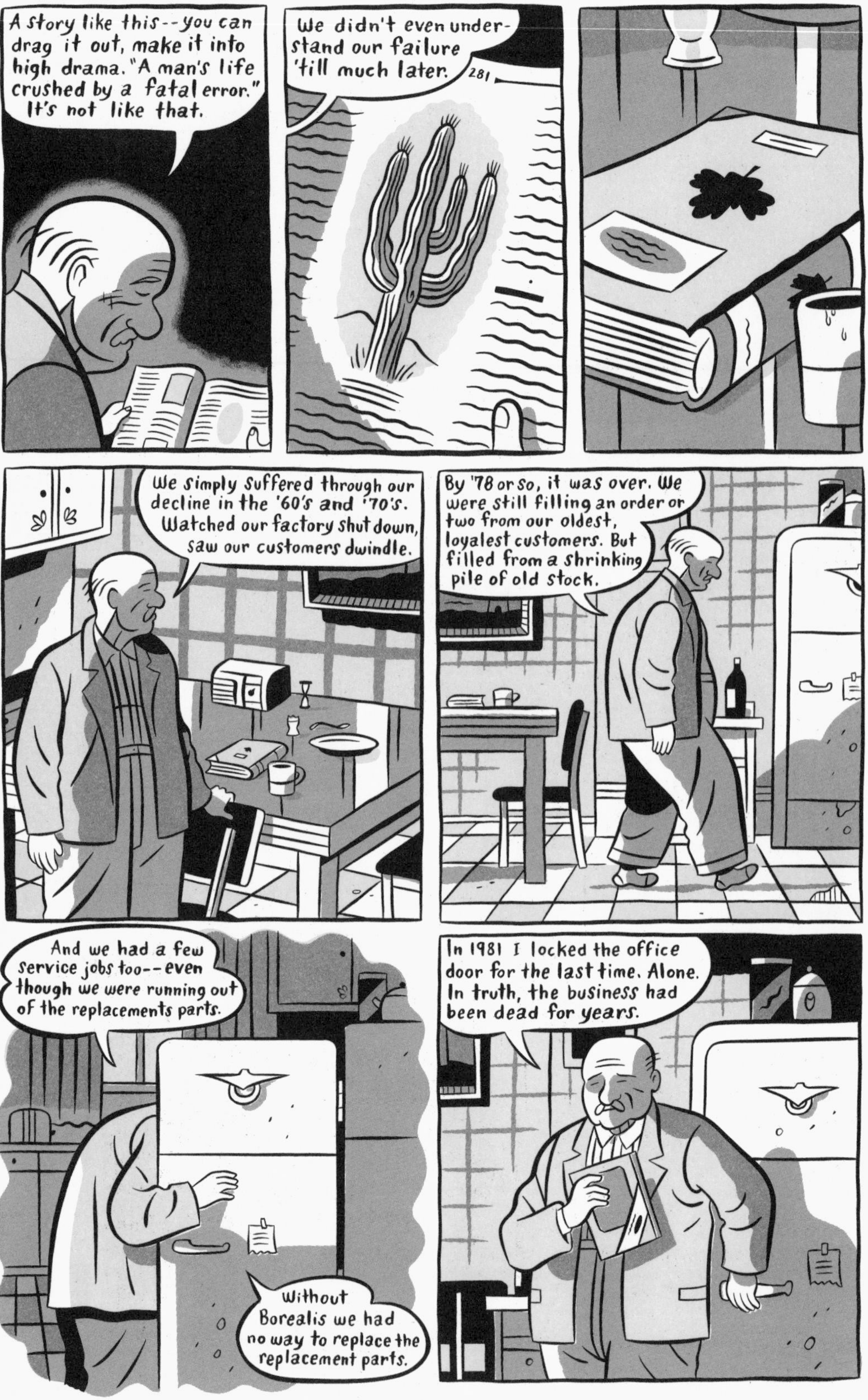
A story like this--you can drag it out, make it into high drama. "A man's life crushed by a fatal error." It's not like that.
We didn't even understand our failure 'till much later.
281
We simply suffered through our decline in the '60's and '70's. Watched our factory shut down, saw our customers dwindle.
By '78 or so, it was over. We were still filling an order or two from our oldest, loyalest customers. But filled from a shrinking pile of old stock.
And we had a few service jobs too--even though we were running out of the replacements parts.
Without Borealis we had no way to replace the replacement parts.
In 1981 I locked the office door for the last time. Alone. In truth, the business had been dead for years.

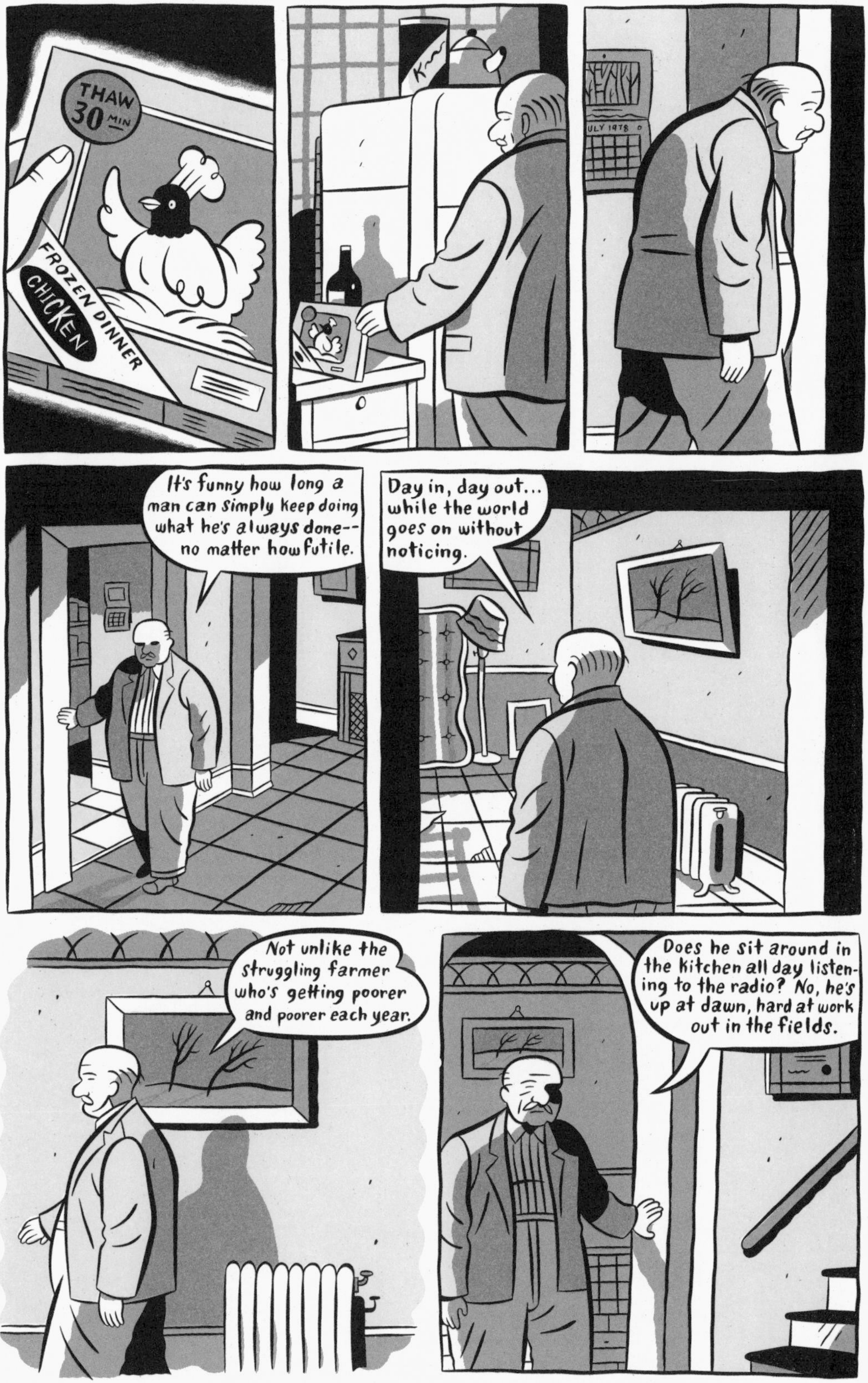
THAW 30 MIN
FROZEN DINNER
CHICKEN
JULY 1978
It's funny how long a man can simply keep doing what he's always done-- no matter how futile.
Day in, day out... while the world goes on without noticing.
Not unlike the struggling farmer who's getting poorer and poorer each year.
Does he sit around in the kitchen all day listening to the radio? No, he's up at dawn, hard at work out in the fields.

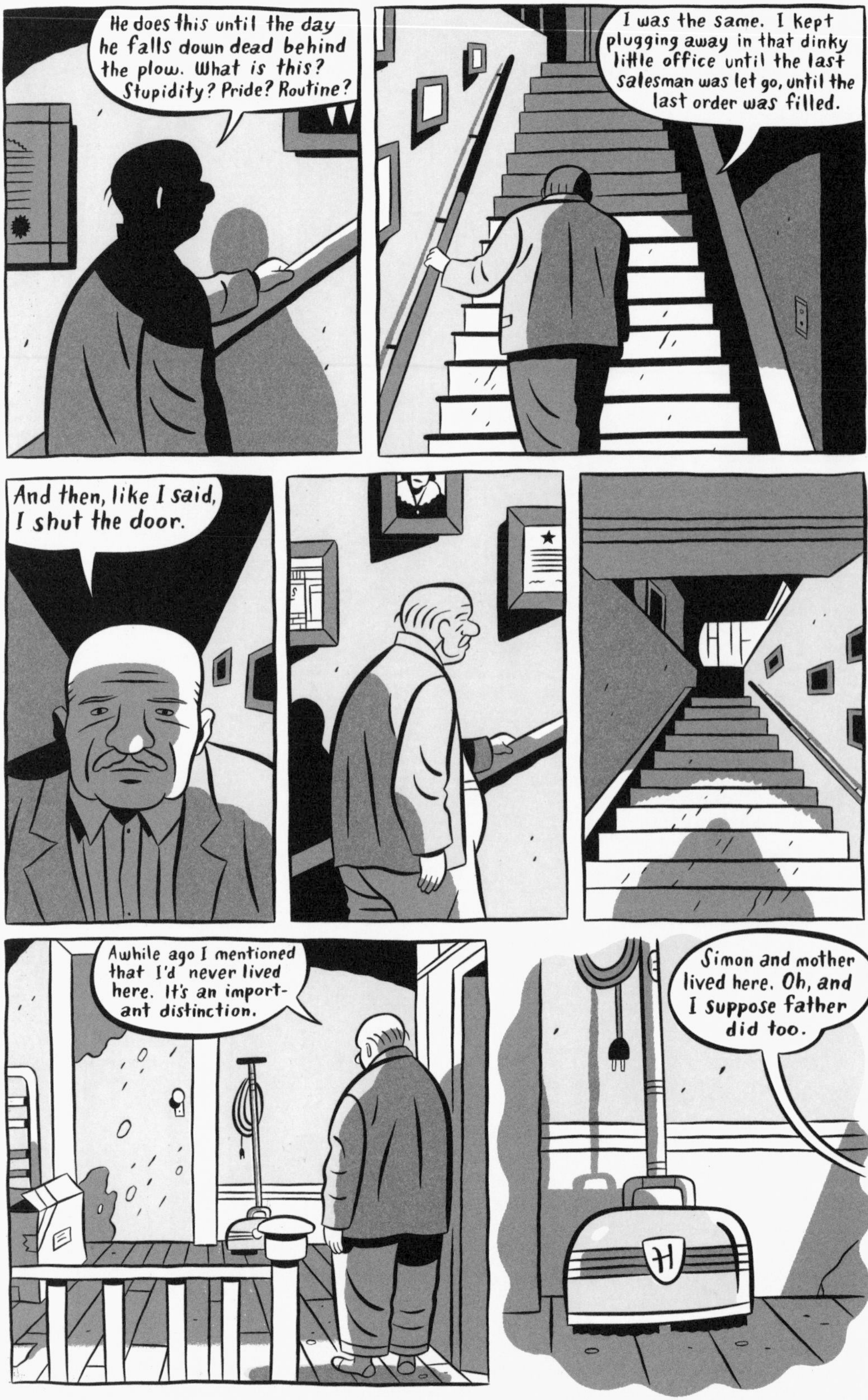

He does this until the day he falls down dead behind the plow. What is this? Stupidity? Pride? Routine?
I was the same. I kept plugging away in that dinky little office until the last salesman was let go, until the last order was filled.
And then, like I said, I shut the door.
Awhile ago I mentioned that I'd never lived here. It's an important distinction.
Simon and mother lived here. Oh, and I suppose father did too.

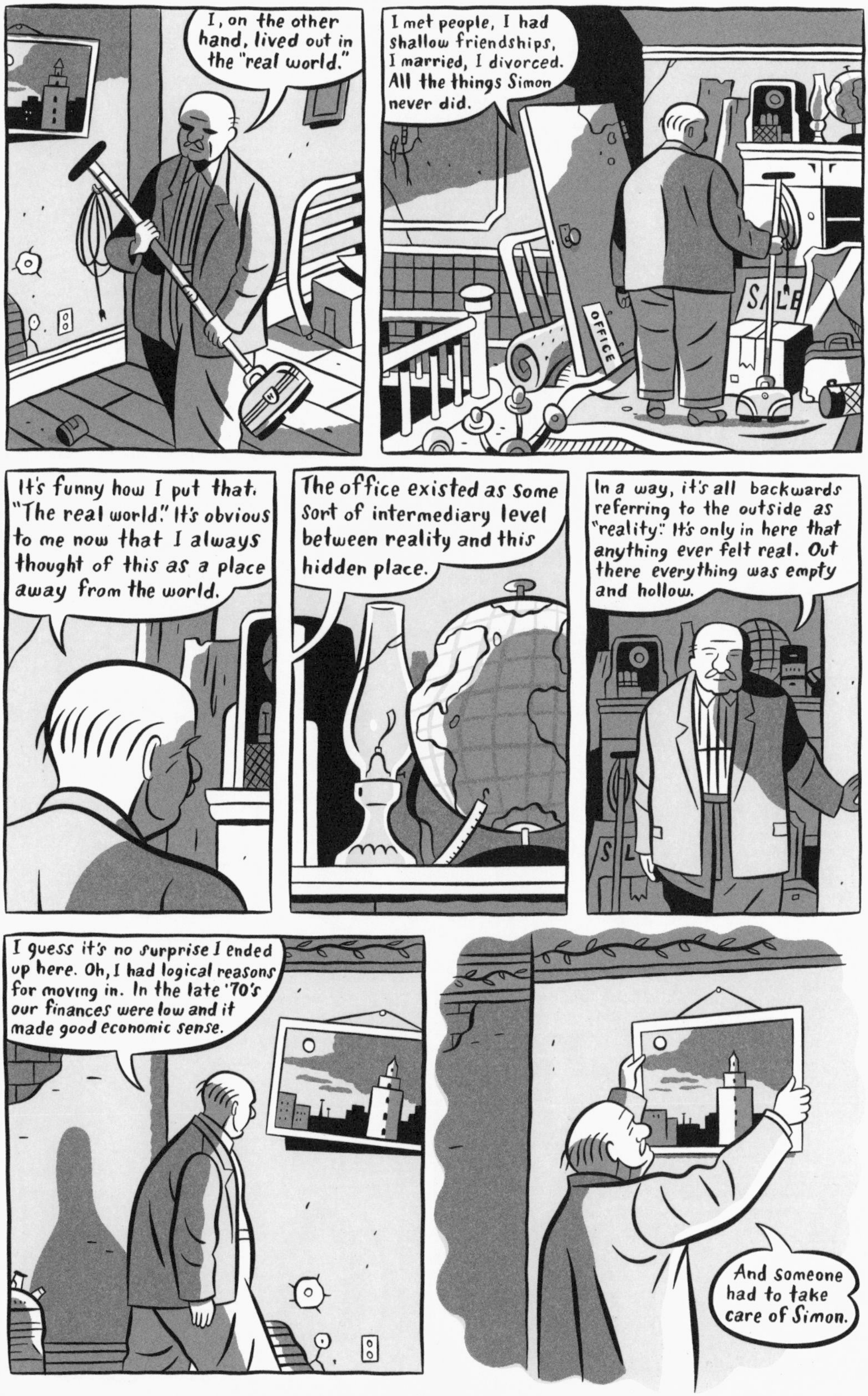
I, on the other hand, lived out in the "real world."
I met people, I had shallow friendships, I married, I divorced. All the things Simon never did.
OFFICE
SALE
It's funny how I put that. "The real world." It's obvious to me now that I always thought of this as a place away from the world.
The office existed as some sort of intermediary level between reality and this hidden place.
In a way, it's all backwards referring to the outside as "reality." It's only in here that anything ever felt real. Out there everything was empty and hollow.
I guess it's no surprise I ended up here. Oh, I had logical reasons for moving in. In the late '70's our finances were low and it made good economic sense.
And someone had to take care of Simon.

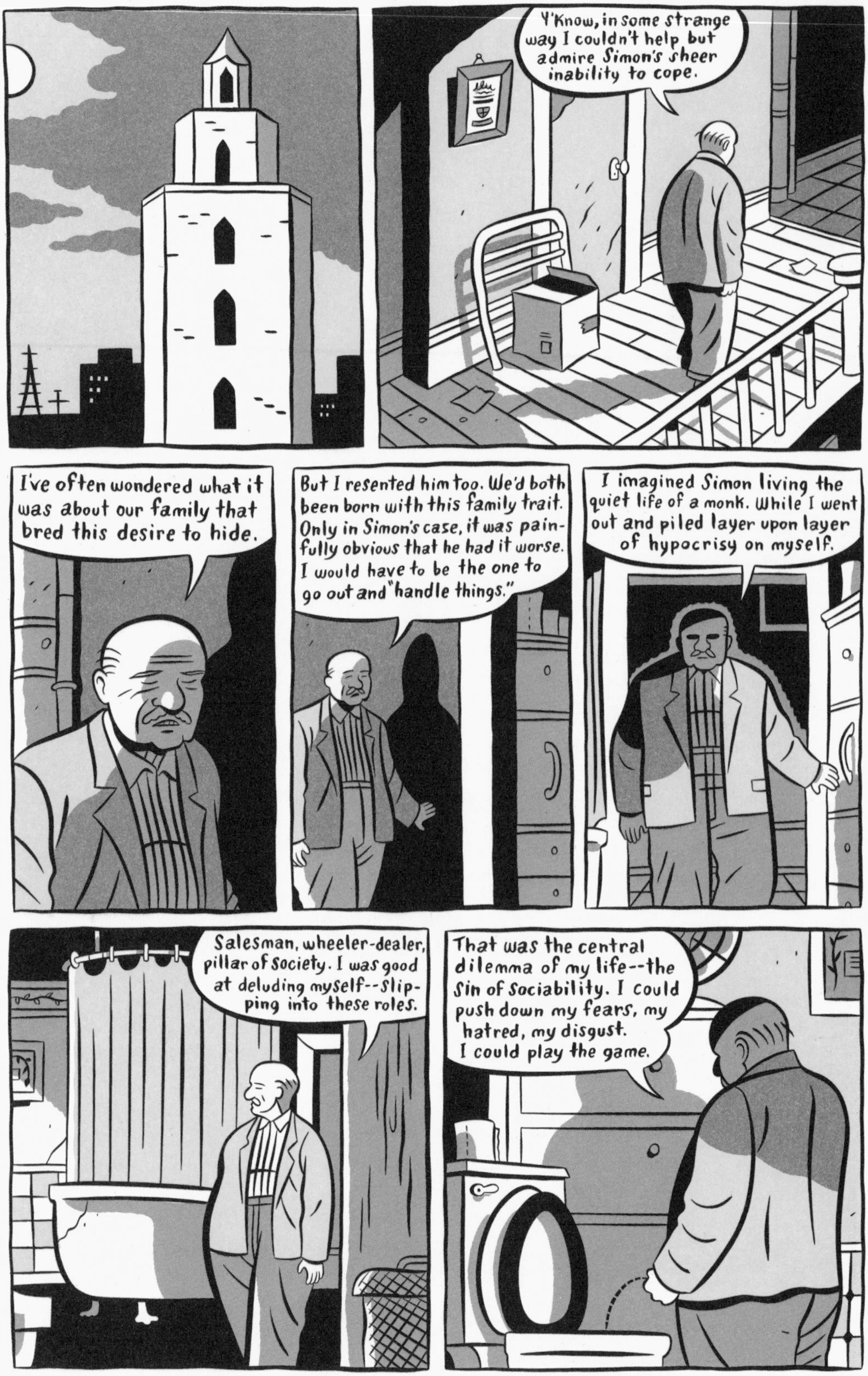

Y'Know, in some strange way I couldn't help but admire Simon's sheer inability to cope.
I've often wondered what it was about our family that bred this desire to hide.
But I resented him too. We'd both been born with this family trait. Only in Simon's case, it was painfully obvious that he had it worse. I would have to be the one to go out and "handle things."
I imagined Simon living the quiet life of a monk. While I went out and piled layer upon layer of hypocrisy on myself.
Salesman, wheeler-dealer, pillar of society. I was good at deluding myself--slipping into these roles.
That was the central dilemma of my life--the Sin of Sociability. I could push down my fears, my hatred, my disgust. I could play the game.

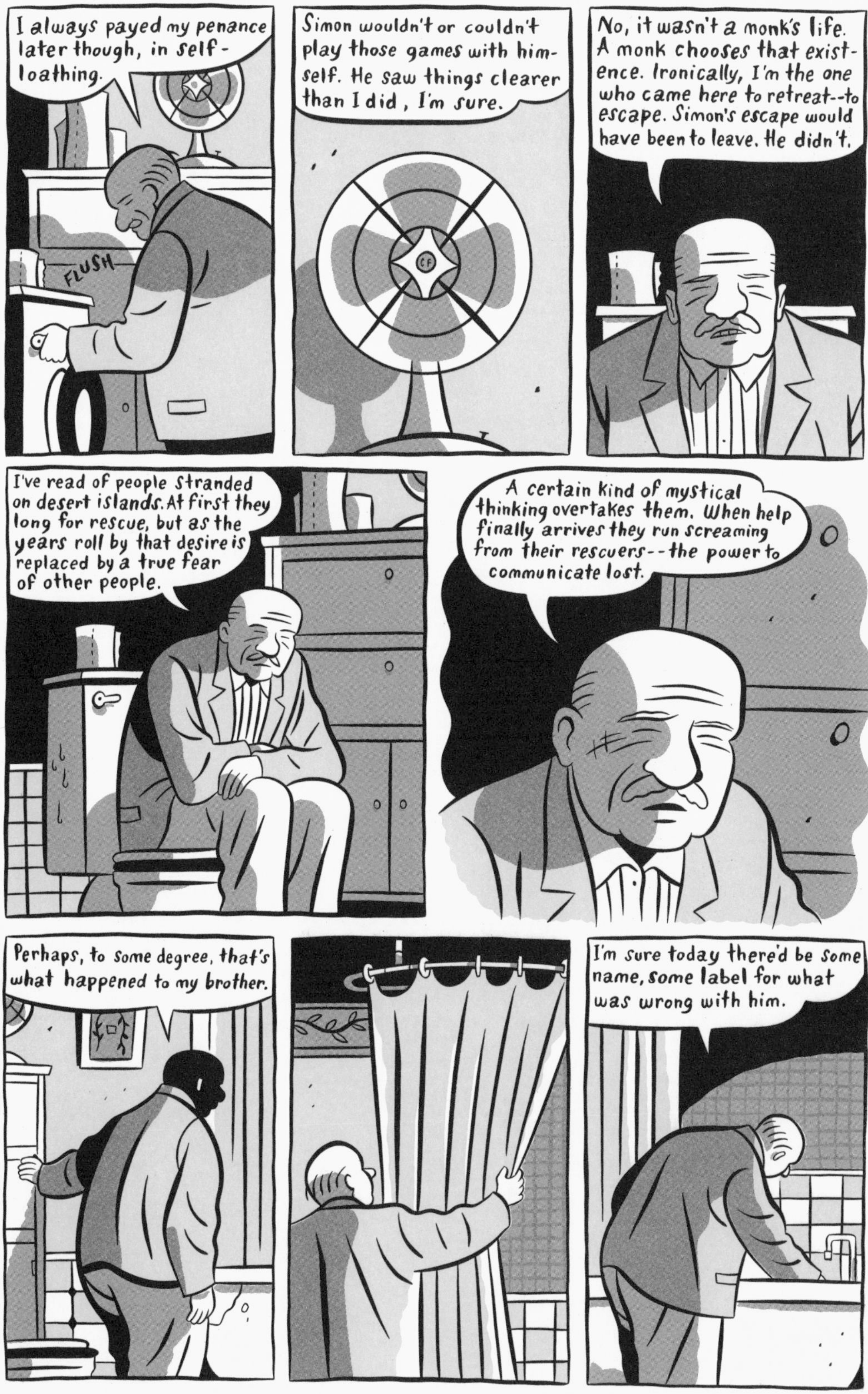
I always payed my penance later though, in self-loathing.
FLUSH
Simon wouldn't or couldn't play those games with himself. He saw things clearer than I did, I'm sure.
No, it wasn't a monk's life. A monk chooses that existence. Ironically, I'm the one who came here to retreat--to escape. Simon's escape would have been to leave. He didn't.
I've read of people stranded on desert islands. At first they long for rescue, but as the years roll by that desire is replaced by a true fear of other people.
A certain kind of mystical thinking overtakes them. When help finally arrives they run screaming from their rescuers--the power to communicate lost.
Perhaps, to some degree, that's what happened to my brother.
I'm sure today there'd be some name, some label for what was wrong with him.

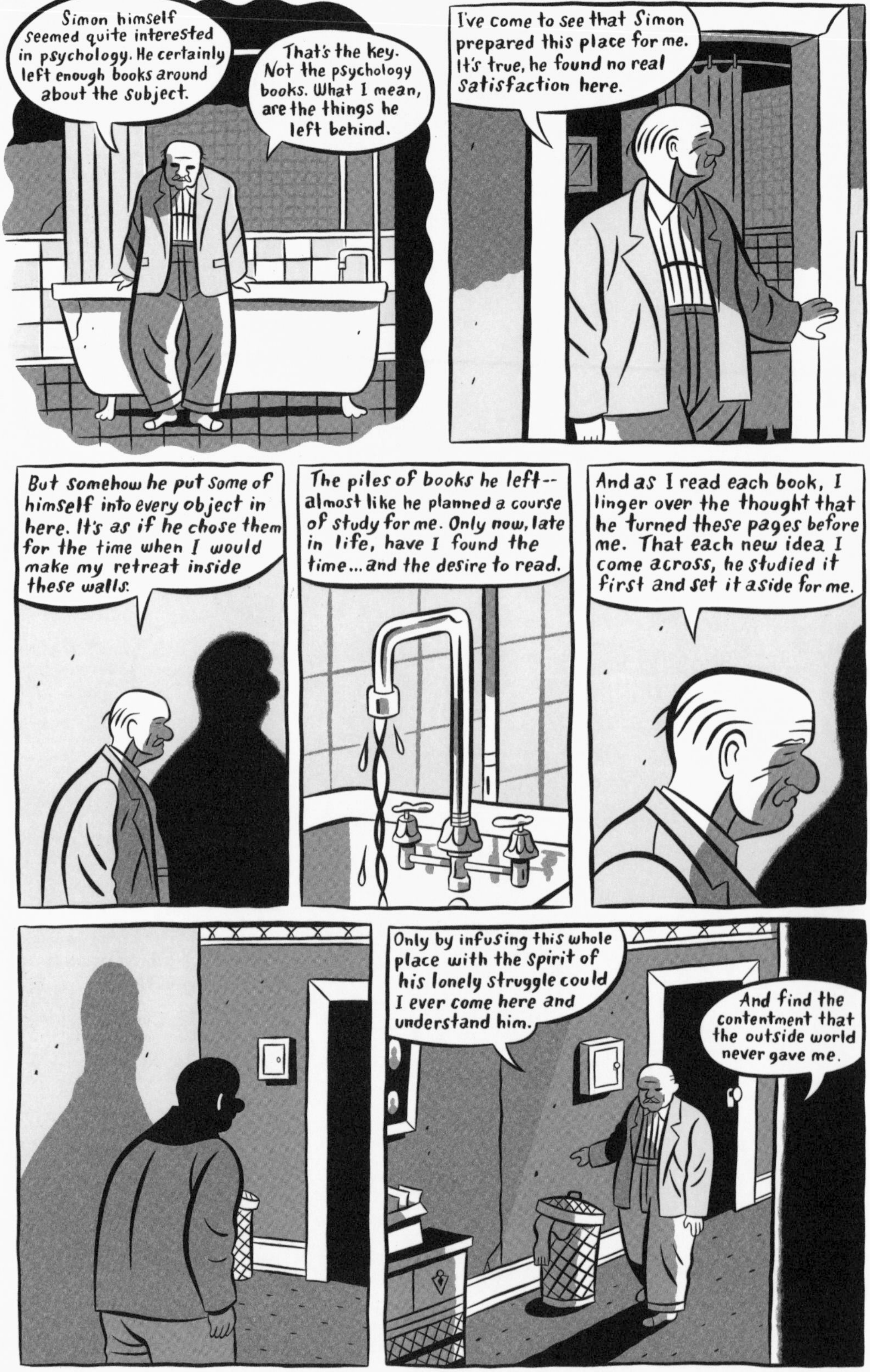
Simon himself seemed quite interested in psychology. He certainly left enough books around about the subject.
That's the key. Not the psychology books. What I mean, are the things he left behind.
I've come to see that Simon prepared this place for me. It's true, he found no real satisfaction here.
But somehow he put some of himself into every object in here. It's as if he chose them for the time when I would make my retreat inside these walls.
The piles of books he left-- almost like he planned a course of study for me. Only now, late in life, have I found the time... and the desire to read.
And as I read each book, I linger over the thought that he turned these pages before me. That each new idea I come across, he studied it first and set it aside for me.
Only by infusing this whole place with the spirit of his lonely struggle could I ever come here and understand him.
And find the contentment that the outside world never gave me.

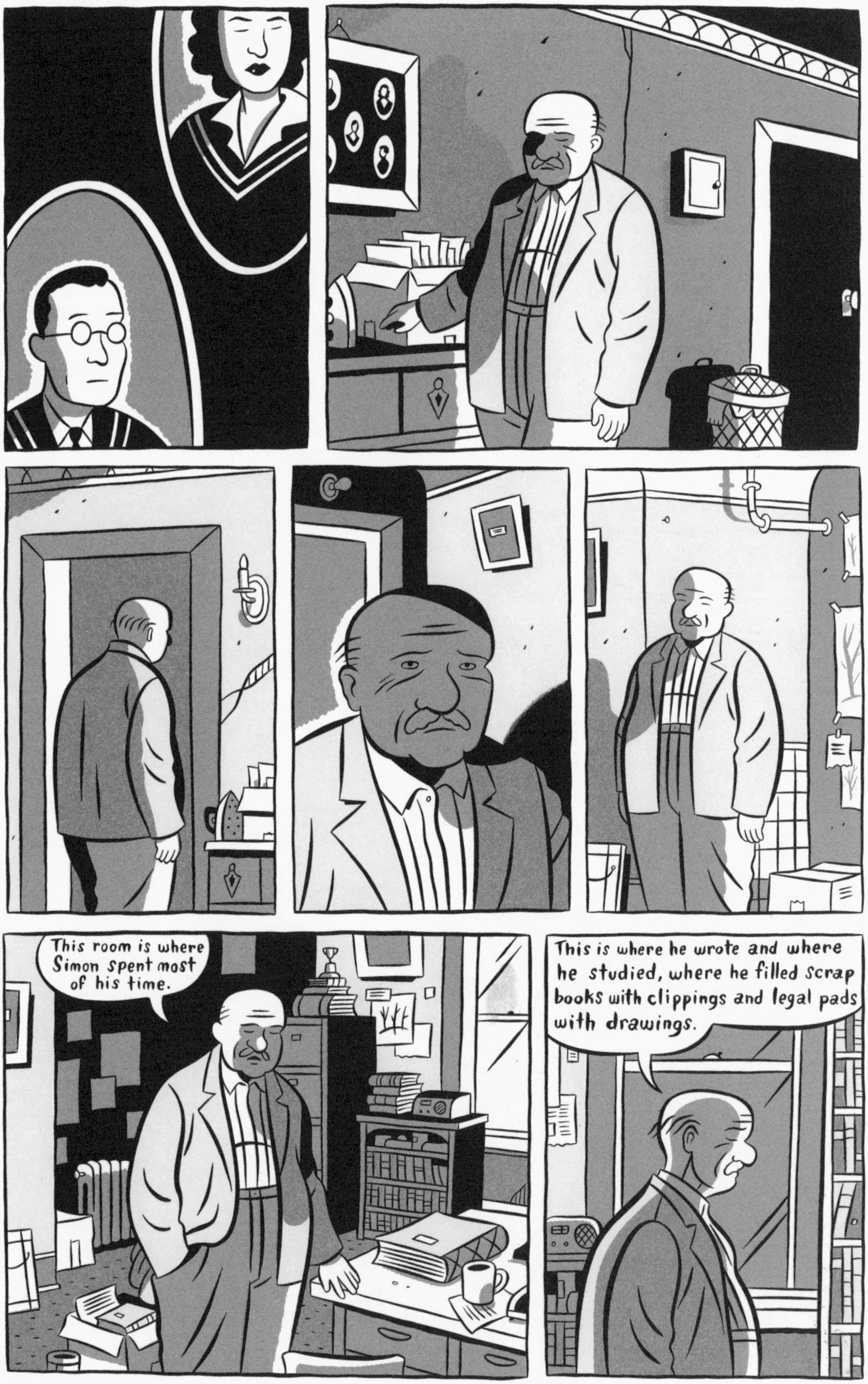
This room is where Simon spent most of his time.
This is where he wrote and where he studied, where he filled scrap books with clippings and legal pads with drawings.

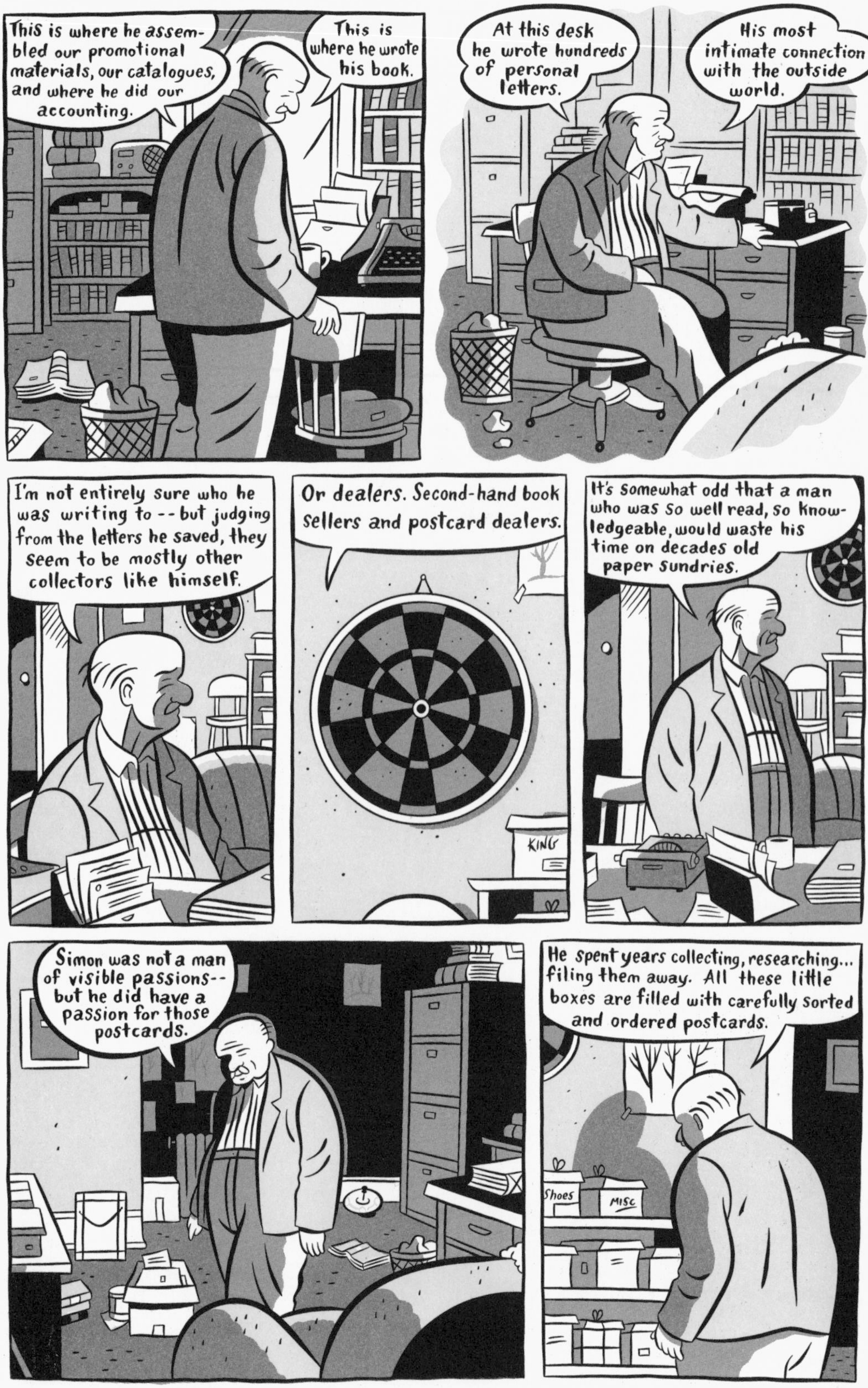
This is where he assembled our promotional materials, our catalogues, and where he did our accounting.
This is where he wrote his book.
At this desk he wrote hundreds of personal letters.
His most intimate connection with the outside world.
I'm not entirely sure who he was writing to -- but judging from the letters he saved, they seem to be mostly other collectors like himself.
Or dealers. Second-hand book sellers and postcard dealers.
KING
It's somewhat odd that a man who was so well read, so knowledgeable, would waste his time on decades old paper sundries.
Simon was not a man of visible passions-- but he did have a passion for those postcards.
He spent years collecting, researching... filing them away. All these little boxes are filled with carefully sorted and ordered postcards.
Shoes
MISC

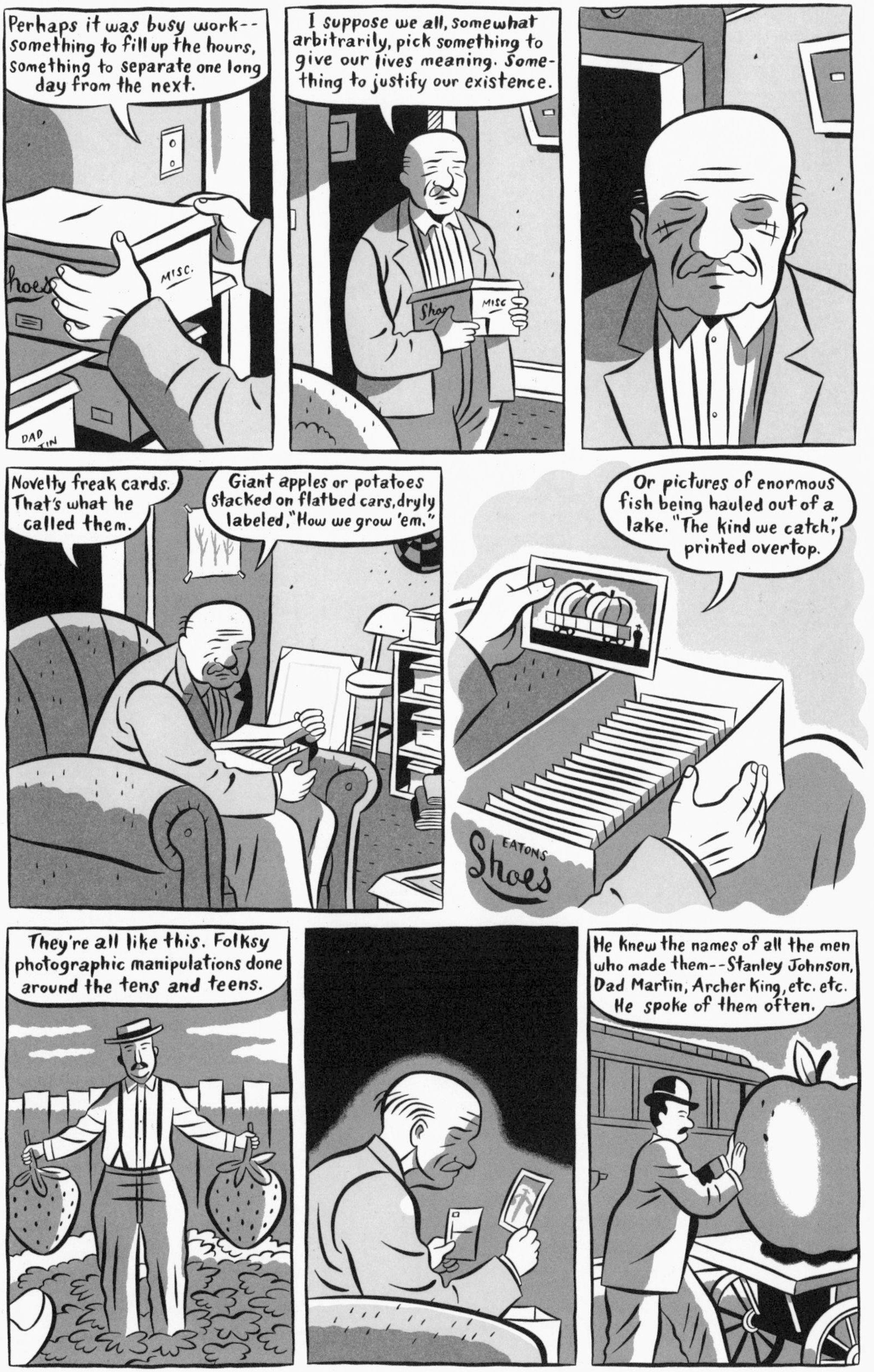
Perhaps it was busy work--something to fill up the hours, something to separate one long day from the next.
Shoes
MISC.
DAD TIN
I suppose we all, somewhat arbitrarily, pick something to give our lives meaning. Something to justify our existence.
Shoes
MISC
Novelty freak cards. That's what he called them.
Giant apples or potatoes stacked on flatbed cars, dryly labeled, "How we grow 'em."
Or pictures of enormous fish being hauled out of a lake. "The kind we catch," printed overtop.
EATONS
Shoes
They're all like this. Folksy photographic manipulations done around the tens and teens.
He knew the names of all the men who made them--Stanley Johnson, Dad Martin, Archer King, etc. etc. He spoke of them often.

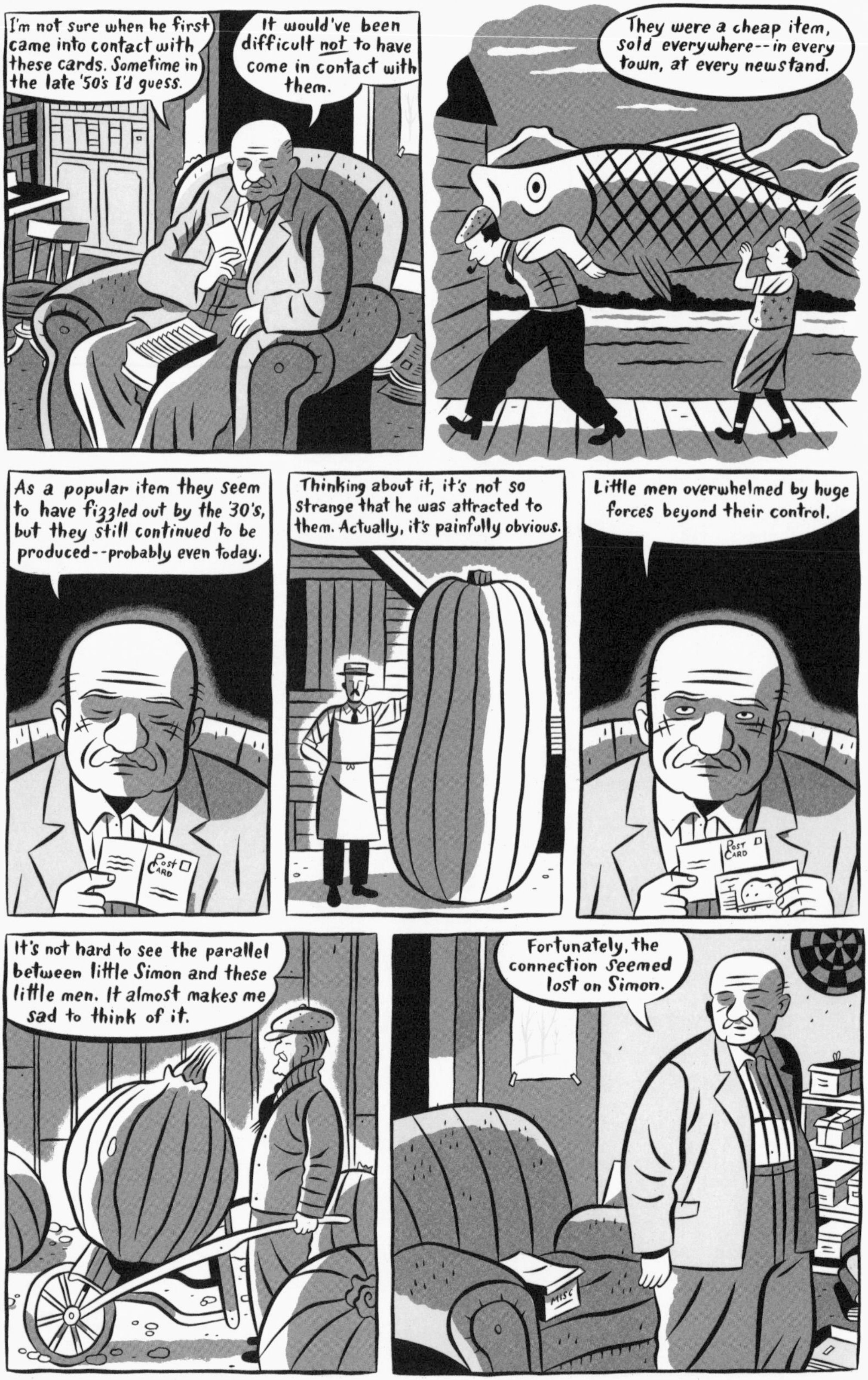

I'm not sure when he first came into contact with these cards. Sometime in the late '50's I'd guess.
It would've been difficult not to have come in contact with them.
They were a cheap item, sold everywhere--in every town, at every newstand.
As a popular item they seem to have fizzled out by the '30's, but they still continued to be produced--probably even today.
Thinking about it, it's not so strange that he was attracted to them. Actually, it's painfully obvious.
Little men overwhelmed by huge forces beyond their control.
It's not hard to see the parallel between little Simon and these little men. It almost makes me sad to think of it.
Fortunately, the connection seemed lost on Simon.

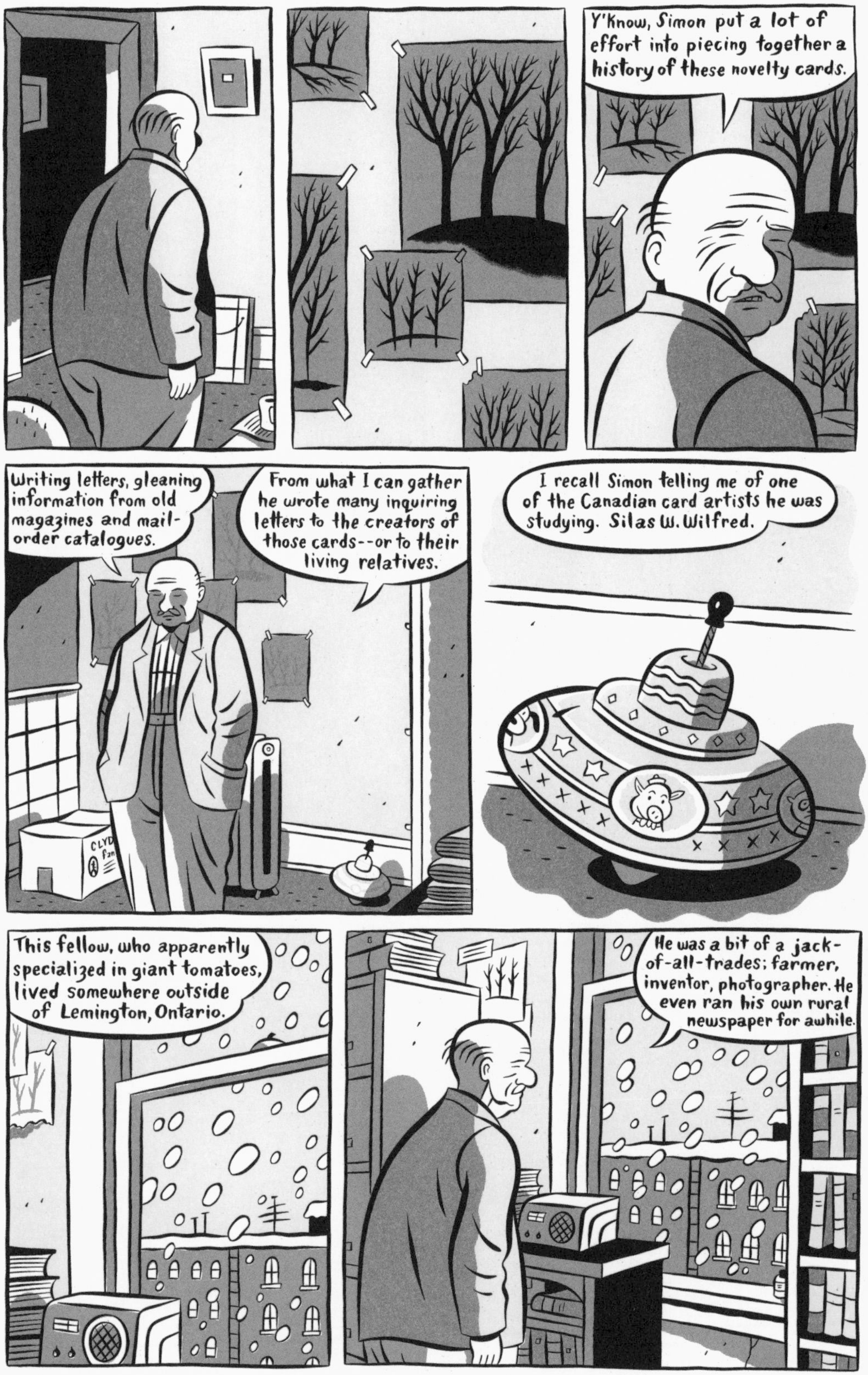

Y'Know, Simon put a lot of effort into piecing together a history of these novelty cards.
Writing letters, gleaning information from old magazines and mail-order catalogues.
From what I can gather he wrote many inquiring letters to the creators of those cards--or to their living relatives.
I recall Simon telling me of one of the Canadian card artists he was studying. Silas W. Wilfred.
This fellow, who apparently specialized in giant tomatoes, lived somewhere outside of Lemington, Ontario.
He was a bit of a jack-of-all-trades; farmer, inventor, photographer. He even ran his own rural newspaper for awhile.

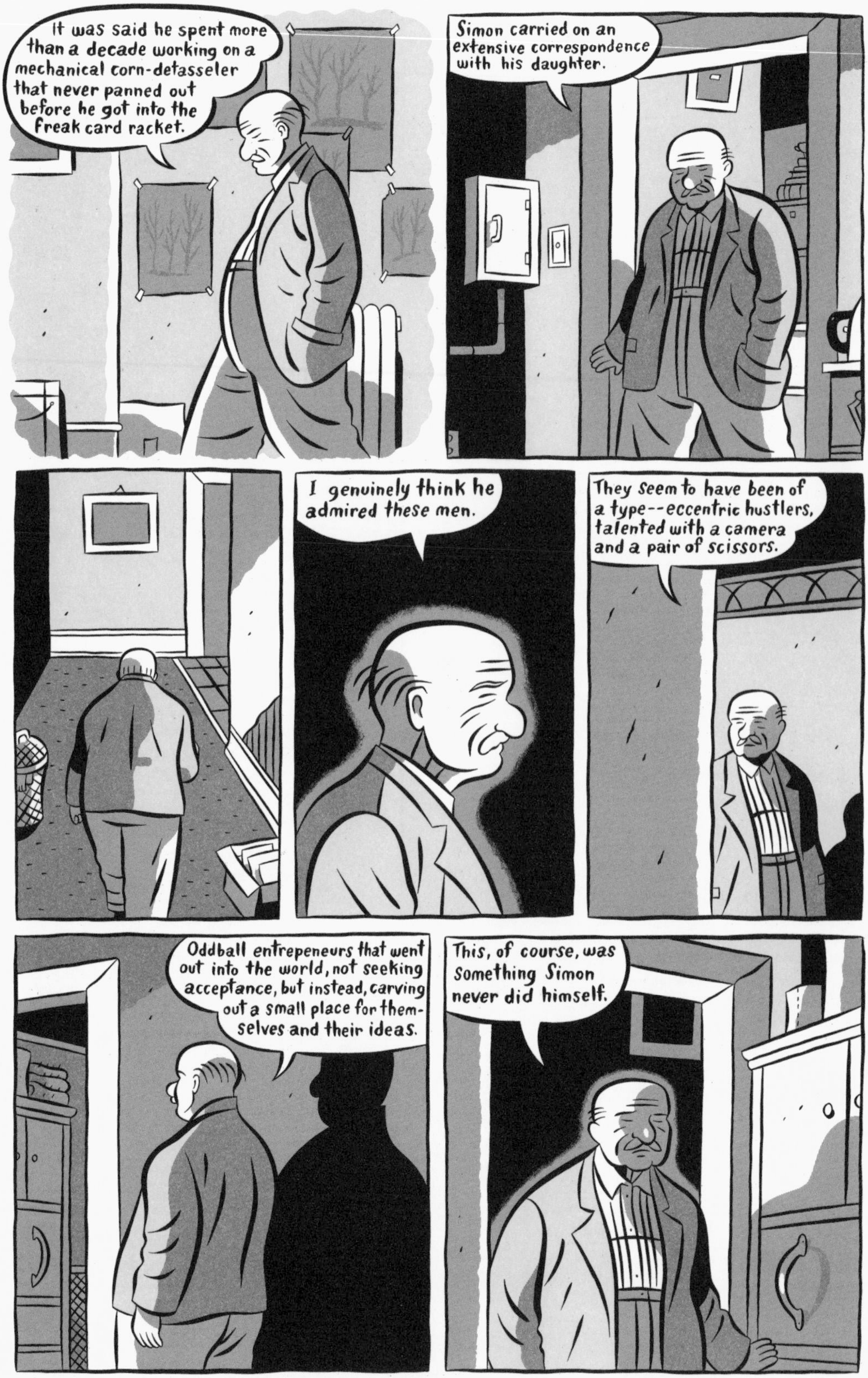

It was said he spent more than a decade working on a mechanical corn-detasseler that never panned out before he got into the freak card racket.
Simon carried on an extensive correspondence with his daughter.
I genuinely think he admired these men.
They seem to have been of a type--eccentric hustlers, talented with a camera and a pair of scissors.
Oddball entrepeneurs that went out into the world, not seeking acceptance, but instead, carving out a small place for themselves and their ideas.
This, of course, was something Simon never did himself.

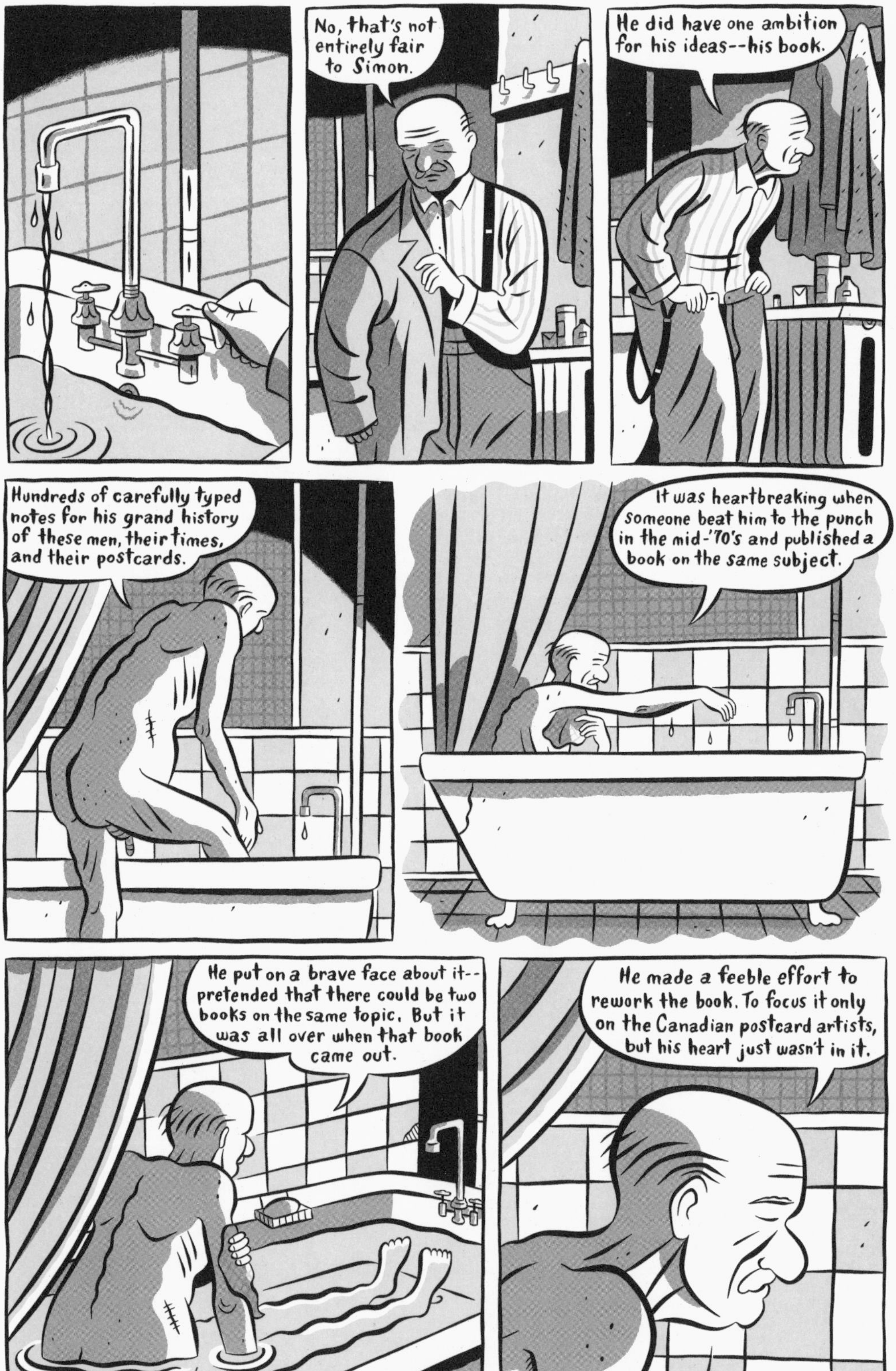
No, that's not entirely fair to Simon.
He did have one ambition for his ideas--his book.
Hundreds of carefully typed notes for his grand history of these men, their times, and their postcards.
It was heartbreaking when someone beat him to the punch in the mid-'70's and published a book on the same subject.
He put on a brave face about it--pretended that there could be two books on the same topic. But it was all over when that book came out.
He made a feeble effort to rework the book. To focus it only on the Canadian postcard artists, but his heart just wasn't in it.

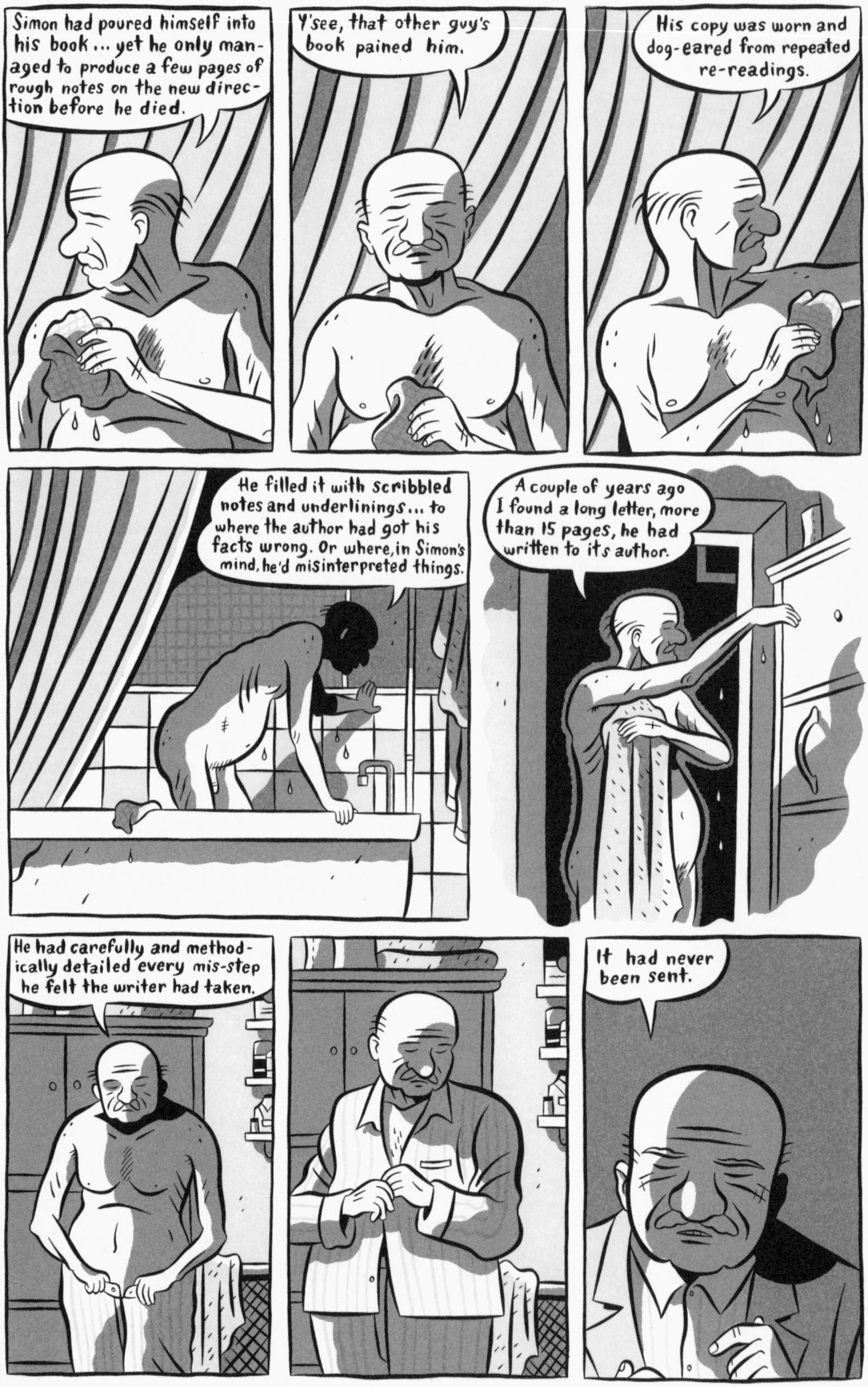
Simon had poured himself into his book... yet he only managed to produce a few pages of rough notes on the new direction before he died.
Y'see, that other guy's book pained him.
His copy was worn and dog-eared from repeated re-readings.
He filled it with scribbled notes and underlinings... to where the author had got his facts wrong. Or where, in Simon's mind, he'd misinterpreted things.
A couple of years ago I found a long letter, more than 15 pages, he had written to its author.
He had carefully and methodically detailed every mis-step he felt the writer had taken.
It had never been sent.

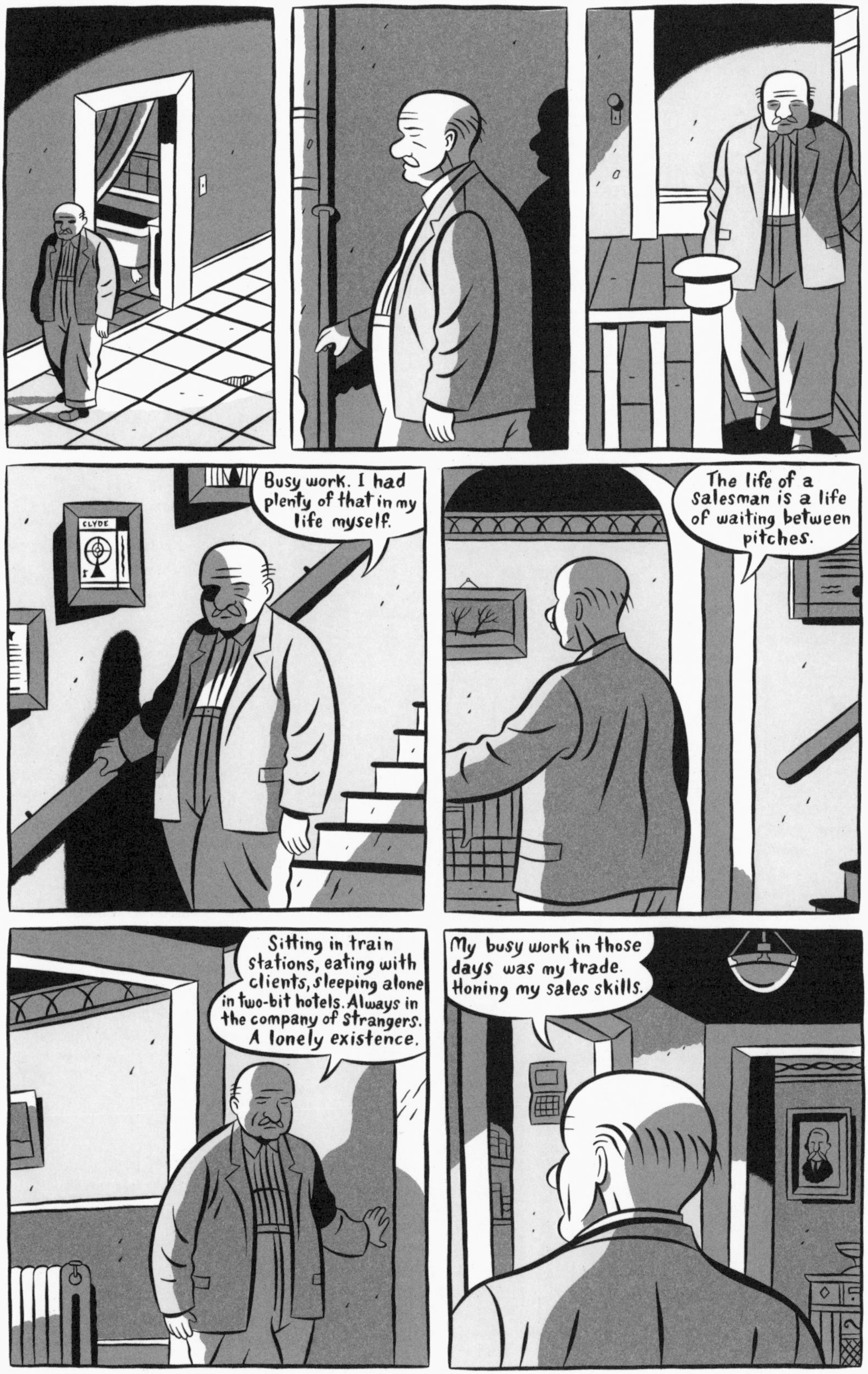
Busy work. I had plenty of that in my life myself.
CLYDE
The life of a salesman is a life of waiting between pitches.
Sitting in train stations, eating with clients, sleeping alone in two-bit hotels. Always in the company of strangers. A lonely existence.
My busy work in those days was my trade. Honing my sales skills.

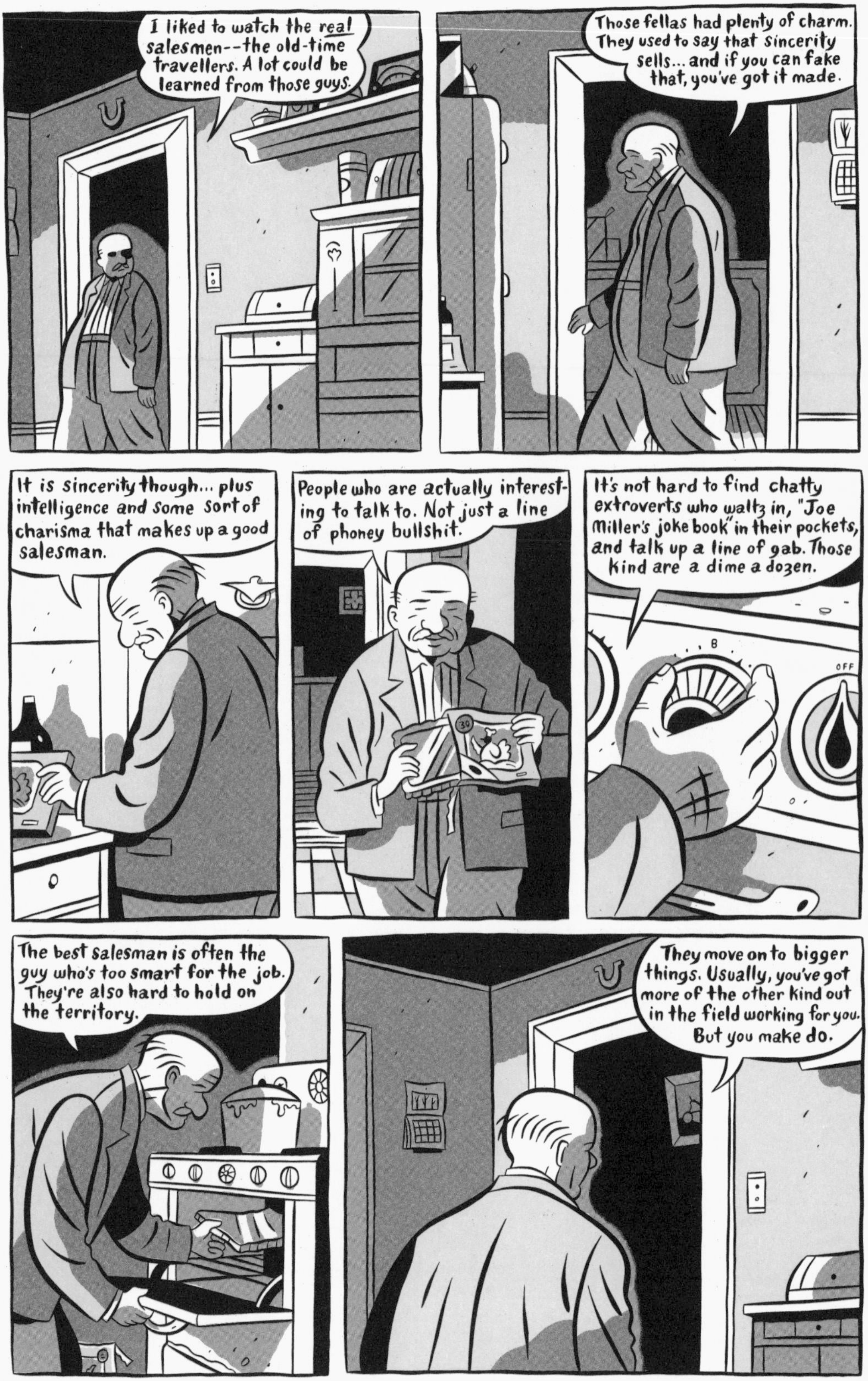
I liked to watch the real salesmen--the old-time travellers. A lot could be learned from those guys.
Those fellas had plenty of charm. They used to say that sincerity sells... and if you can fake that, you've got it made.
It is sincerity though... plus intelligence and some sort of charisma that makes up a good salesman.
People who are actually interesting to talk to. Not just a line of phoney bullshit.
It's not hard to find chatty extroverts who waltz in, "Joe Miller's joke book" in their pockets, and talk up a line of gab. Those kind are a dime a dozen.
B
OFF
The best salesman is often the guy who's too smart for the job. They're also hard to hold on the territory.
They move on to bigger things. Usually, you've got more of the other kind out in the field working for you. But you make do.

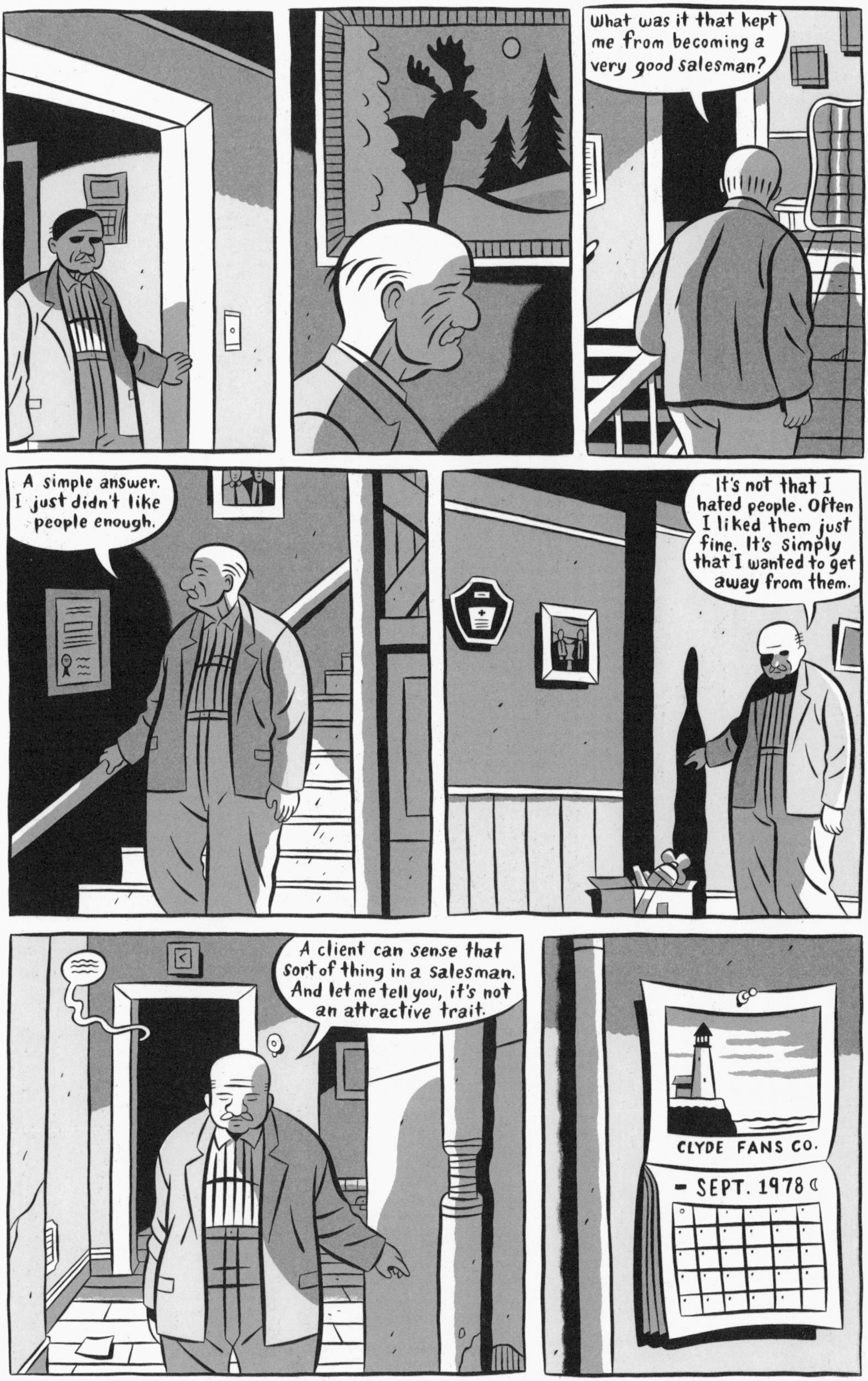
What was it that kept me from becoming a very good salesman?
A simple answer. I just didn't like people enough.
It's not that I hated people. Often I liked them just fine. It's simply that I wanted to get away from them.
A client can sense that sort of thing in a salesman. And let me tell you, it's not an attractive trait.
CLYDE FANS CO.
SEPT. 1978

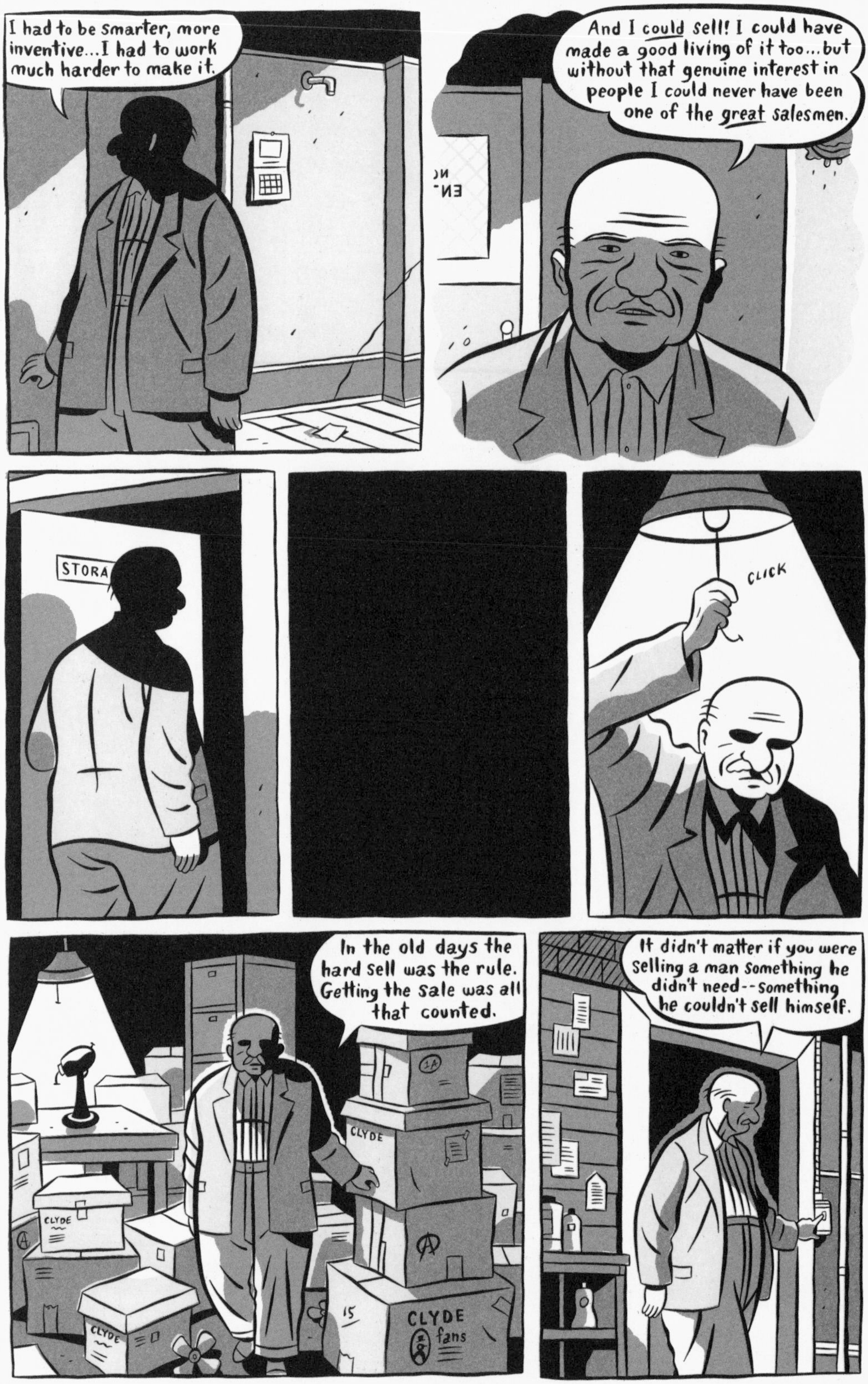
I had to be smarter, more inventive...I had to work much harder to make it.
And I could sell! I could have made a good living of it too...but without that genuine interest in people I could never have been one of the great salesmen.
STORA
CLICK
In the old days the hard sell was the rule. Getting the sale was all that counted.
CLYDE
CLYDE
CLYDE
CLYDE fans
It didn't matter if you were selling a man something he didn't need--something he couldn't sell himself.

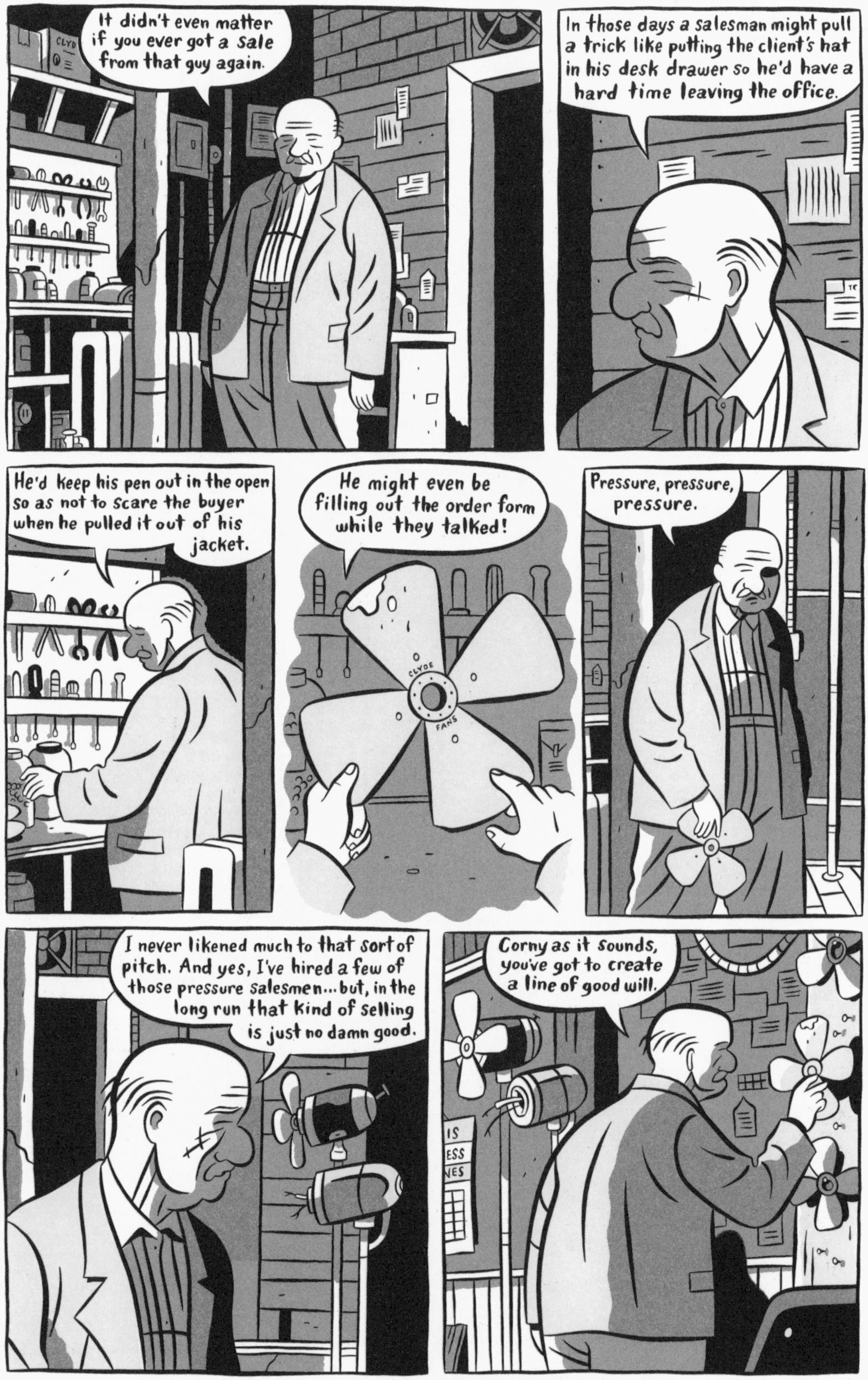
It didn't even matter if you ever got a sale from that guy again.
In those days a salesman might pull a trick like putting the client's hat in his desk drawer so he'd have a hard time leaving the office.
He'd keep his pen out in the open so as not to scare the buyer when he pulled it out of his jacket.
He might even be filling out the order form while they talked!
CLYDE FANS
Pressure, pressure, pressure.
I never likened much to that sort of pitch. And yes, I've hired a few of those pressure salesmen... but, in the long run that kind of selling is just no damn good.
Corny as it sounds, you've got to create a line of good will.

You must sell according to the needs of your customer-- you want return orders. That's where the real money is. Not the quick buck.

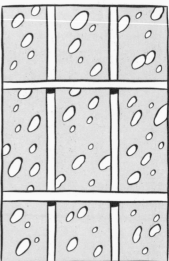

The quality salesman seems to be vanishing from the world.

Another thing--the level of manufacturing has gotten cheaper and cheaper every year.

Today's consumer is so used to shoddy goods that he's willing to repeatedly buy products that break within a year or so.

I guess they've become so cynical that they expect to be cheated. These modern companies have things rigged to their advantage.

68

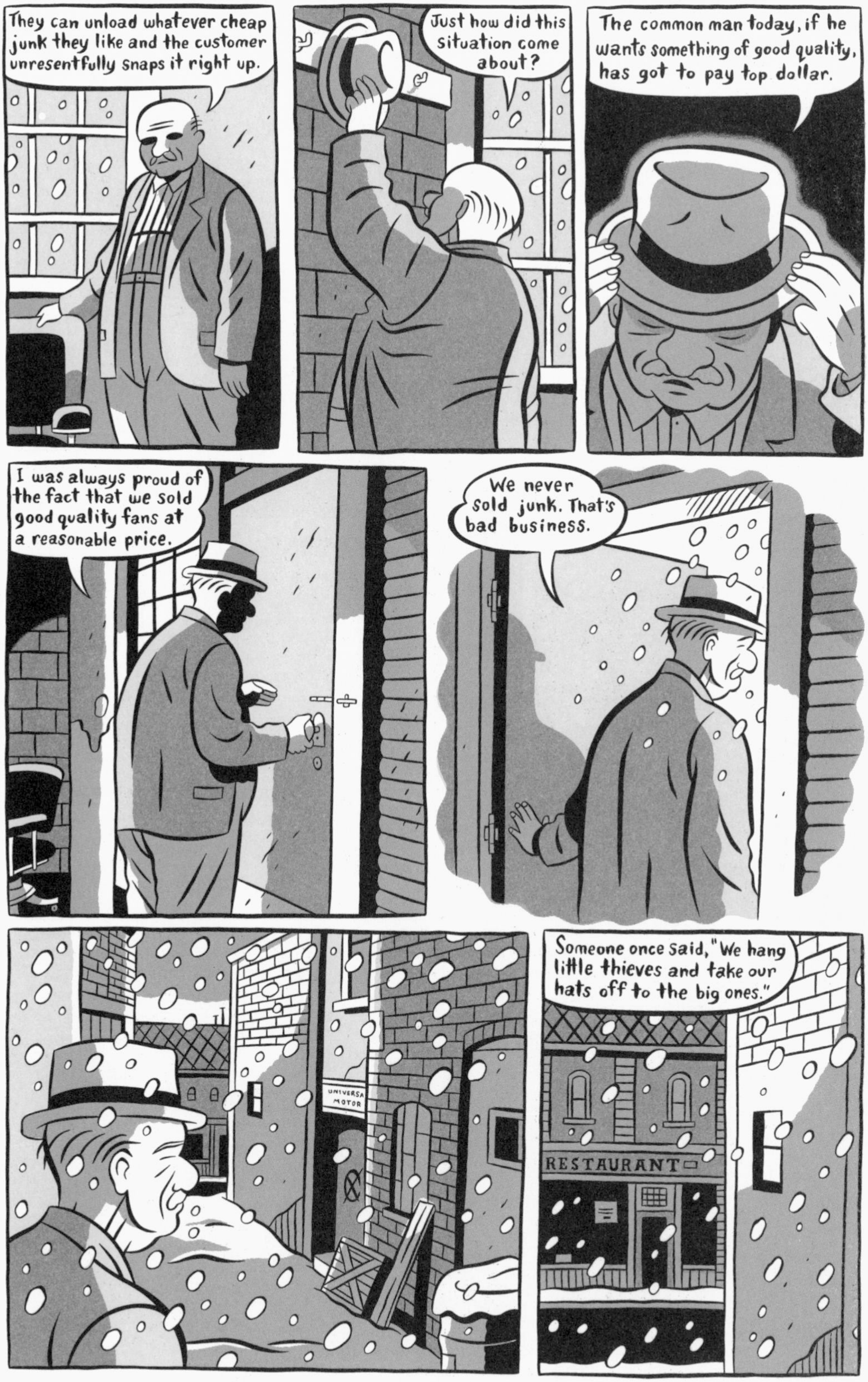

They can unload whatever cheap junk they like and the customer unresentfully snaps it right up.
Just how did this situation come about?
The common man today, if he wants something of good quality, has got to pay top dollar.
I was always proud of the fact that we sold good quality fans at a reasonable price.
We never sold junk. That's bad business.
UNIVERSA MOTOR
Someone once said, "We hang little thieves and take our hats off to the big ones."
RESTAURANT

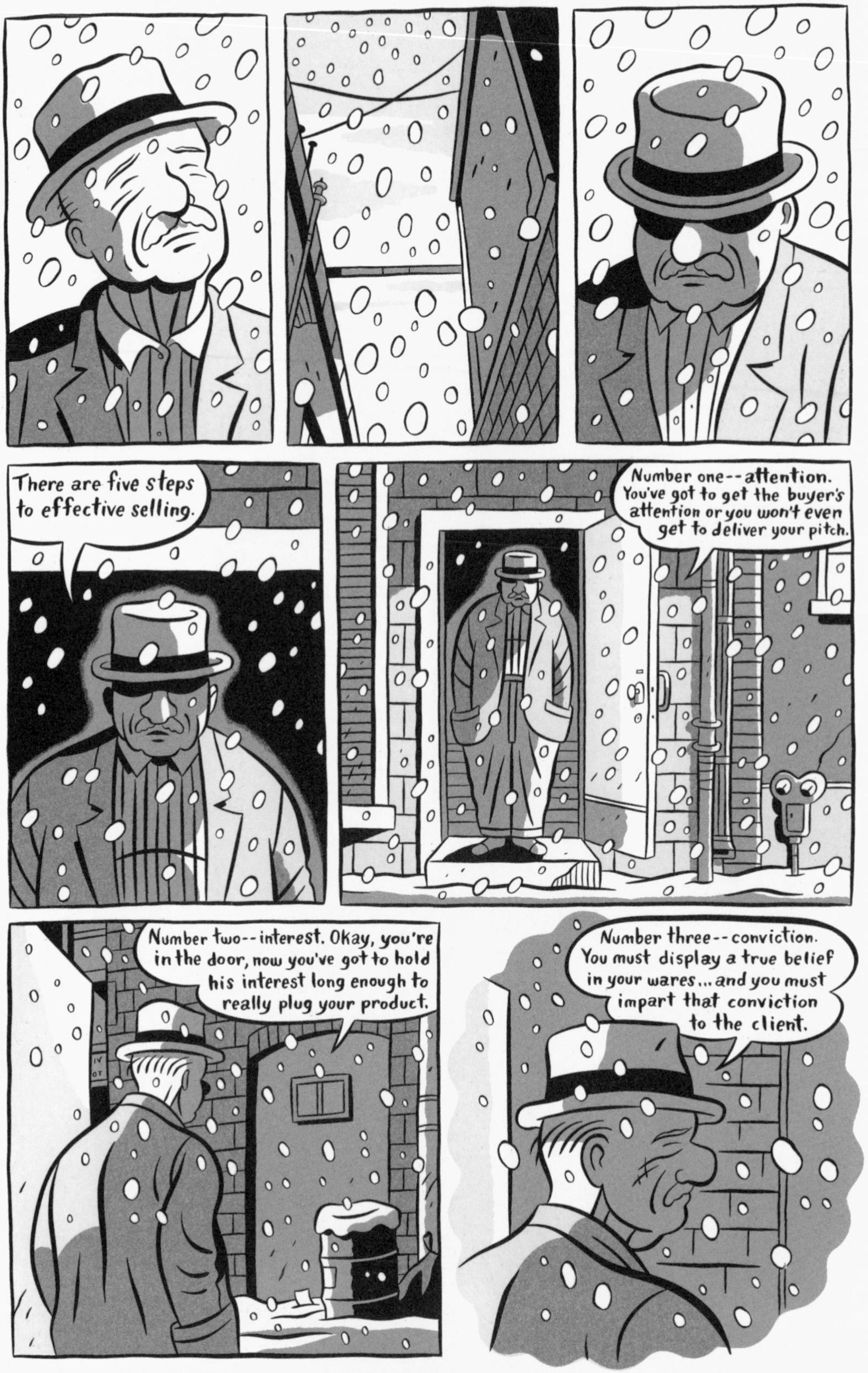
There are five steps to effective selling.
Number one--attention. You've got to get the buyer's attention or you won't even get to deliver your pitch.
Number two--interest. Okay, you're in the door, now you've got to hold his interest long enough to really plug your product.
Number three--conviction. You must display a true belief in your wares...and you must impart that conviction to the client.

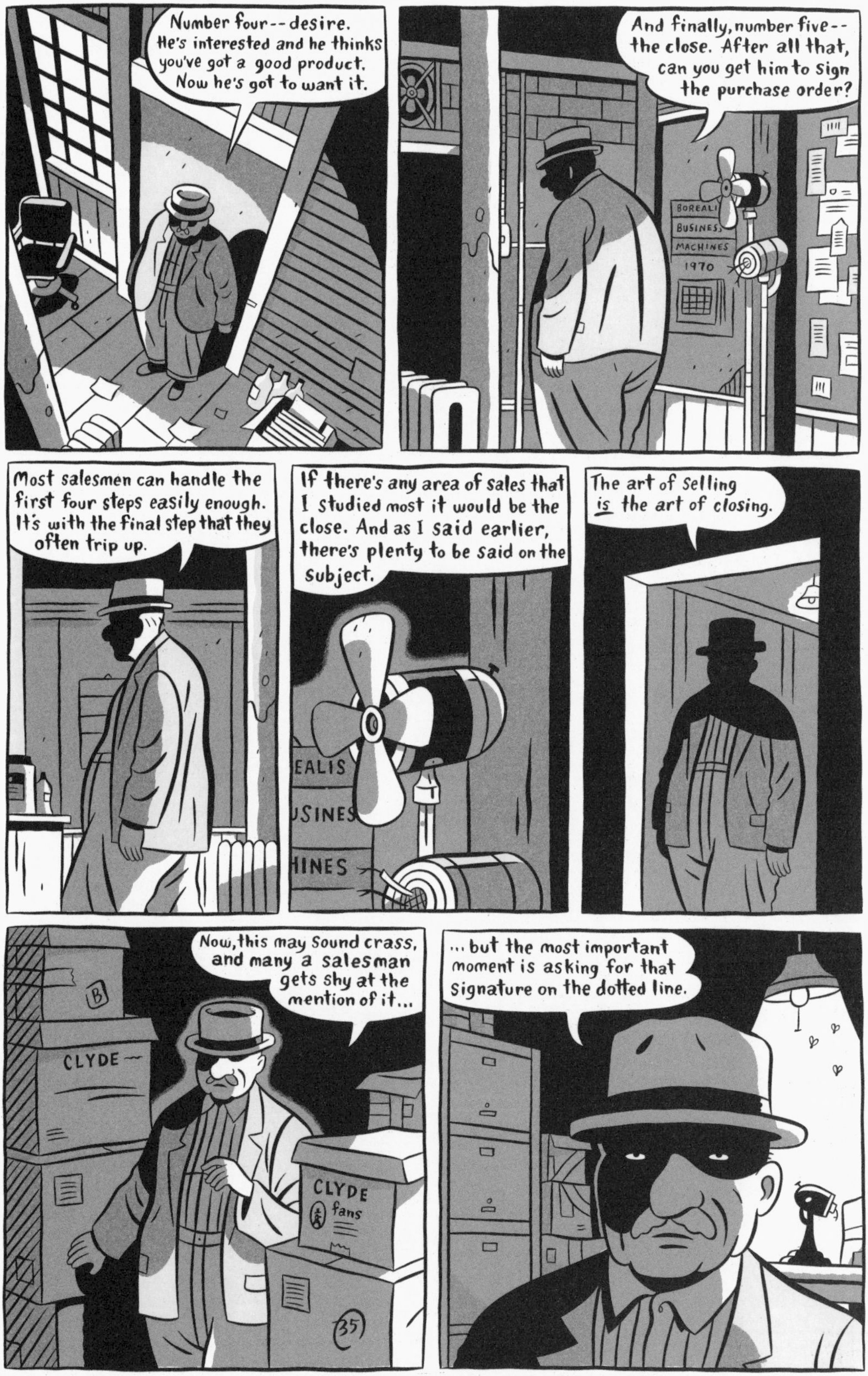
Number four -- desire. He's interested and he thinks you've got a good product. Now he's got to want it.
And finally, number five -- the close. After all that, can you get him to sign the purchase order?
BOREALI
BUSINESS
MACHINES
1970
Most salesmen can handle the first four steps easily enough. It's with the final step that they often trip up.
If there's any area of sales that I studied most it would be the close. And as I said earlier, there's plenty to be said on the subject.
EALIS
USINES
HINES
The art of selling is the art of closing.
Now, this may sound crass, and many a salesman gets shy at the mention of it...
B
CLYDE
CLYDE
fans
35
... but the most important moment is asking for that signature on the dotted line.

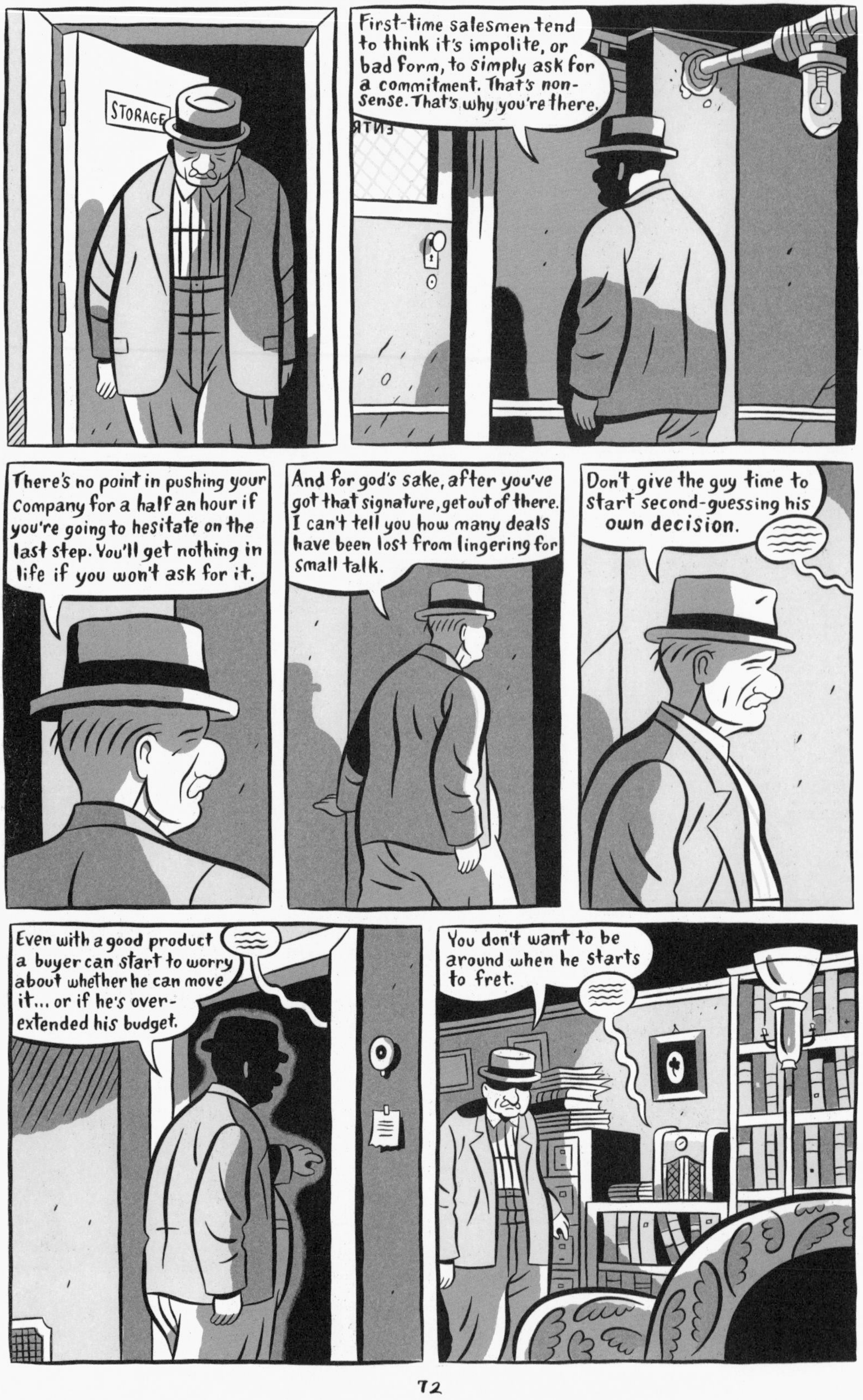
STORAGE
First-time salesmen tend to think it's impolite, or bad form, to simply ask for a commitment. That's non-sense. That's why you're there.
There's no point in pushing your Company for a half an hour if you're going to hesitate on the last step. You'll get nothing in life if you won't ask for it.
And for god's sake, after you've got that signature, get out of there. I can't tell you how many deals have been lost from lingering for small talk.
Don't give the guy time to start second-guessing his own decision.
Even with a good product a buyer can start to worry about whether he can move it... or if he's over-extended his budget.
You don't want to be around when he starts to fret.

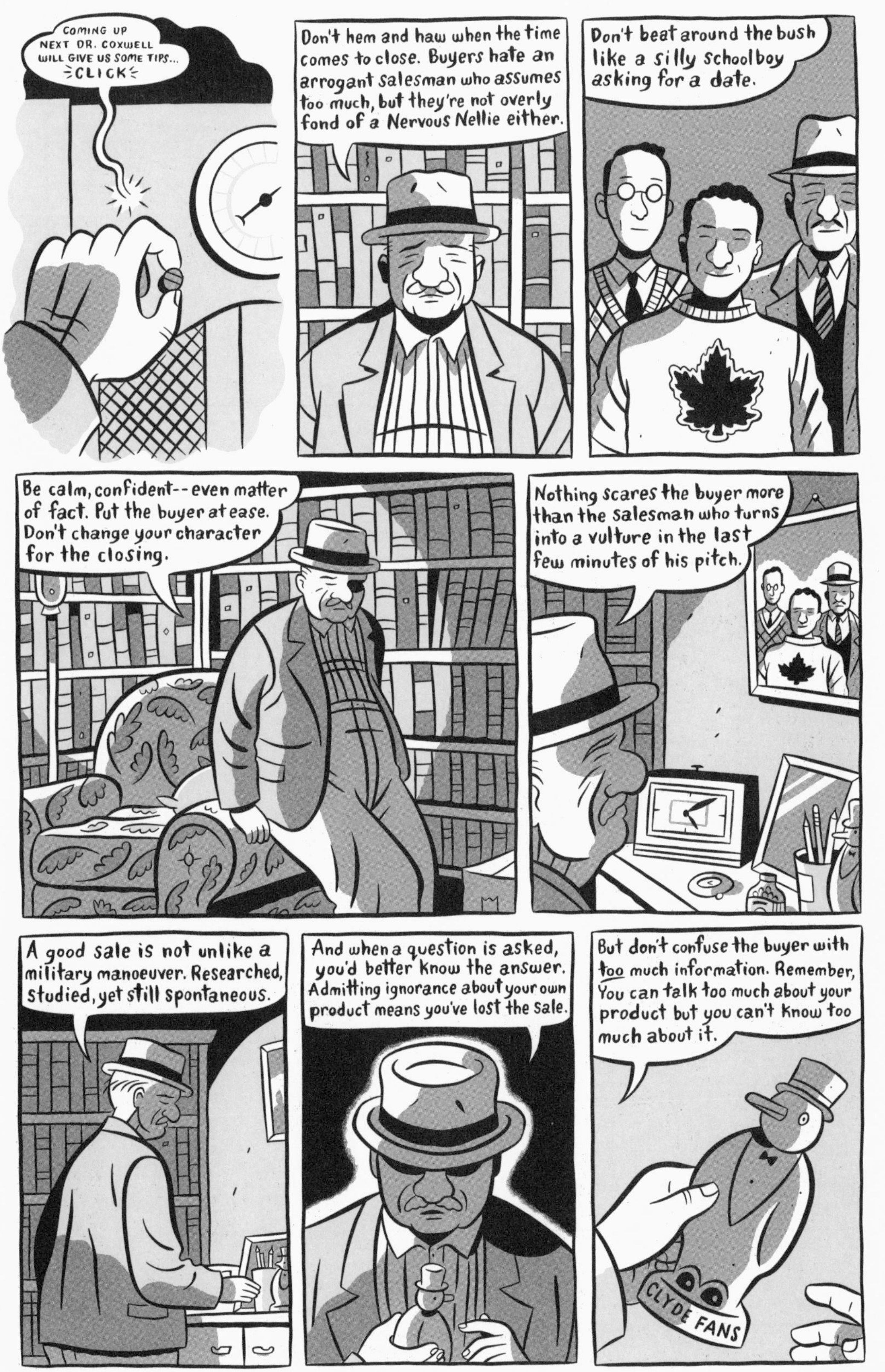
COMING UP NEXT DR. COXWELL WILL GIVE US SOME TIPS...
CLICK
Don't hem and haw when the time comes to close. Buyers hate an arrogant salesman who assumes too much, but they're not overly fond of a Nervous Nellie either.
Don't beat around the bush like a silly schoolboy asking for a date.
Be calm, confident--even matter of fact. Put the buyer at ease. Don't change your character for the closing.
Nothing scares the buyer more than the salesman who turns into a vulture in the last few minutes of his pitch.
A good sale is not unlike a military manoeuver. Researched, studied, yet still spontaneous.
And when a question is asked, you'd better know the answer. Admitting ignorance about your own product means you've lost the sale.
But don't confuse the buyer with too much information. Remember, You can talk too much about your product but you can't know too much about it.
CLYDE FANS

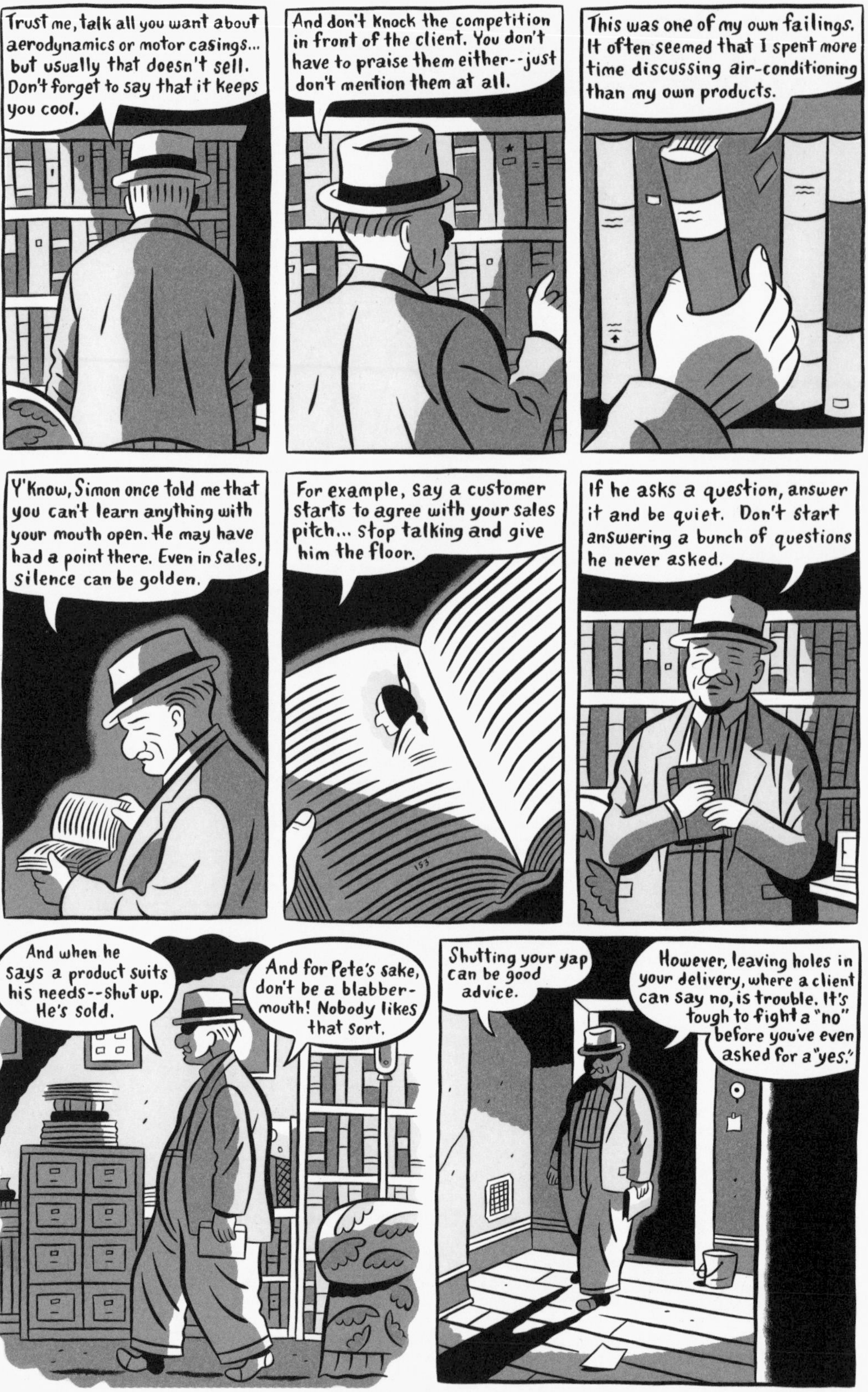
Trust me, talk all you want about aerodynamics or motor casings... but usually that doesn't sell. Don't forget to say that it keeps you cool.
And don't knock the competition in front of the client. You don't have to praise them either--just don't mention them at all.
This was one of my own failings. It often seemed that I spent more time discussing air-conditioning than my own products.
Y'Know, Simon once told me that you can't learn anything with your mouth open. He may have had a point there. Even in sales, silence can be golden.
For example, say a customer starts to agree with your sales pitch... stop talking and give him the floor.
If he asks a question, answer it and be quiet. Don't start answering a bunch of questions he never asked.
And when he says a product suits his needs--shut up. He's sold.
And for Pete's sake, don't be a blabber-mouth! Nobody likes that sort.
Shutting your yap can be good advice.
However, leaving holes in your delivery, where a client can say no, is trouble. It's tough to fight a "no" before you've even asked for a "yes."

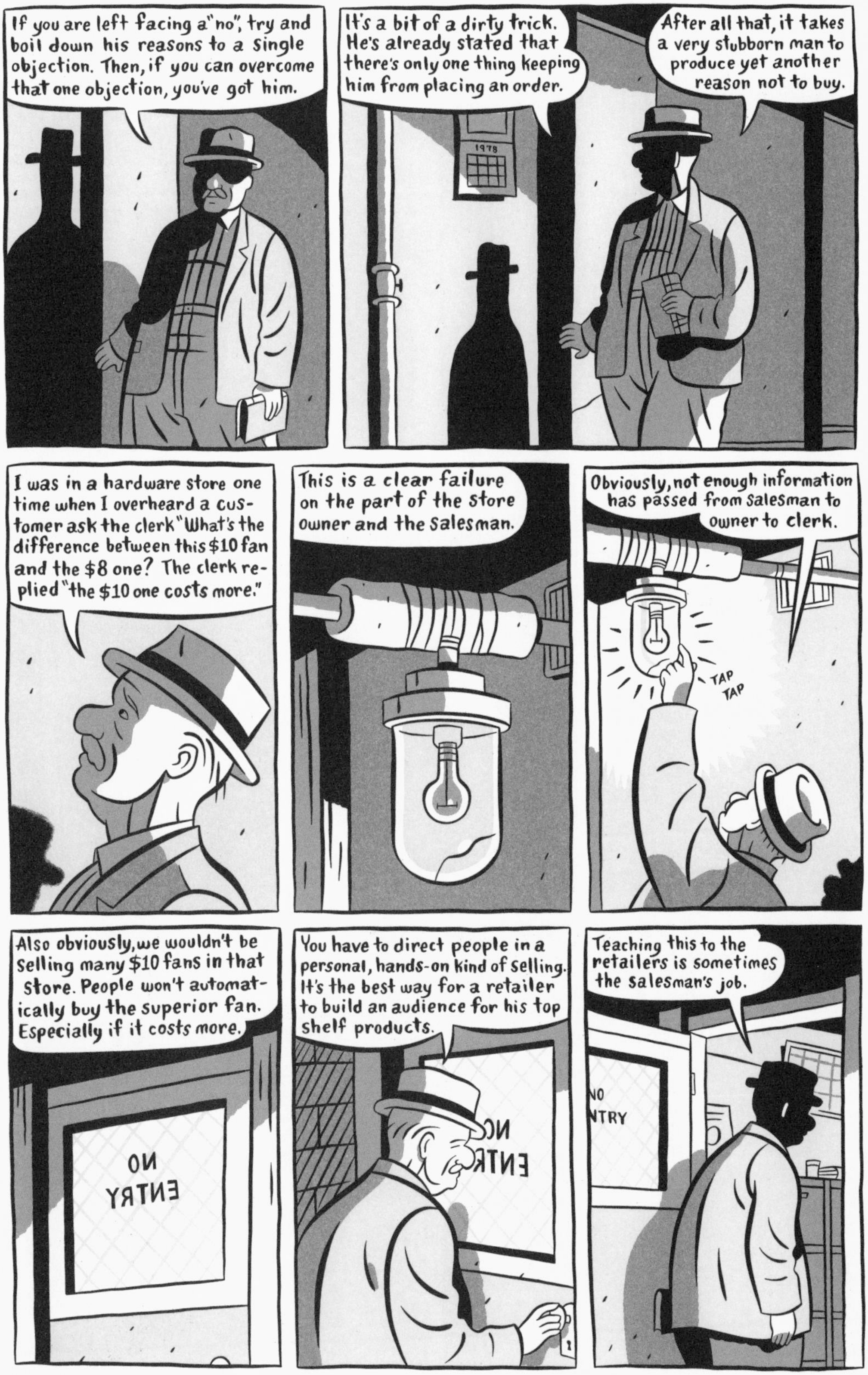
If you are left facing a "no", try and boil down his reasons to a single objection. Then, if you can overcome that one objection, you've got him.
It's a bit of a dirty trick. He's already stated that there's only one thing keeping him from placing an order.
1978
After all that, it takes a very stubborn man to produce yet another reason not to buy.
I was in a hardware store one time when I overheard a customer ask the clerk "What's the difference between this $10 fan and the $8 one? The clerk replied "the $10 one costs more."
This is a clear failure on the part of the store owner and the salesman.
Obviously, not enough information has passed from salesman to owner to clerk.
TAP TAP
Also obviously, we wouldn't be selling many $10 fans in that store. People won't automatically buy the superior fan. Especially if it costs more.
NO ENTRY
You have to direct people in a personal, hands-on kind of selling. It's the best way for a retailer to build an audience for his top shelf products.
Teaching this to the retailers is sometimes the salesman's job.

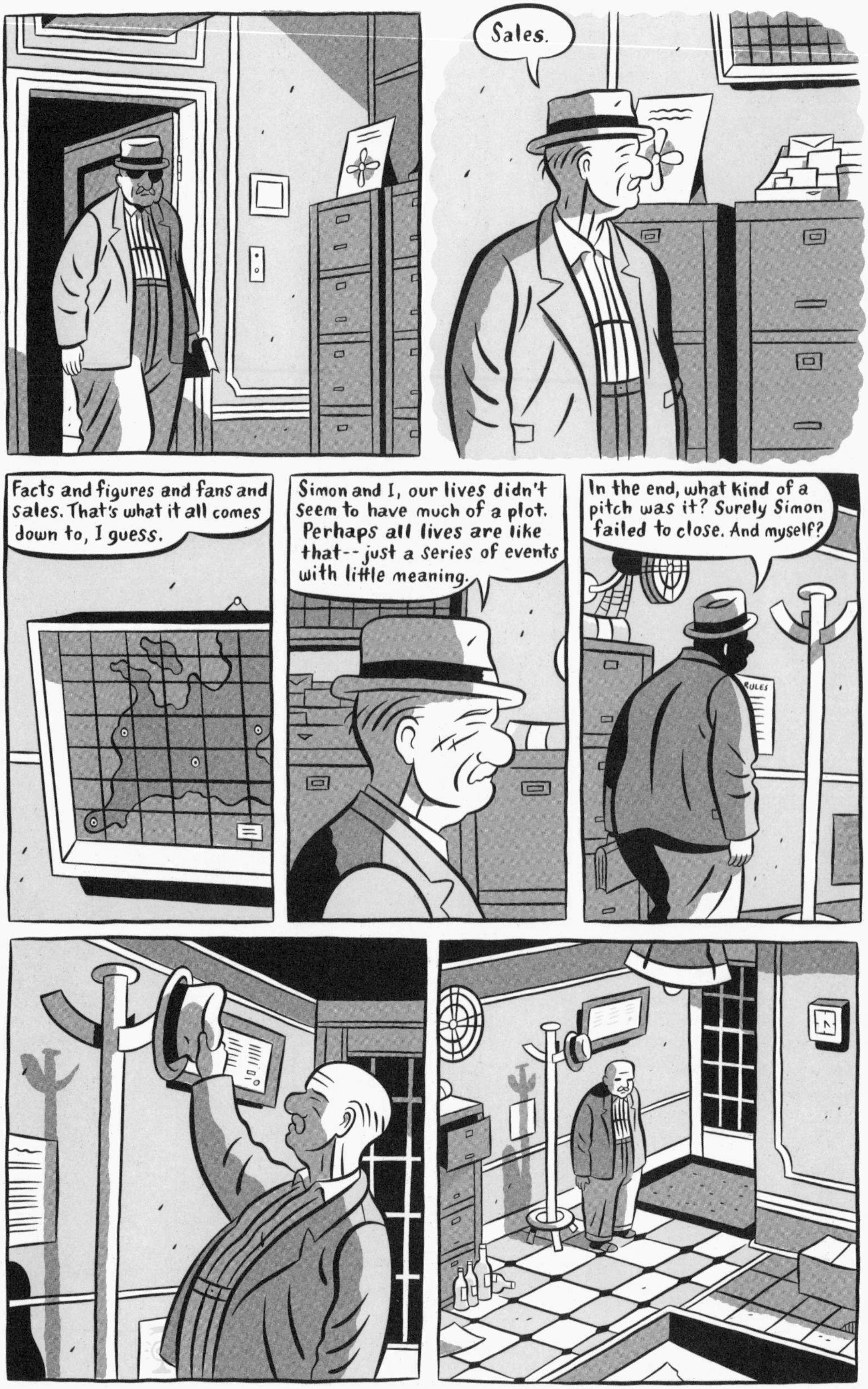

Sales.
Facts and figures and fans and sales. That's what it all comes down to, I guess.
Simon and I, our lives didn't seem to have much of a plot. Perhaps all lives are like that-- just a series of events with little meaning.
In the end, what kind of a pitch was it? Surely Simon failed to close. And myself?
RULES

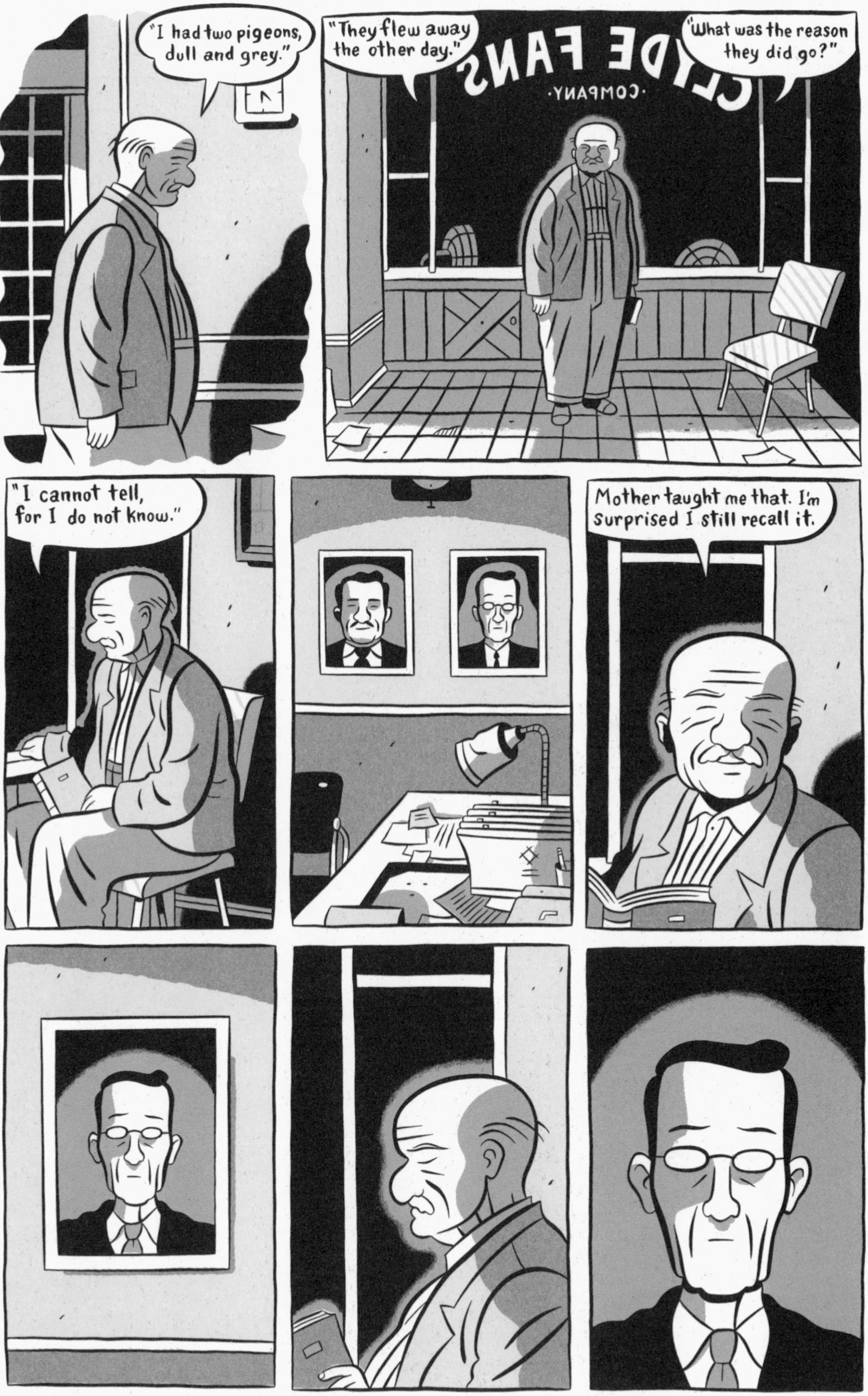
"I had two pigeons, dull and grey."
"They flew away the other day."
CLYDE FANS
·COMPANY·
"What was the reason they did go?"
"I cannot tell, for I do not know."
Mother taught me that. I'm surprised I still recall it.

CLYDE
FANS CO.

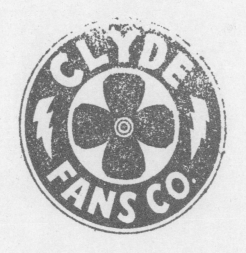

PART TWO

·1957·

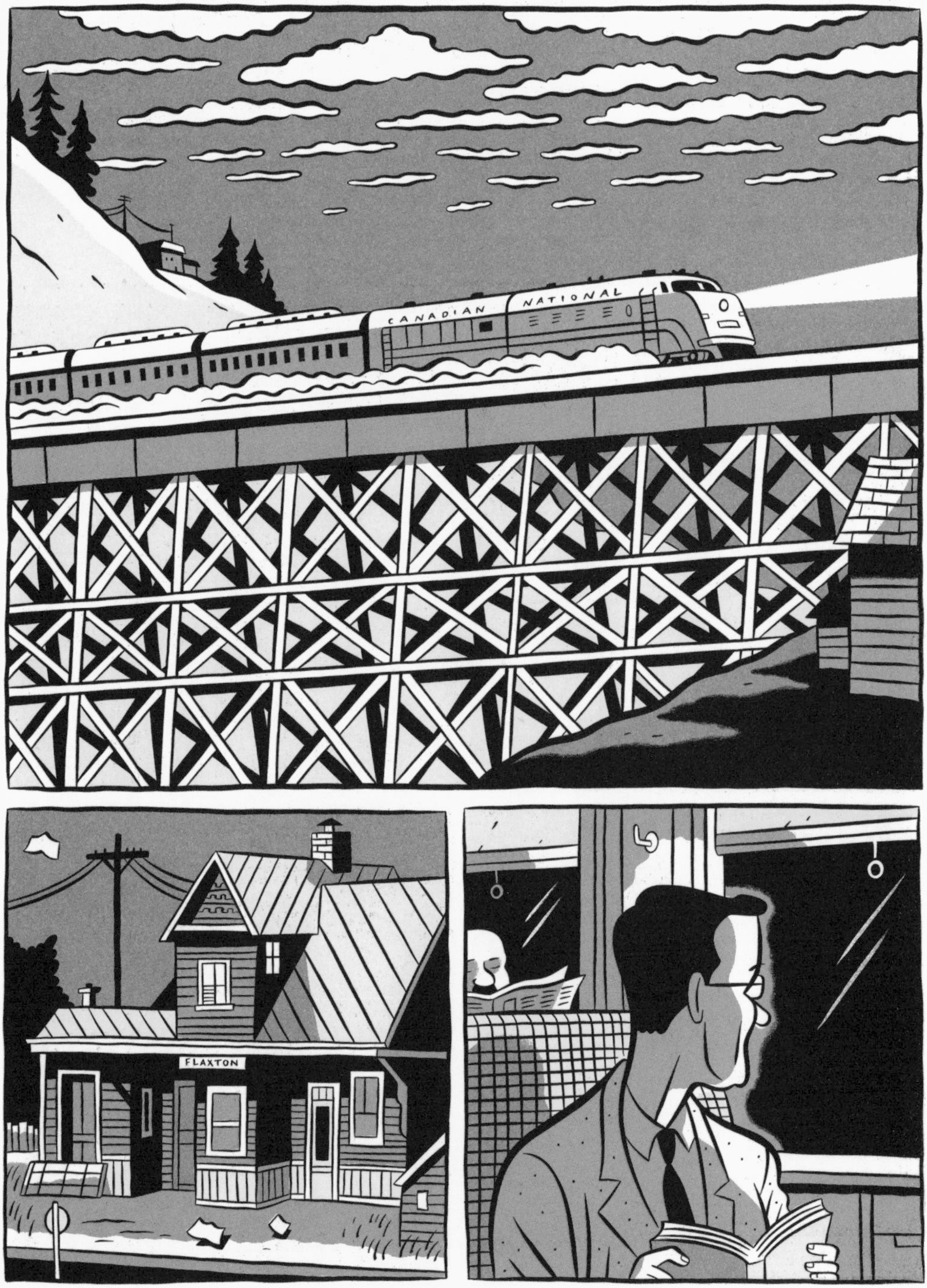
CANADIAN NATIONAL
FLAXTON

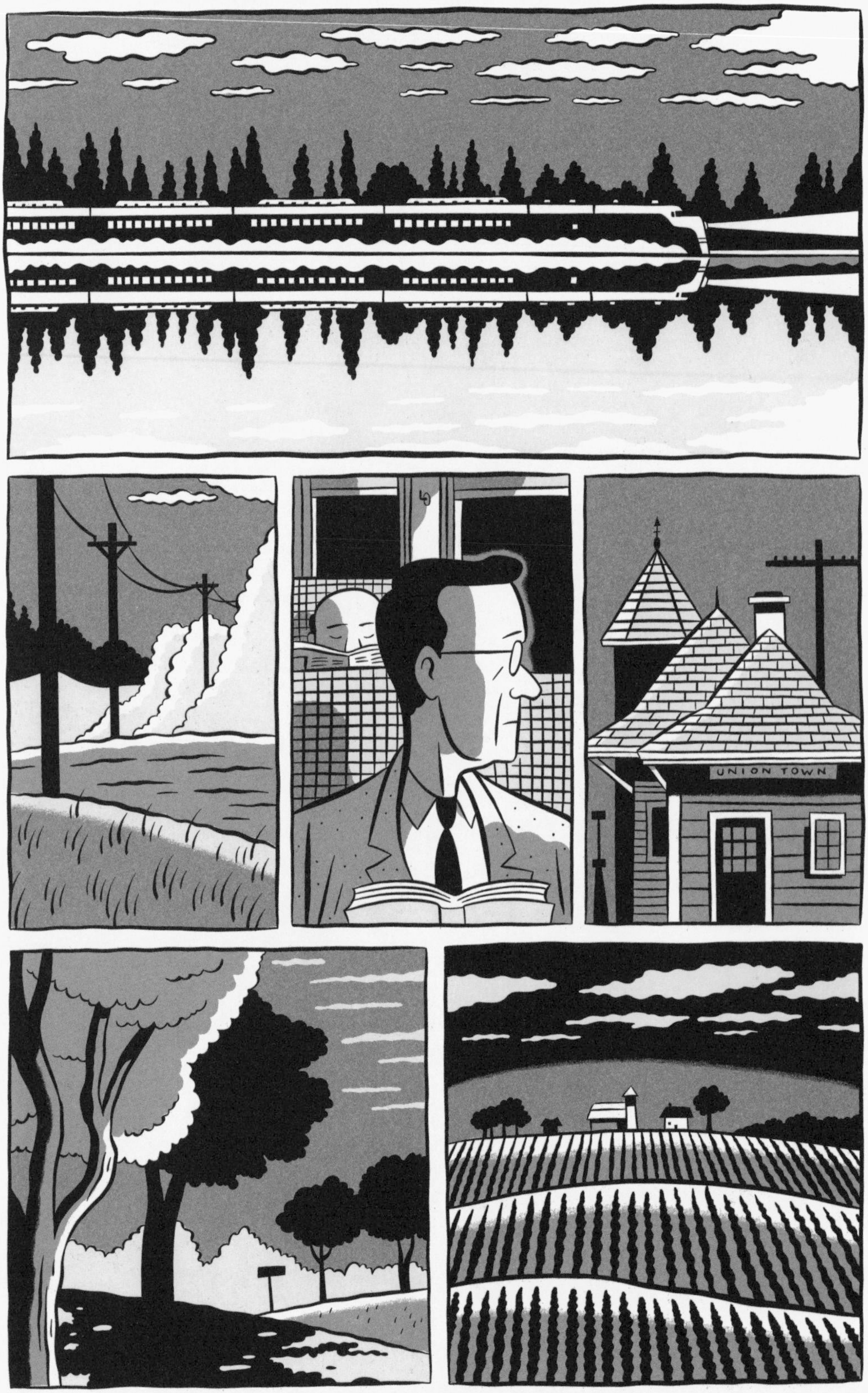
UNION TOWN

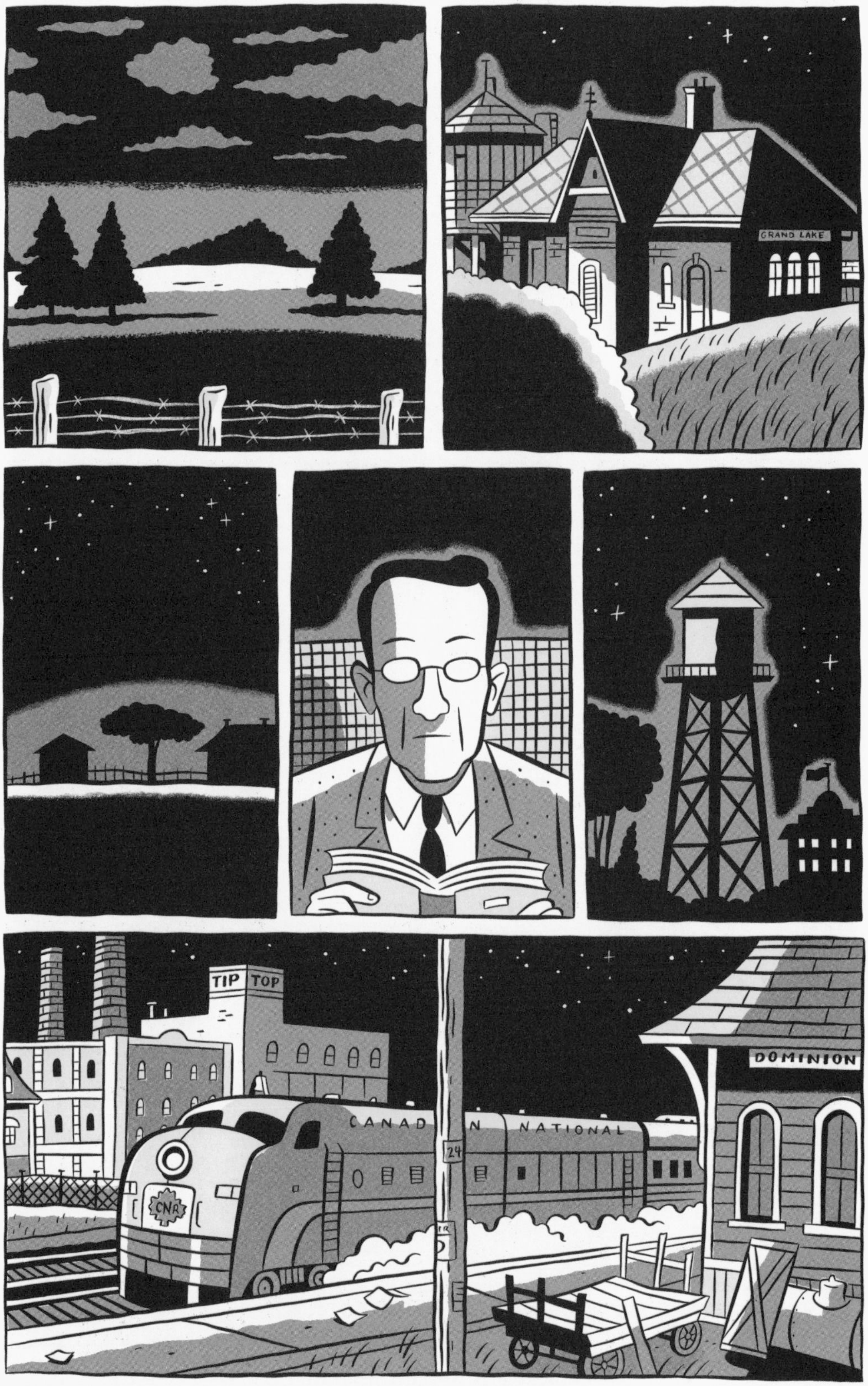
GRAND LAKE
TIP TOP
DOMINION
CANAD
N NATIONAL
CNR
24

Pardon me. Perhaps, um, perhaps you might know a restaurant in town still open at this hour?

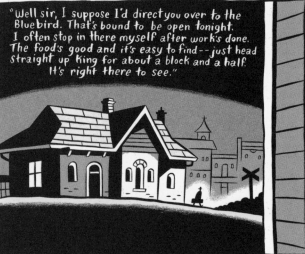

"Well sir, I suppose I'd direct you over to the Bluebird. That's bound to be open tonight. I often stop in there myself after work's done. The food's good and it's easy to find -- just head straight up King for about a block and a half. It's right there to see."

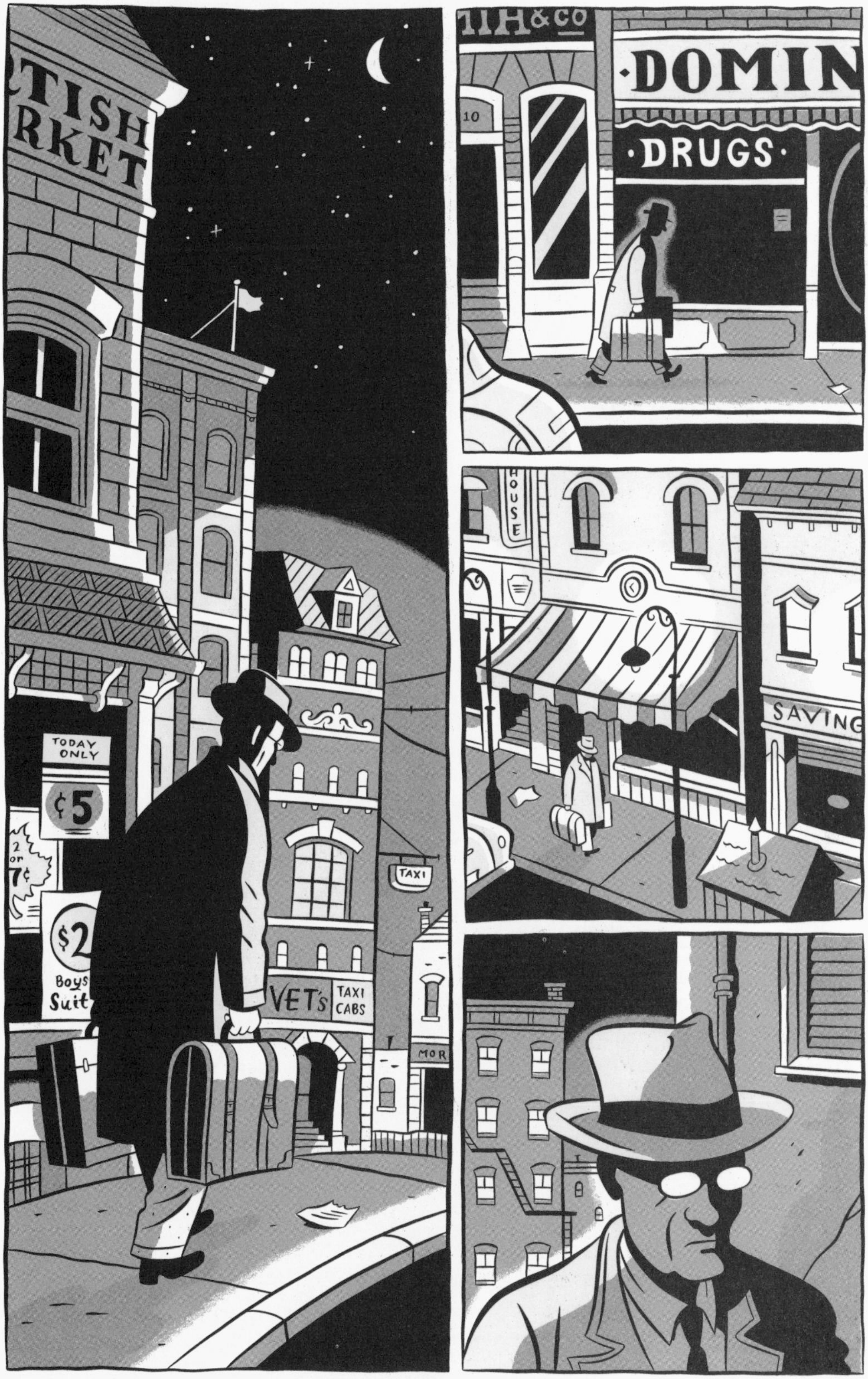
TISH
RKET
TODAY ONLY
¢5
$2
Boys
Suit
VET's
TAXI CABS
TAXI
MOR
TIH&CO
DOMIN
DRUGS
10
HOUSE
SAVING

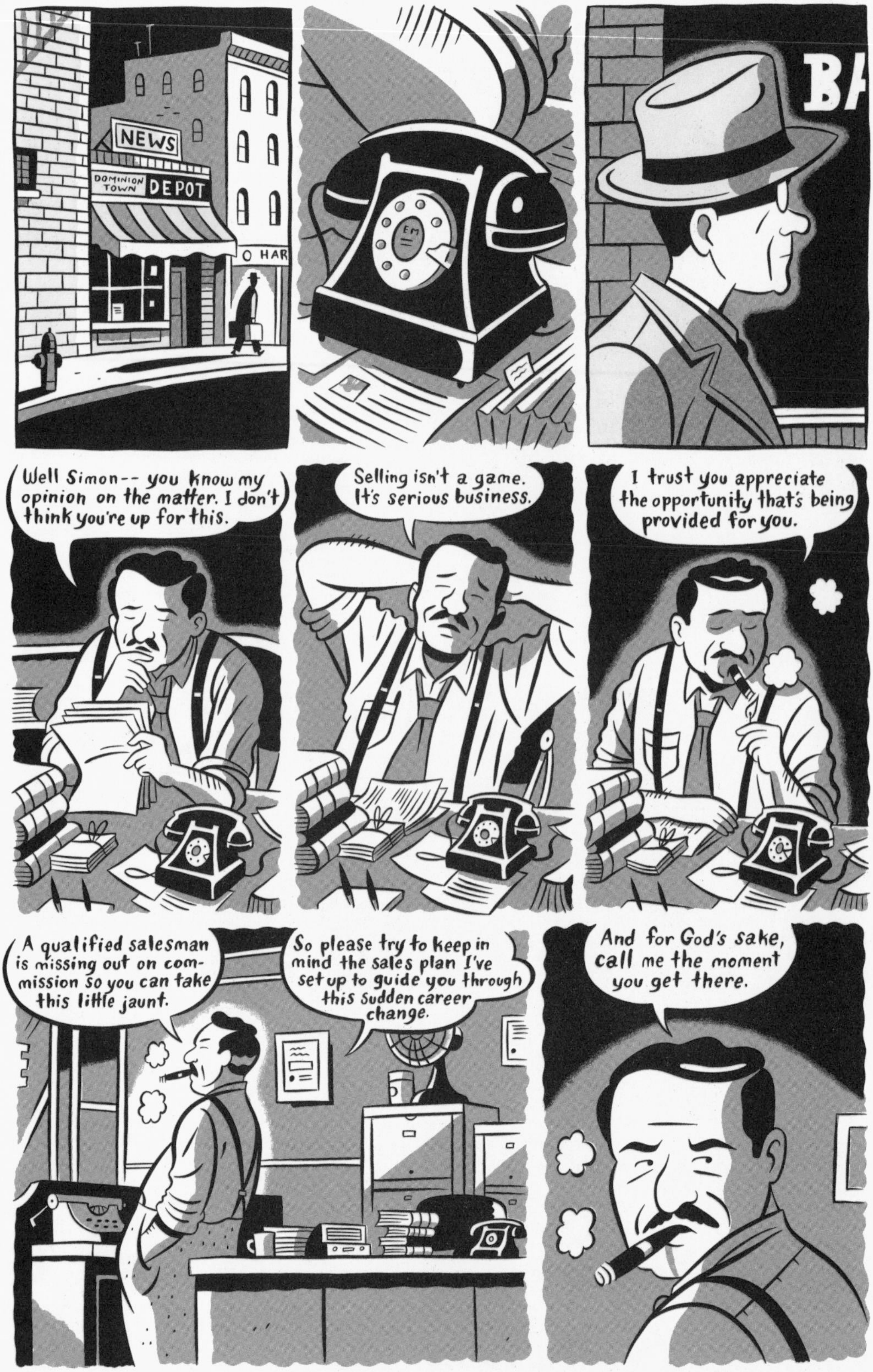
NEWS
DOMINION TOWN
DEPOT
O HAR
BA
Well Simon-- you know my opinion on the matter. I don't think you're up for this.
Selling isn't a game. It's serious business.
I trust you appreciate the opportunity that's being provided for you.
A qualified salesman is missing out on commission so you can take this little jaunt.
So please try to keep in mind the sales plan I've set up to guide you through this sudden career change.
And for God's sake, call me the moment you get there.

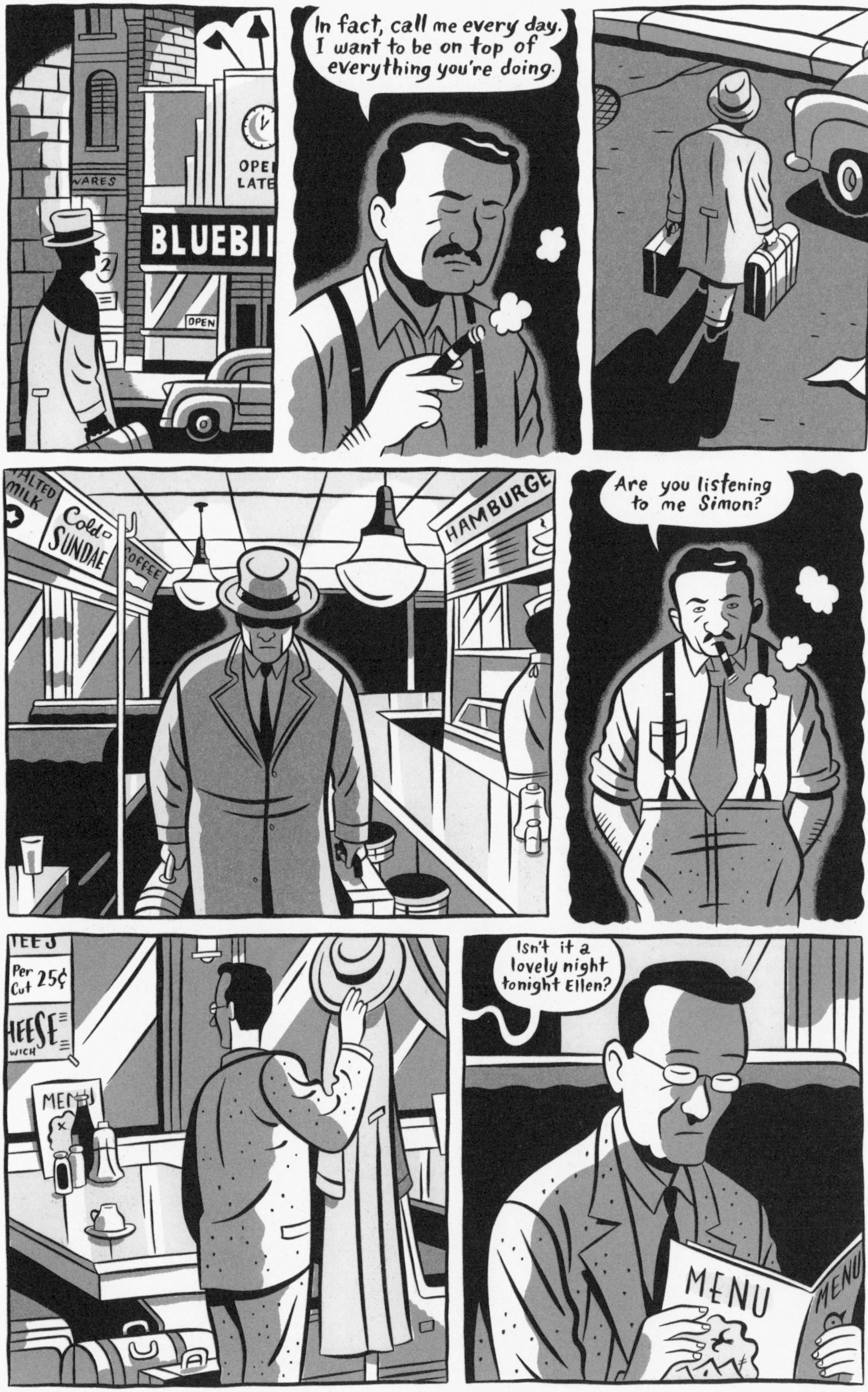
WARES
OPEN LATE
BLUEBI
OPEN
In fact, call me every day. I want to be on top of everything you're doing.
MALTED MILK
Cold SUNDAE
COFFEE
HAMBURGE
Are you listening to me Simon?
Per Cut 25¢
HEESE WICH
MENU
Isn't it a lovely night tonight Ellen?
MENU
MENU

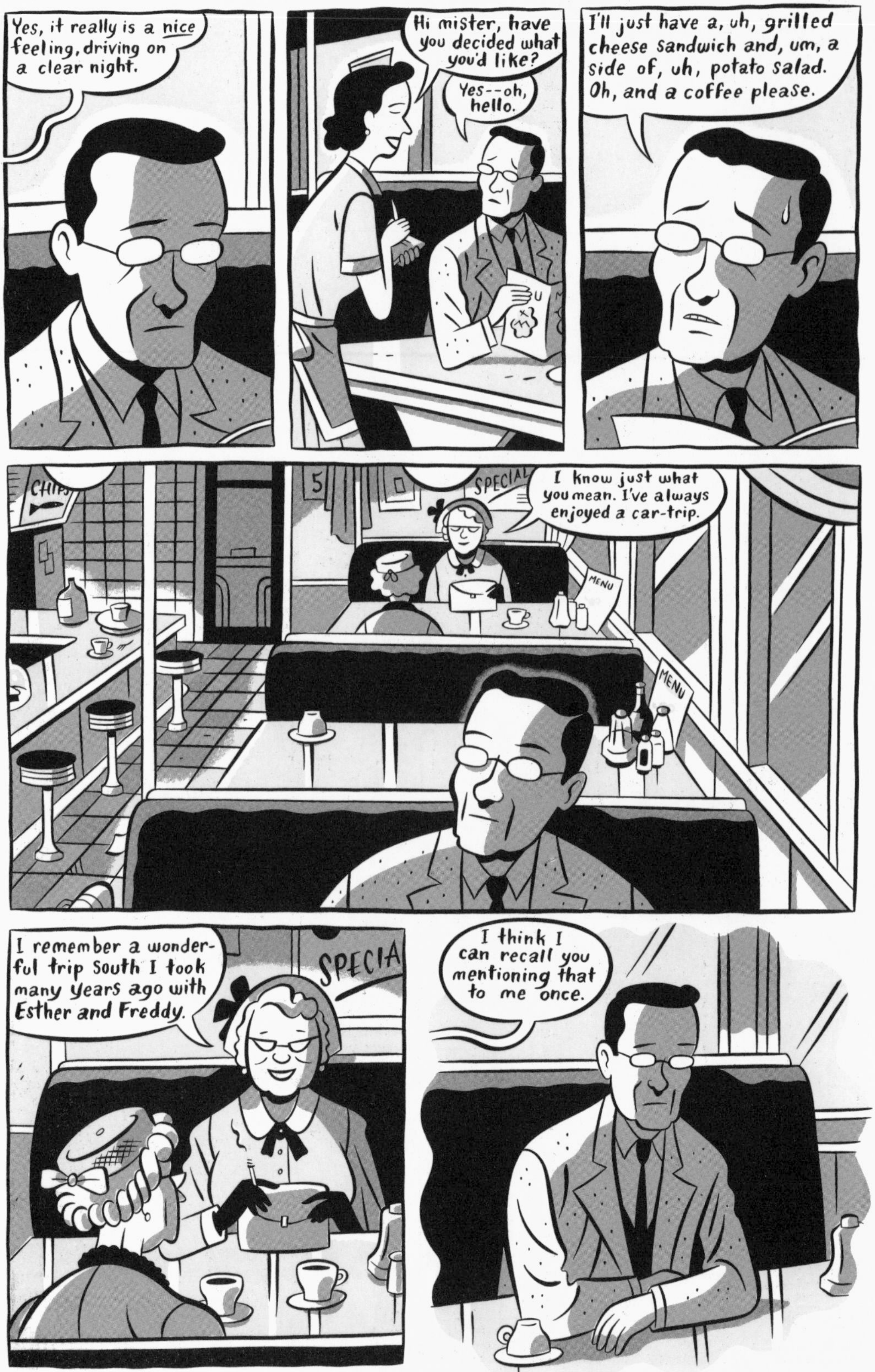
Yes, it really is a nice feeling, driving on a clear night.
Hi mister, have you decided what you'd like?
Yes--oh, hello.
I'll just have a, uh, grilled cheese sandwich and, um, a side of, uh, potato salad. Oh, and a coffee please.
CHIPS
SPECIAL
MENU
MENU
I know just what you mean. I've always enjoyed a car-trip.
I remember a wonderful trip South I took many years ago with Esther and Freddy.
SPECIA
I think I can recall you mentioning that to me once.

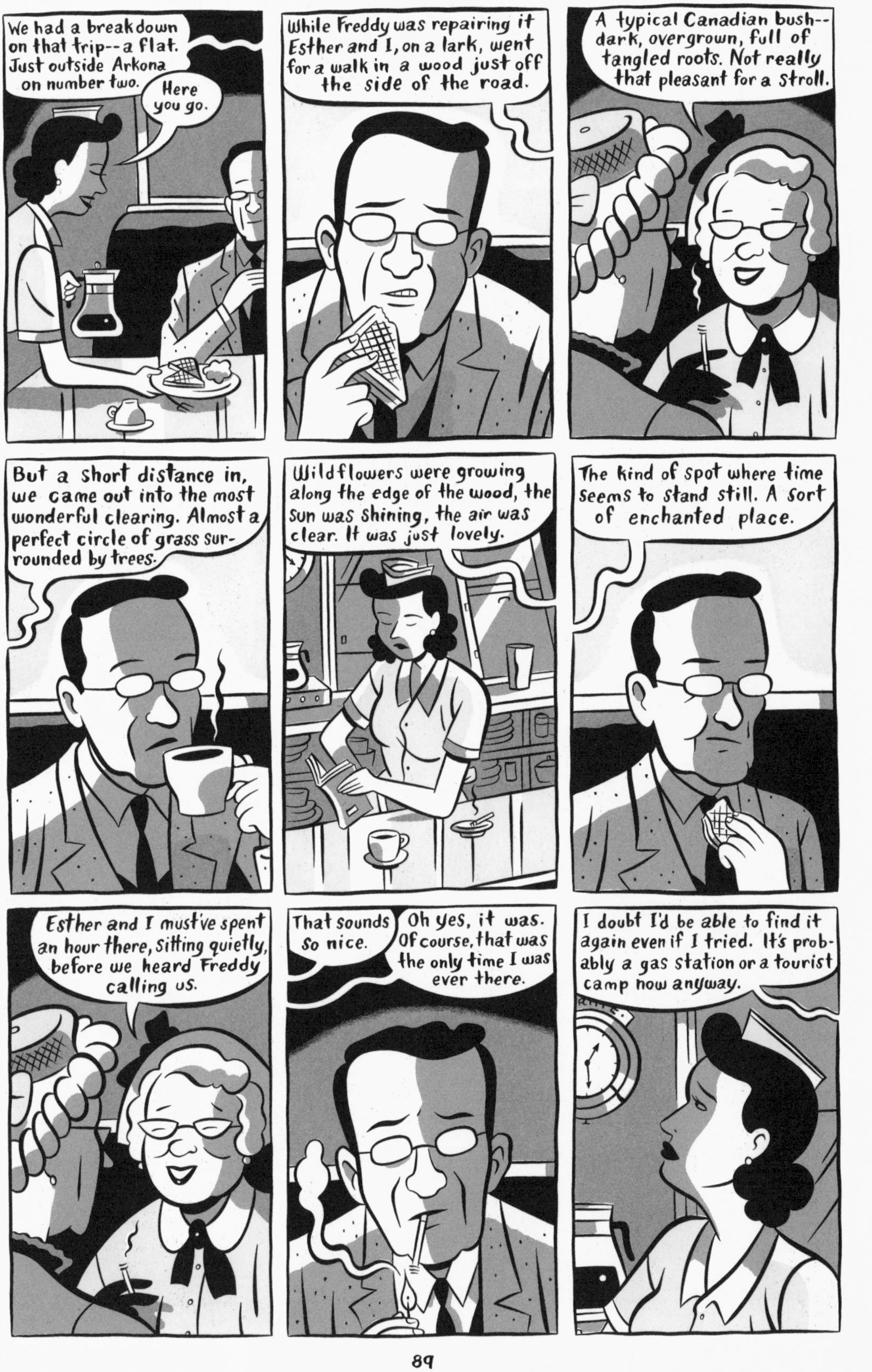
We had a breakdown on that trip--a flat. Just outside Arkona on number two.
Here you go.
While Freddy was repairing it Esther and I, on a lark, went for a walk in a wood just off the side of the road.
A typical Canadian bush--dark, overgrown, full of tangled roots. Not really that pleasant for a stroll.
But a short distance in, we came out into the most wonderful clearing. Almost a perfect circle of grass surrounded by trees.
Wildflowers were growing along the edge of the wood, the sun was shining, the air was clear. It was just lovely.
The kind of spot where time seems to stand still. A sort of enchanted place.
Esther and I must've spent an hour there, sitting quietly, before we heard Freddy calling us.
That sounds so nice.
Oh yes, it was. Of course, that was the only time I was ever there.
I doubt I'd be able to find it again even if I tried. It's probably a gas station or a tourist camp now anyway.

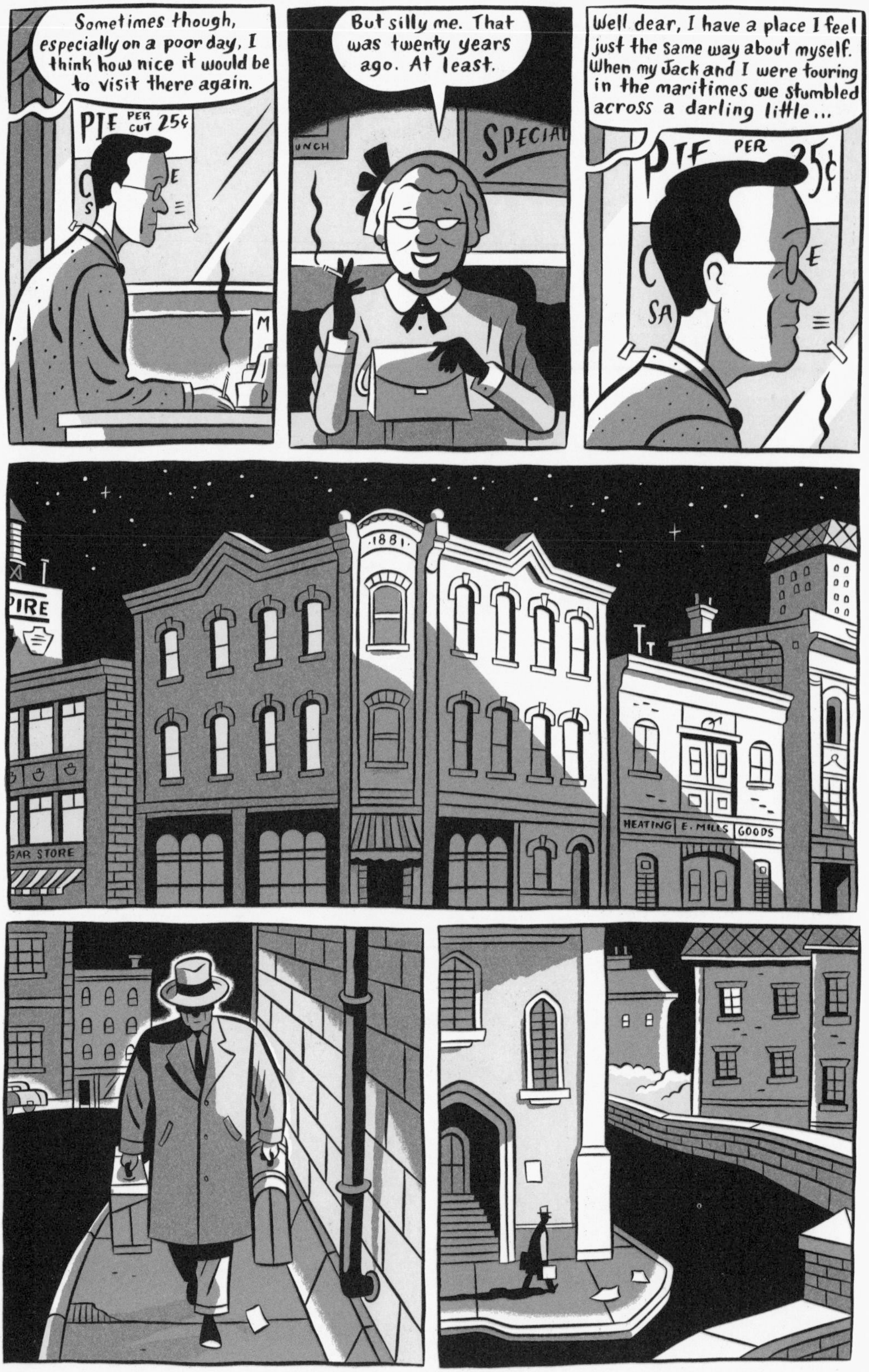
Sometimes though, especially on a poor day, I think how nice it would be to visit there again.
PIE PER CUT 25¢
But silly me. That was twenty years ago. At least.
SPECIAL
Well dear, I have a place I feel just the same way about myself. When my Jack and I were touring in the maritimes we stumbled across a darling little...
1881
PIRE
HEATING
E. MILLS
GOODS
GAR STORE

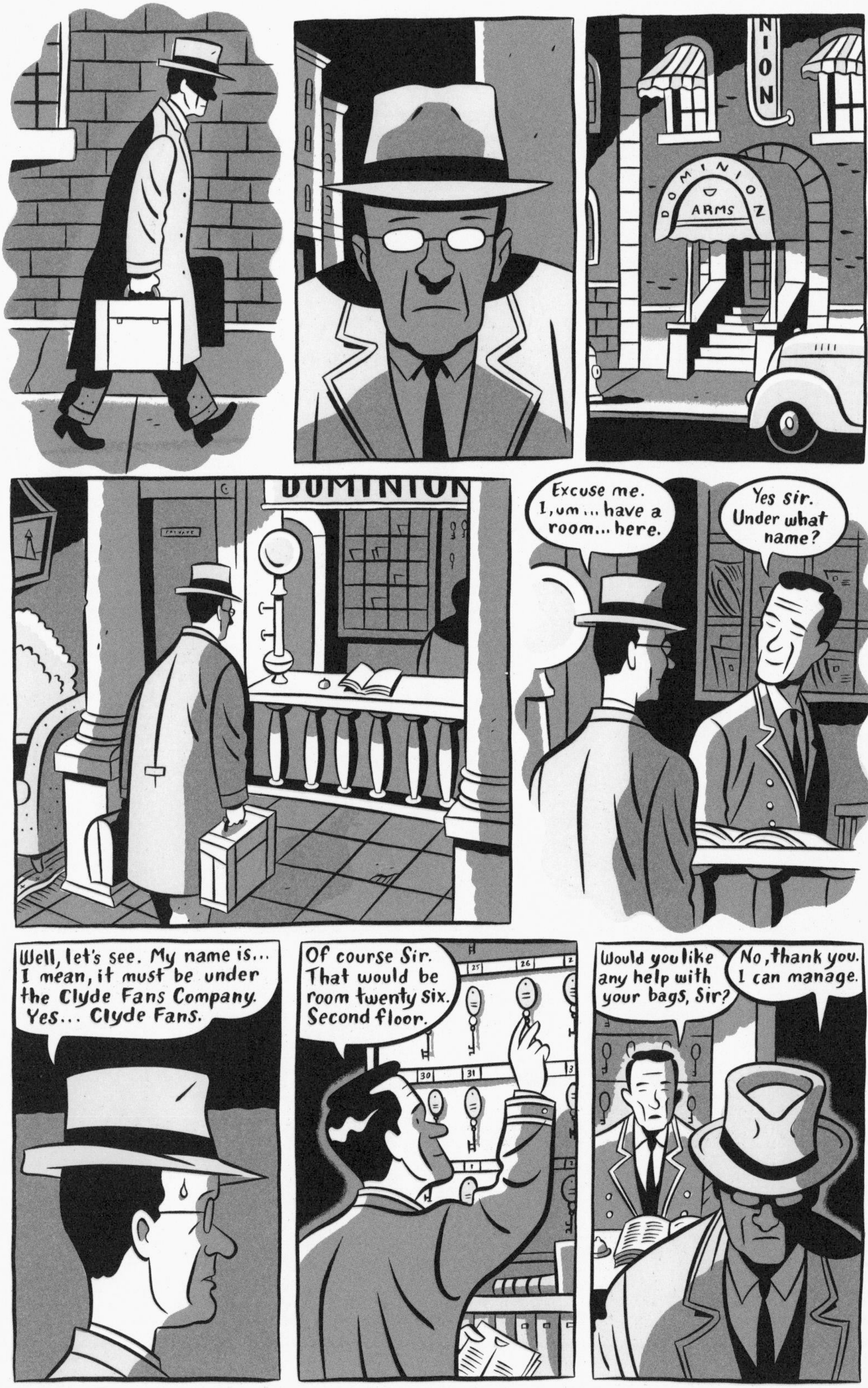
NION
DOMINION
ARMS
DOMINION
Excuse me. I, um... have a room... here.
Yes sir. Under what name?
Well, let's see. My name is... I mean, it must be under the Clyde Fans Company. Yes... Clyde Fans.
Of course Sir. That would be room twenty six. Second floor.
Would you like any help with your bags, Sir?
No, thank you. I can manage.

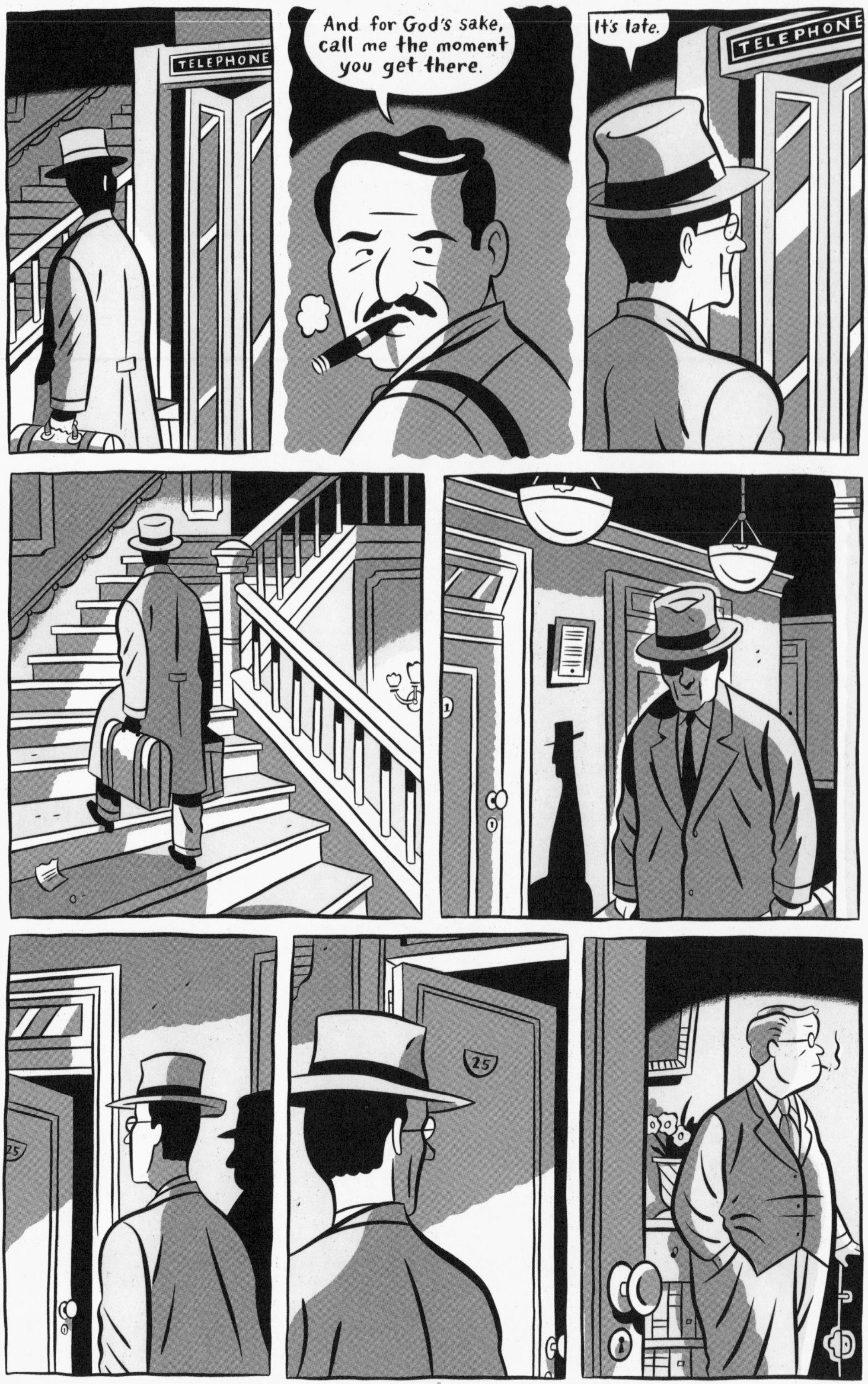
TELEPHONE
And for God's sake, call me the moment you get there.
It's late.
TELEPHONE
25
25

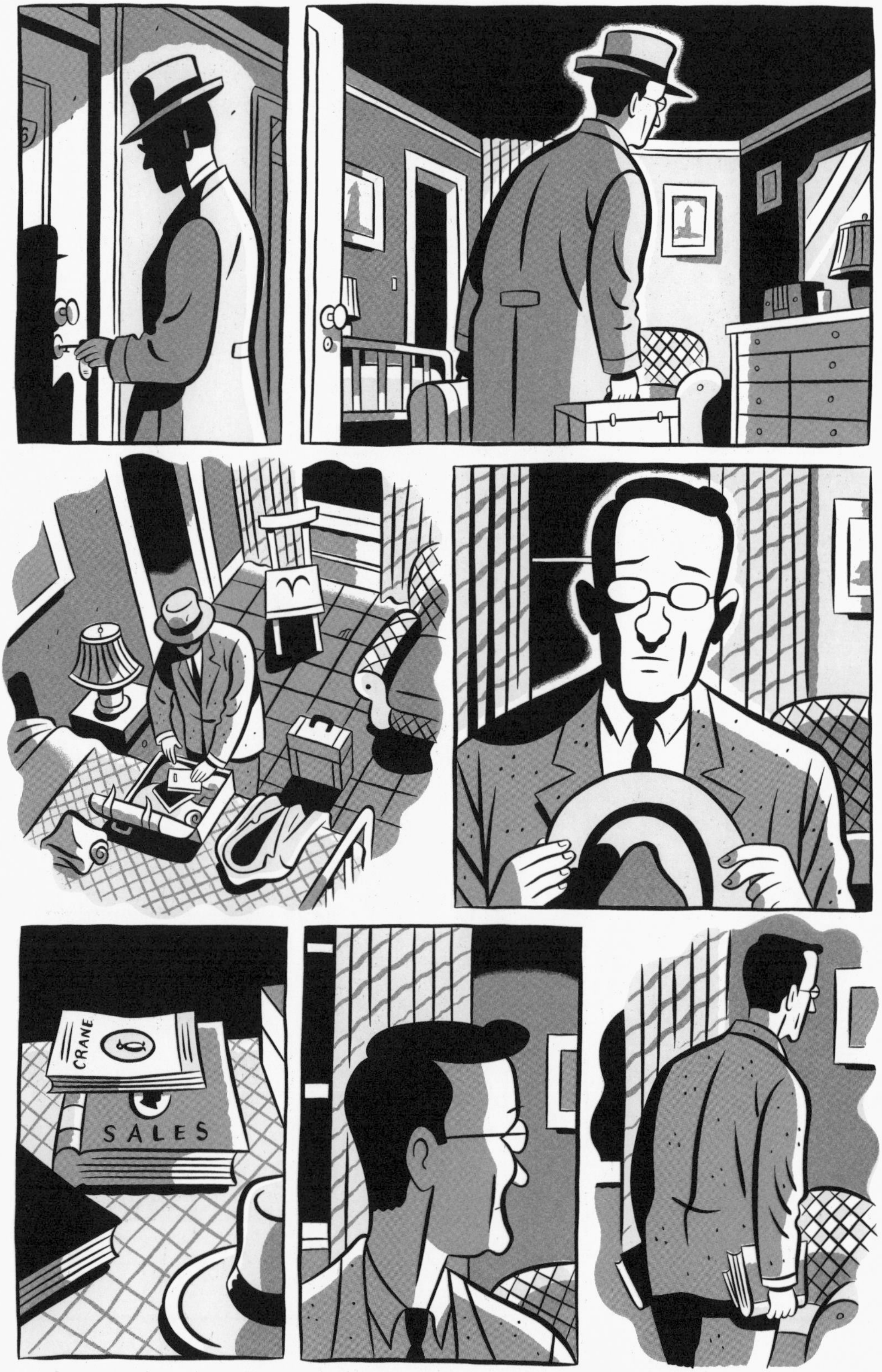
CRANE
SALES

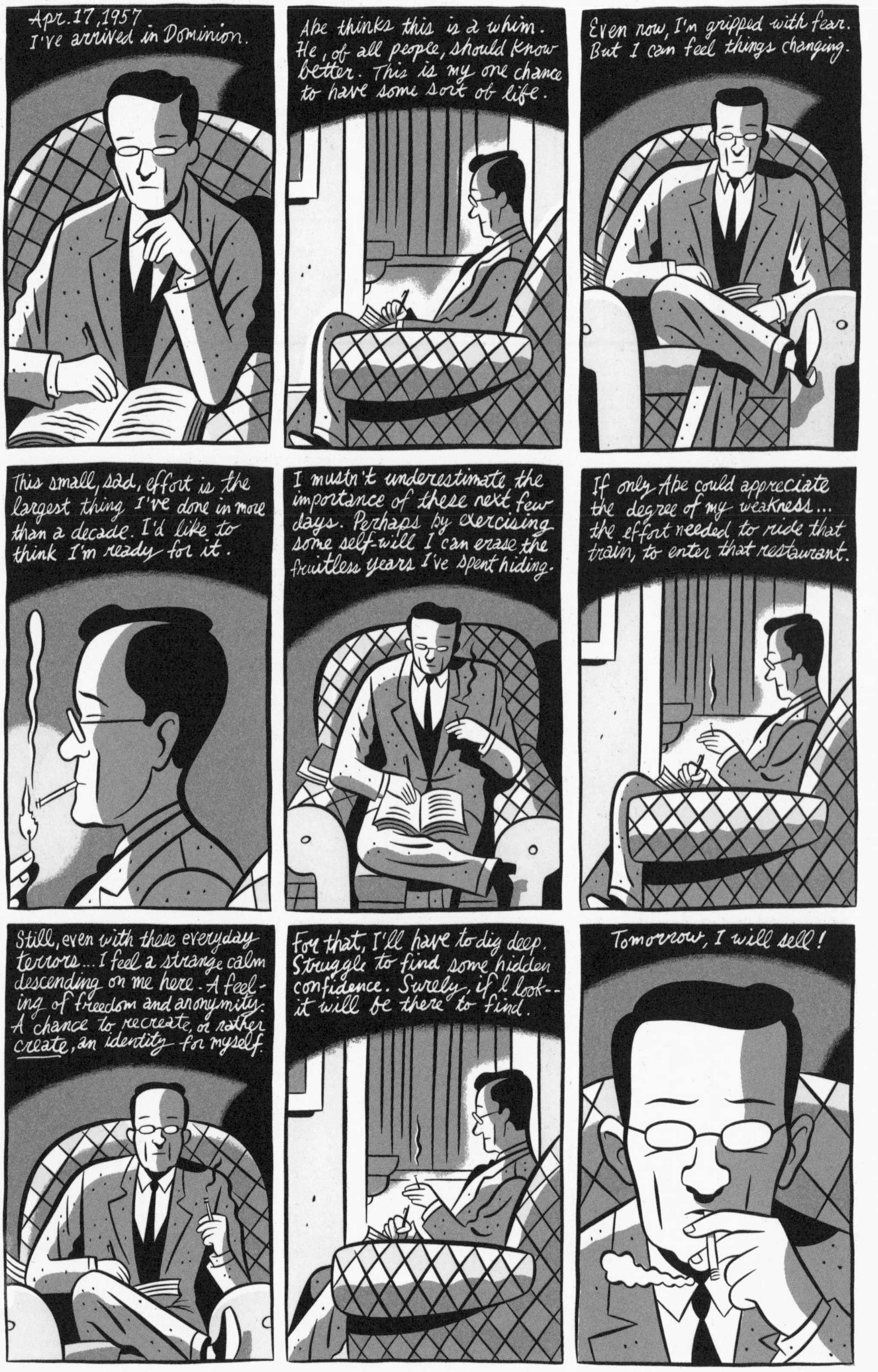
Apr. 17, 1957
I've arrived in Dominion.
Abe thinks this is a whim. He, of all people, should know better. This is my one chance to have some sort of life.
Even now, I'm gripped with fear. But I can feel things changing.
This small, sad, effort is the largest thing I've done in more than a decade. I'd like to think I'm ready for it.
I mustn't underestimate the importance of these next few days. Perhaps by exercising some self-will I can erase the fruitless years I've spent hiding.
If only Abe could appreciate the degree of my weakness... the effort needed to ride that train, to enter that restaurant.
Still, even with these everyday terrors... I feel a strange calm descending on me here. A feeling of freedom and anonymity. A chance to recreate, or rather create, an identity for myself.
For that, I'll have to dig deep. Struggle to find some hidden confidence. Surely, if I look-- it will be there to find.
Tomorrow, I will sell!

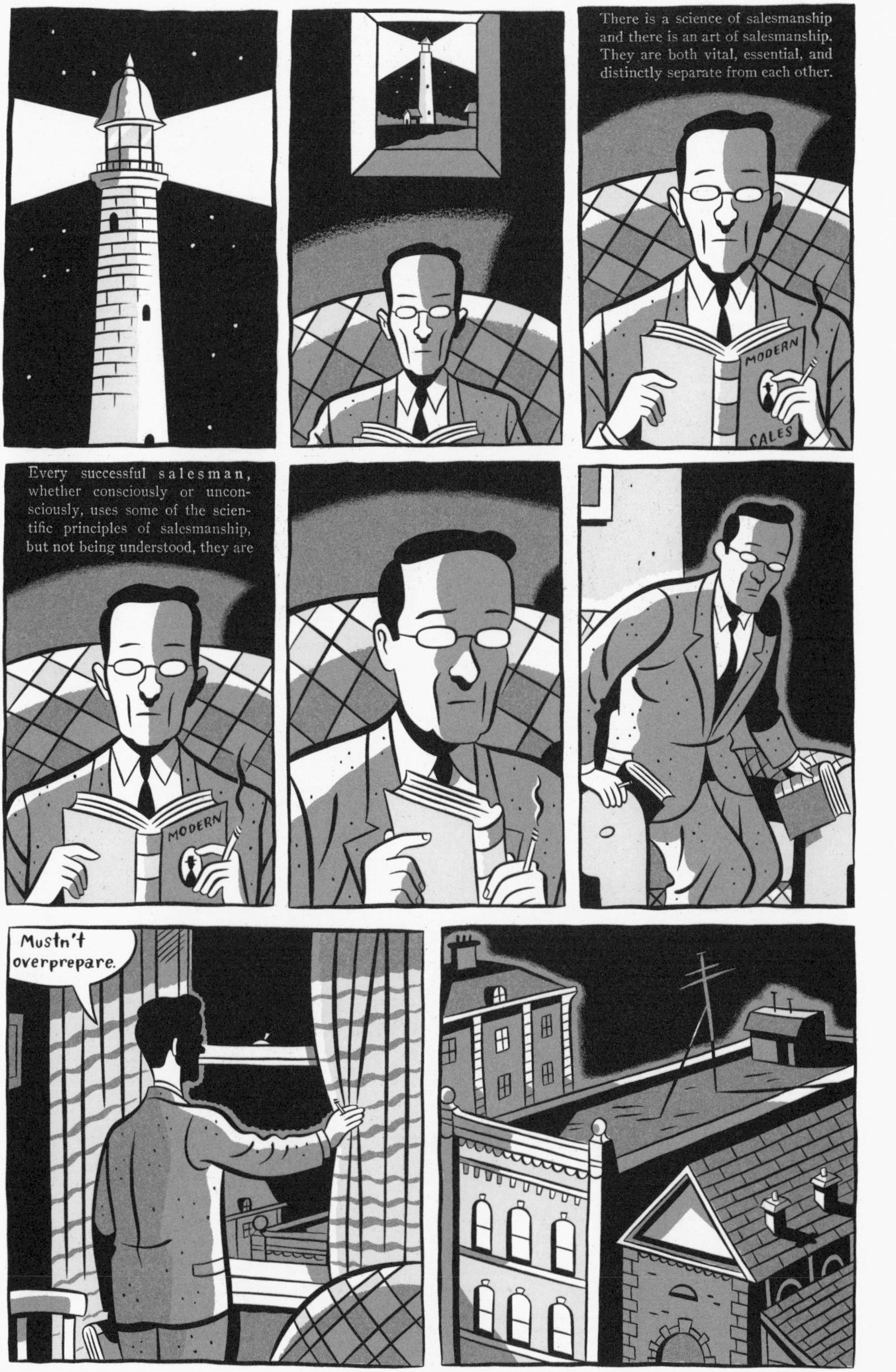
There is a science of salesmanship and there is an art of salesmanship. They are both vital, essential, and distinctly separate from each other.
MODERN
SALES
Every successful salesman, whether consciously or unconsciously, uses some of the scientific principles of salesmanship, but not being understood, they are
MODERN
Mustn't overprepare.

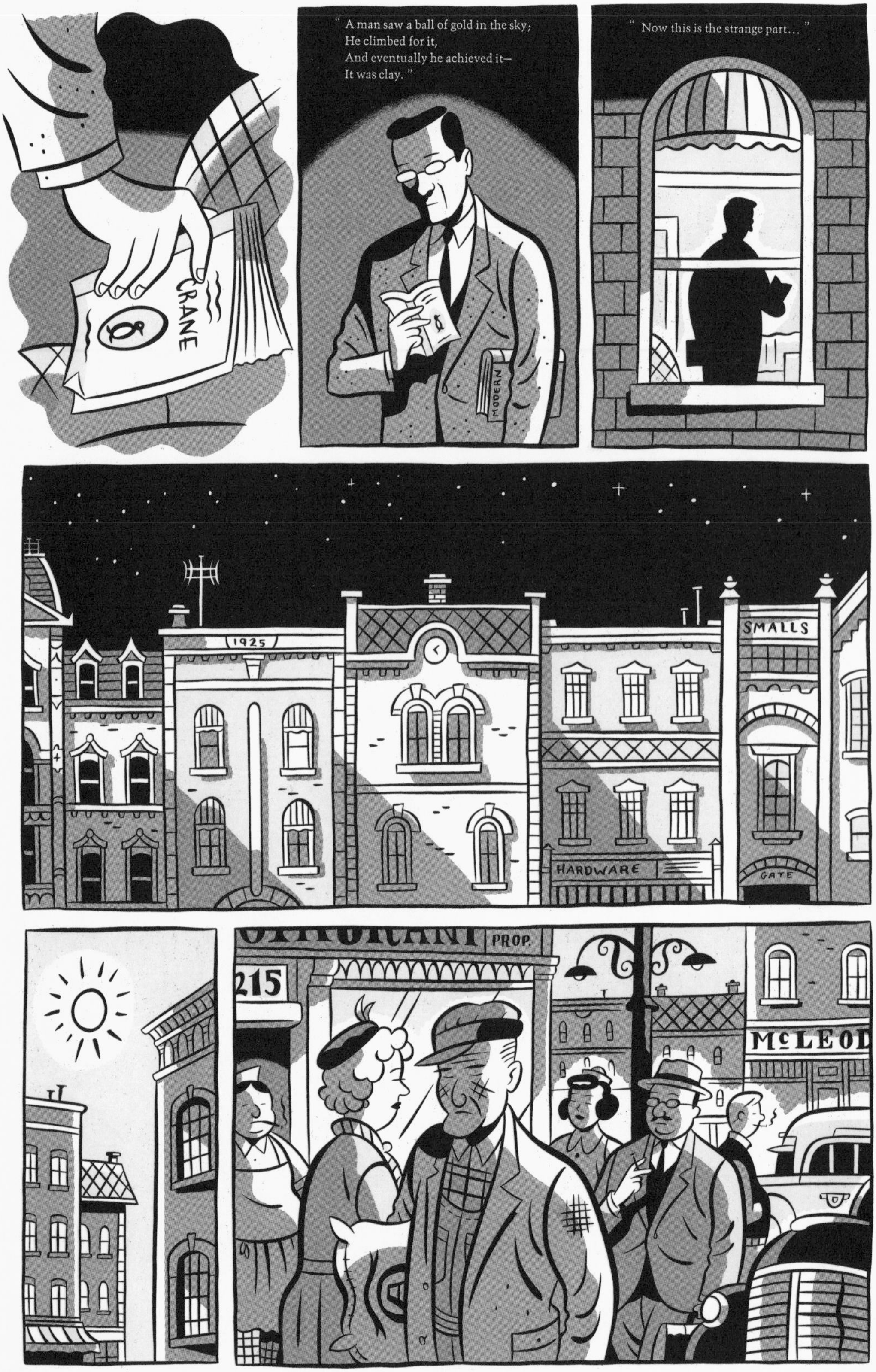
CRANE
" A man saw a ball of gold in the sky;
He climbed for it,
And eventually he achieved it—
It was clay. "
MODERN
" Now this is the strange part... "
1925
SMALLS
HARDWARE
GATE
PROP.
215
McLEOD

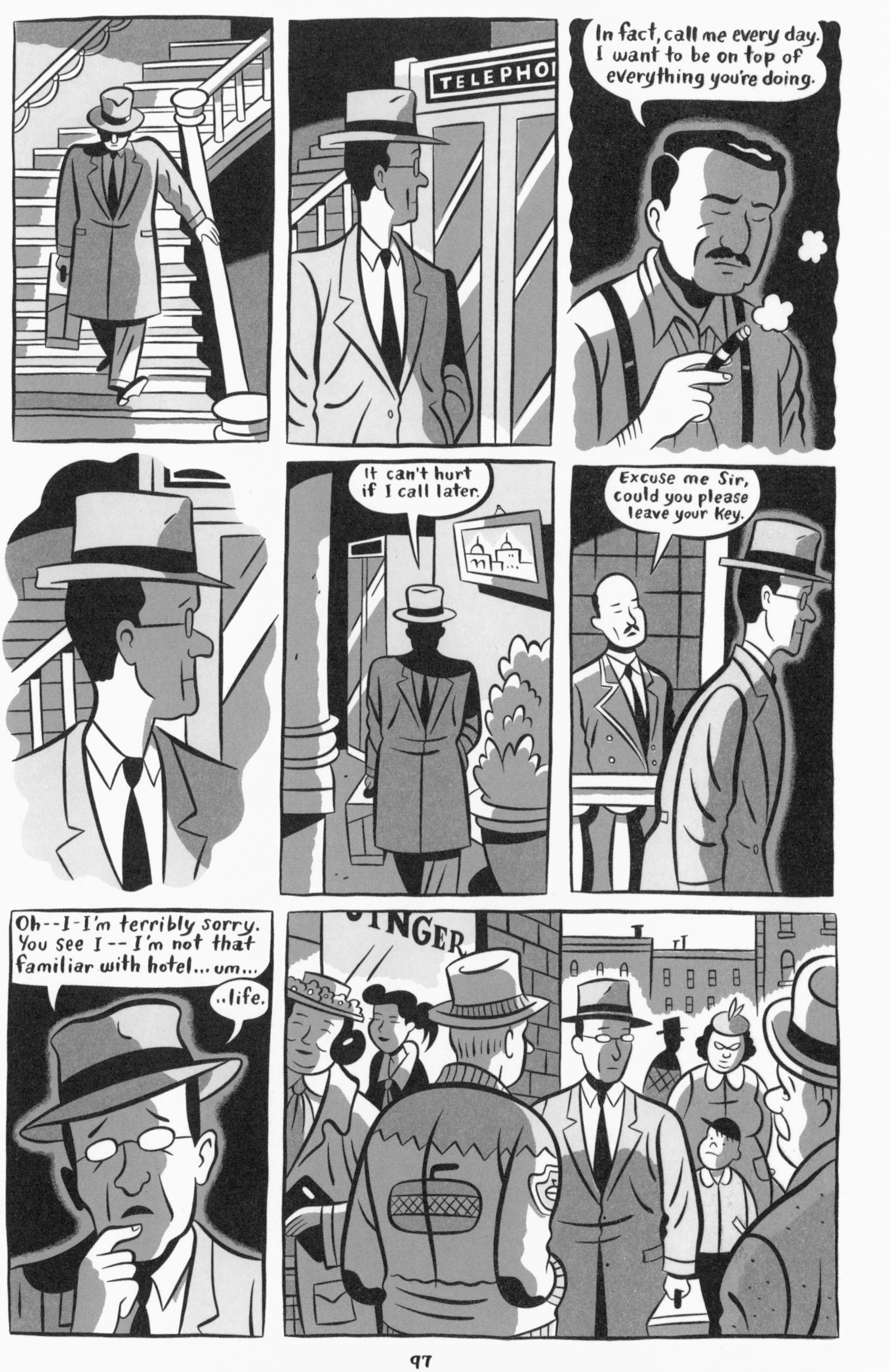
TELEPHO
In fact, call me every day. I want to be on top of everything you're doing.
It can't hurt if I call later.
Excuse me Sir, could you please leave your Key.
Oh--I-I'm terribly sorry. You see I -- I'm not that familiar with hotel... um...
..life.
NGER

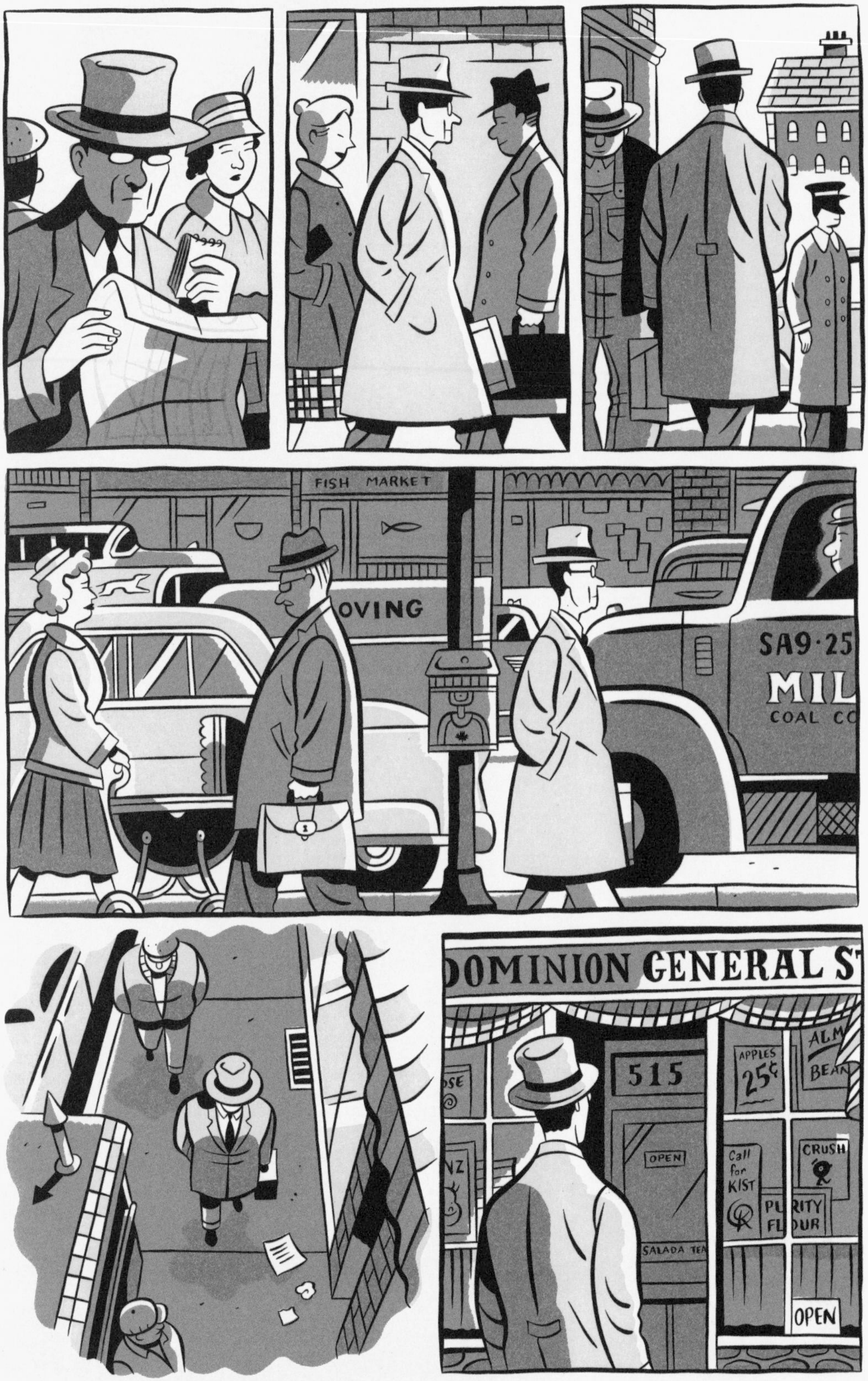

FISH MARKET
OVING
SA9·25
MIL
COAL CO
DOMINION GENERAL ST
515
APPLES 25¢
ALM
BEAN
OSE
OPEN
NZ
Call for KIST
CRUSH
PURITY FLOUR
SALADA TEA
OPEN

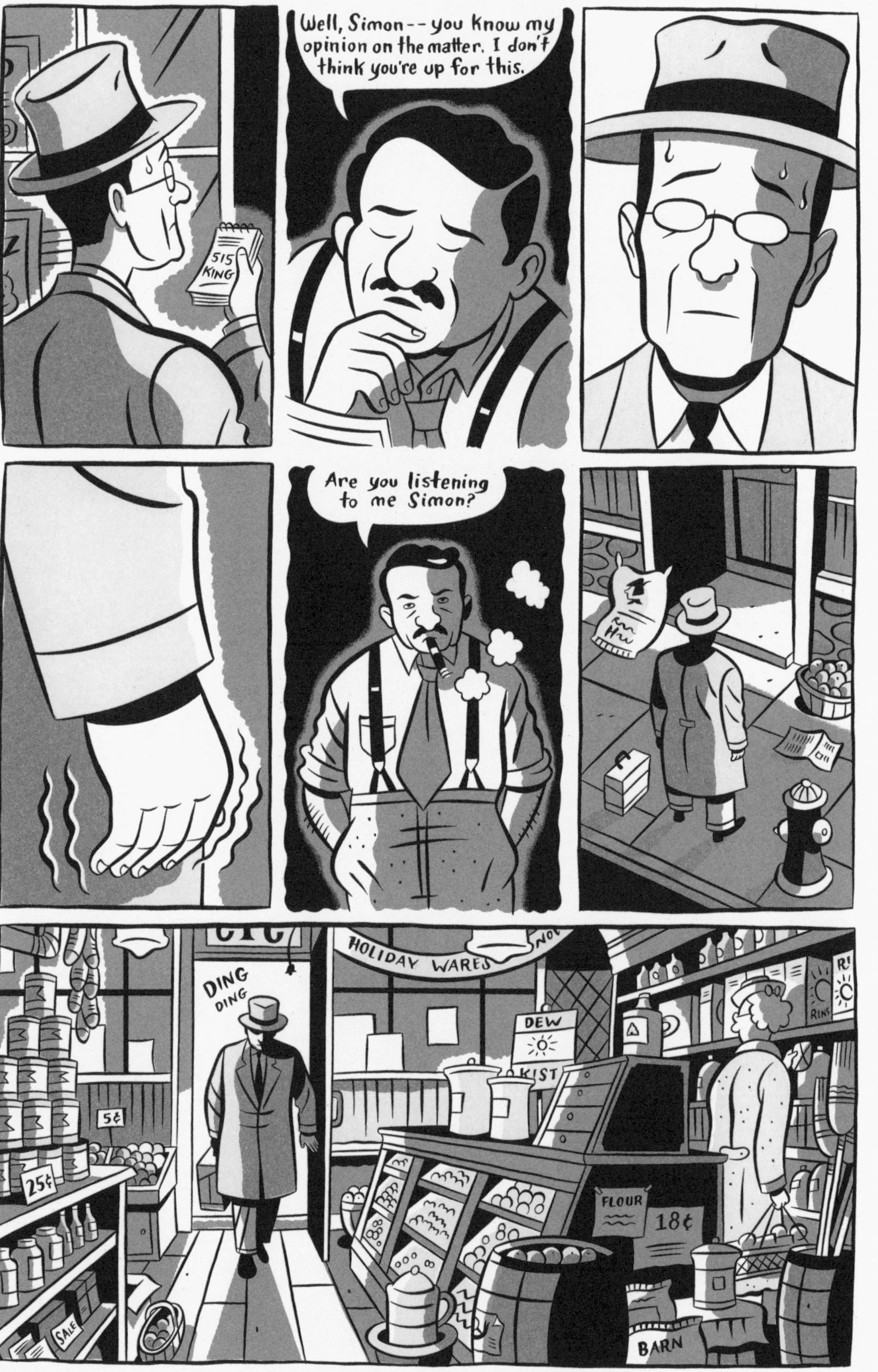
515 KING
Well, Simon-- you know my opinion on the matter. I don't think you're up for this.
Are you listening to me Simon?
HOLIDAY WARES
DING DING
DEW
KIST
5¢
25¢
FLOUR
18¢
SALE
BARN

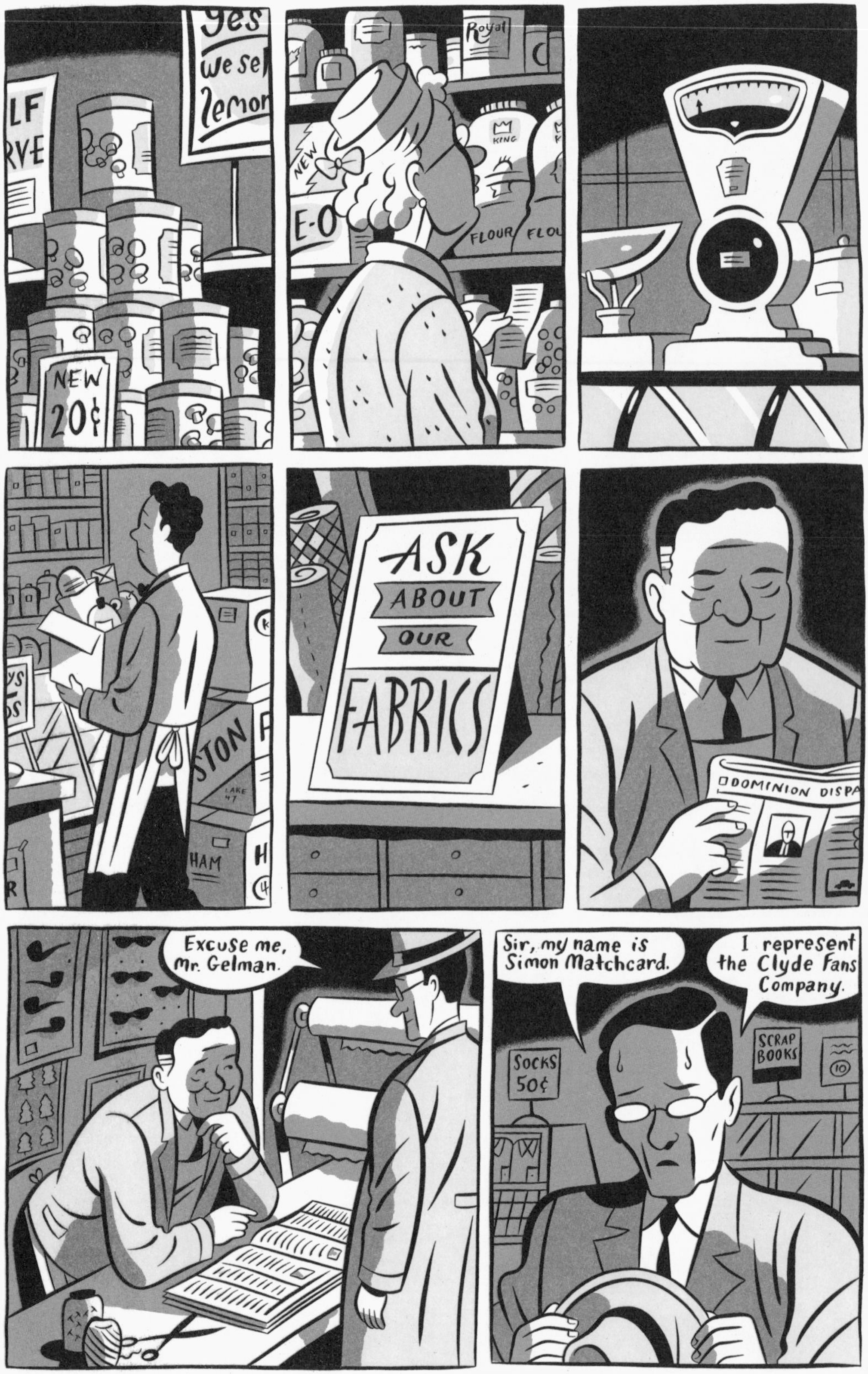

Yes
We sell
lemon
NEW 20¢
NEW
E-O
Royal
KING
FLOUR
FLOUR
ASK
ABOUT
OUR
FABRICS
DOMINION DISPA
Excuse me, Mr. Gelman.
Sir, my name is Simon Matchcard.
I represent the Clyde Fans Company.
SOCKS 50¢
SCRAP BOOKS

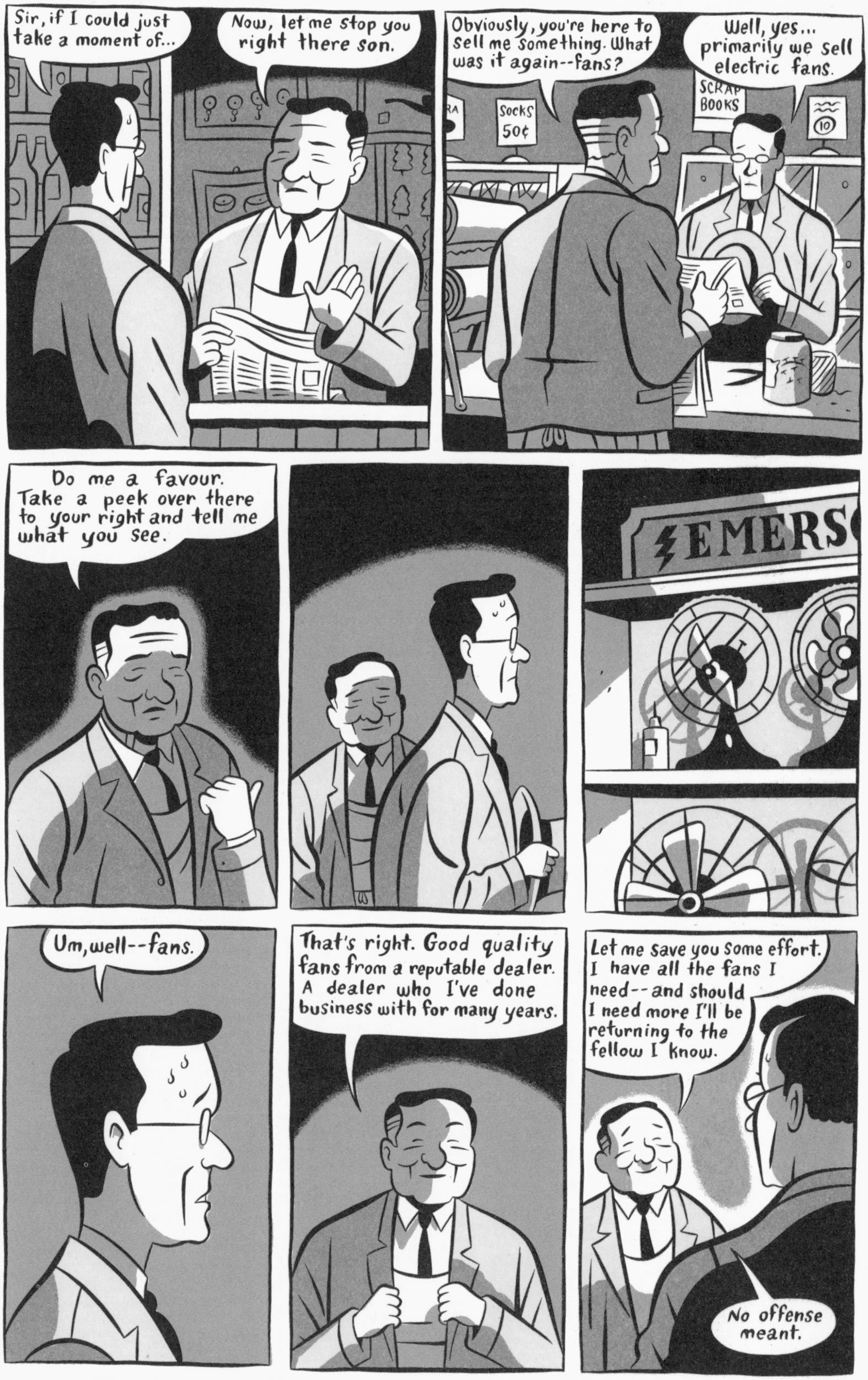
Sir, if I could just take a moment of...
Now, let me stop you right there son.
Obviously, you're here to sell me something. What was it again--fans?
Well, yes... primarily we sell electric fans.
SOCKS 50¢
SCRAP BOOKS
Do me a favour. Take a peek over there to your right and tell me what you see.
EMERS
Um, well--fans.
That's right. Good quality fans from a reputable dealer. A dealer who I've done business with for many years.
Let me save you some effort. I have all the fans I need--and should I need more I'll be returning to the fellow I know.
No offense meant.

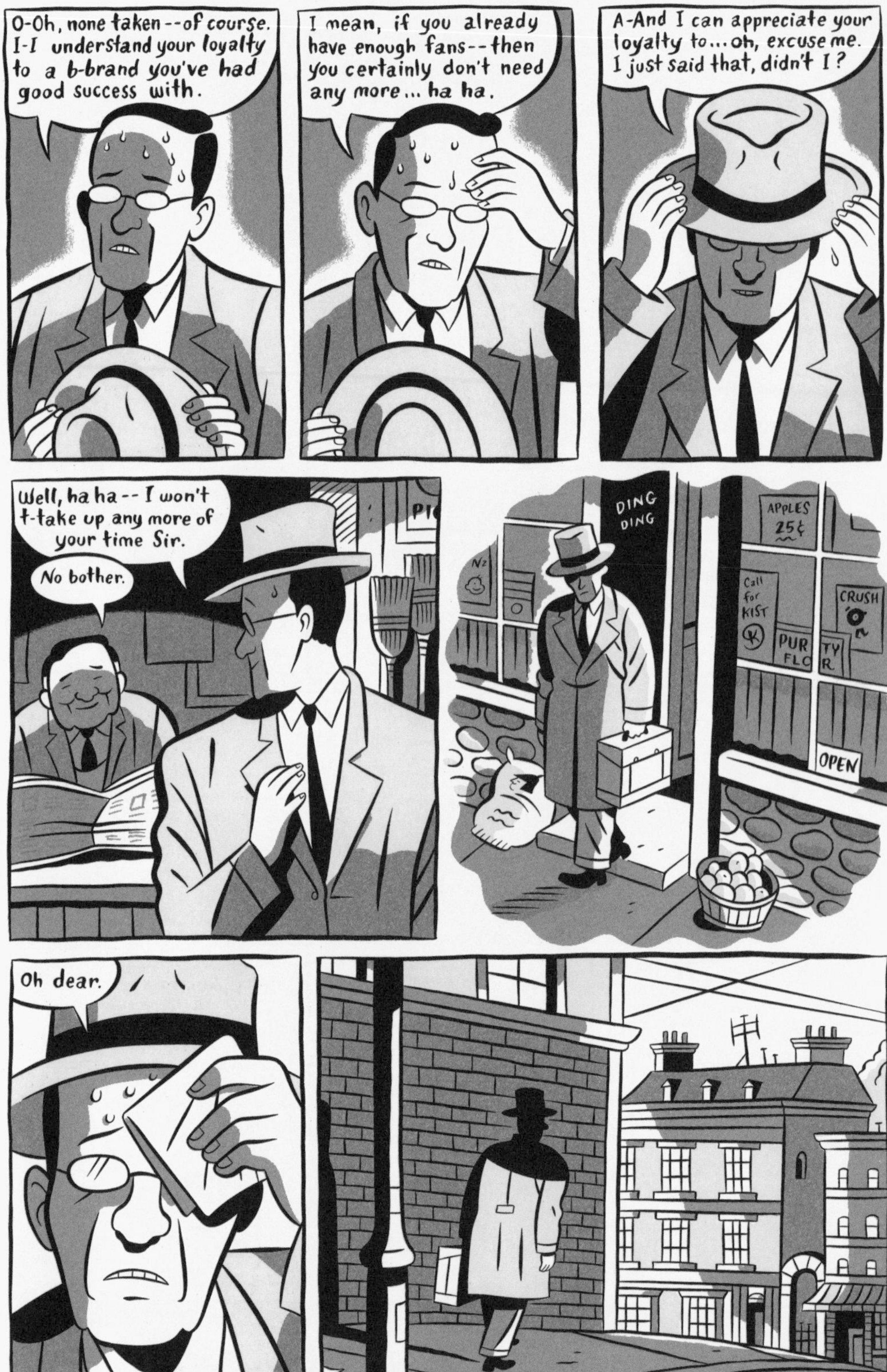

O-Oh, none taken--of course. I-I understand your loyalty to a b-brand you've had good success with.
I mean, if you already have enough fans--then you certainly don't need any more... ha ha.
A-And I can appreciate your loyalty to... oh, excuse me. I just said that, didn't I?
Well, ha ha-- I won't t-take up any more of your time Sir.
No bother.
DING DING
APPLES 25¢
Call for KIST
CRUSH
OPEN
Oh dear.

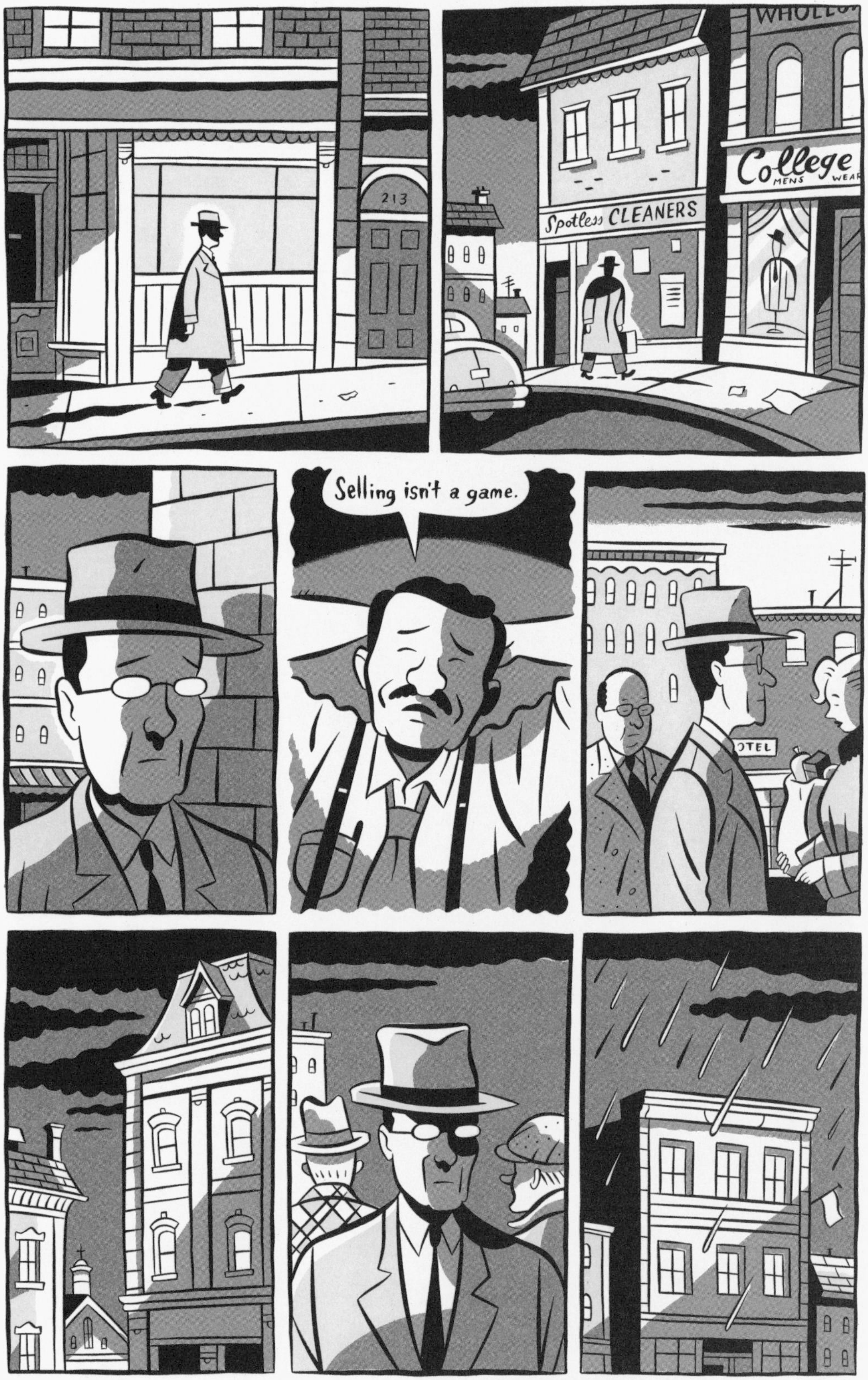
213
WHOLE
College
MENS WEAR
Spotless CLEANERS
Selling isn't a game.
OTEL

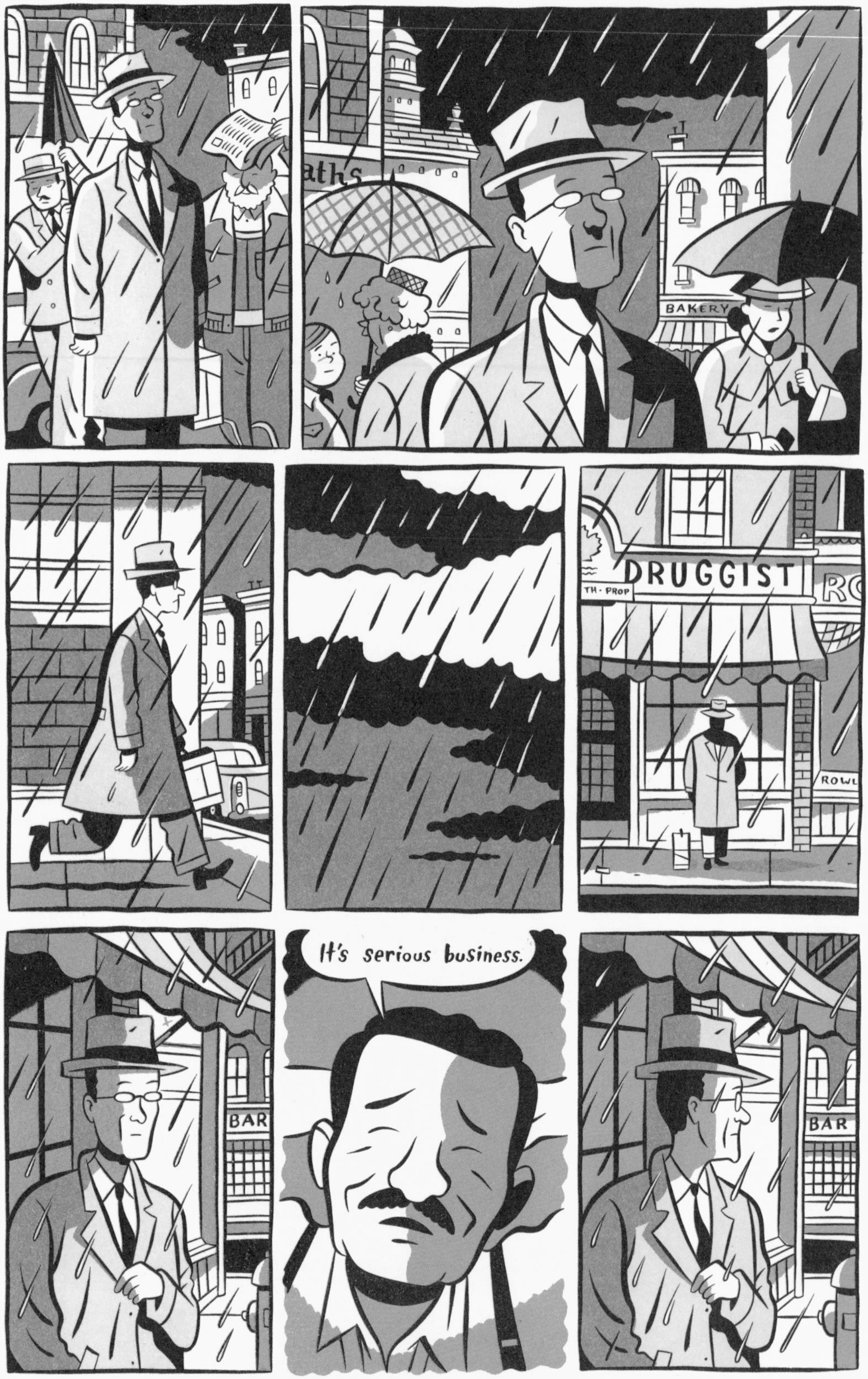
aths
BAKERY
DRUGGIST
TH · PROP
ROWL
BAR
It's serious business.
BAR

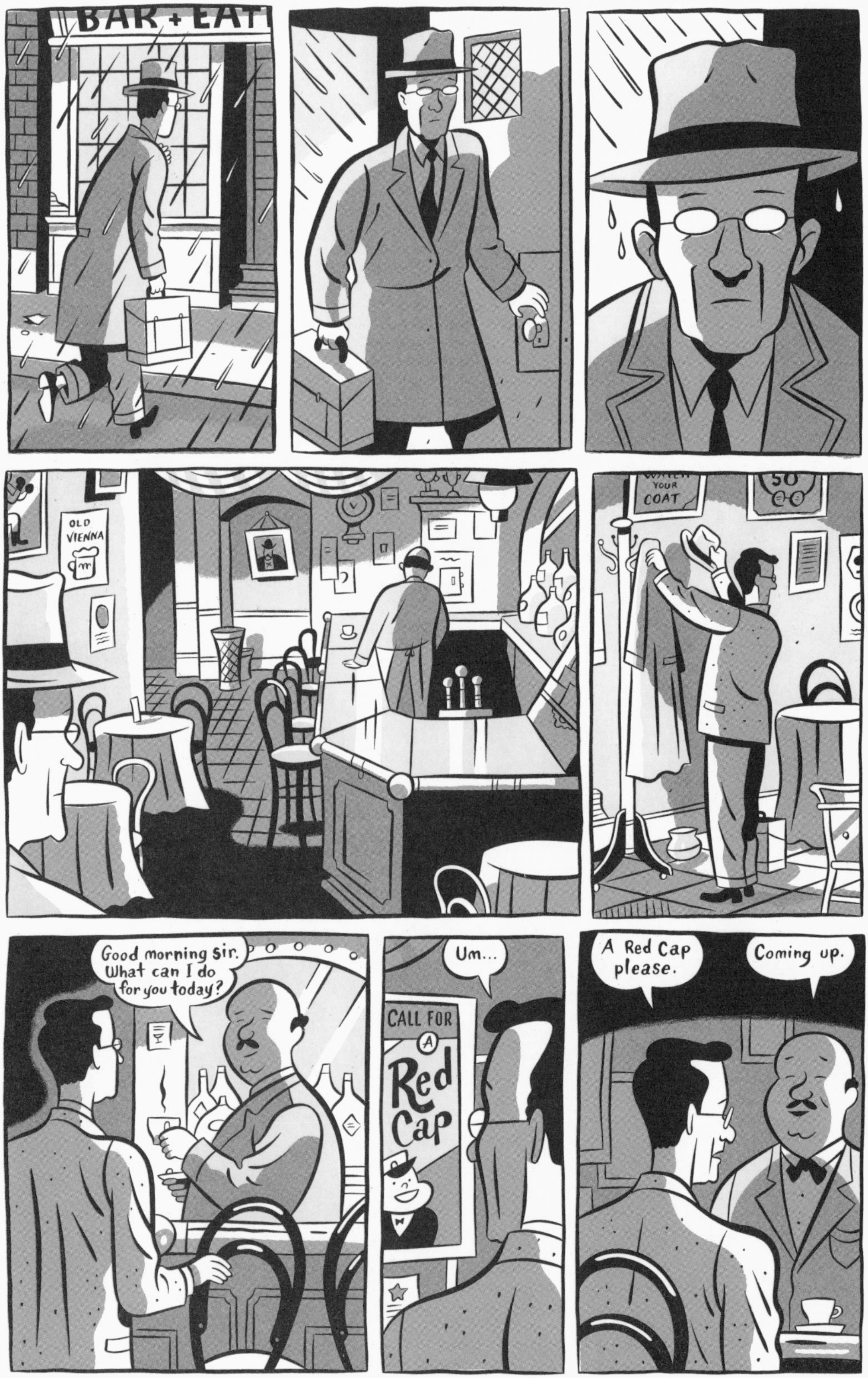
BAR + EAT
OLD VIENNA
YOUR COAT
Good morning sir. What can I do for you today?
Um...
CALL FOR A Red Cap
A Red Cap please.
Coming up.

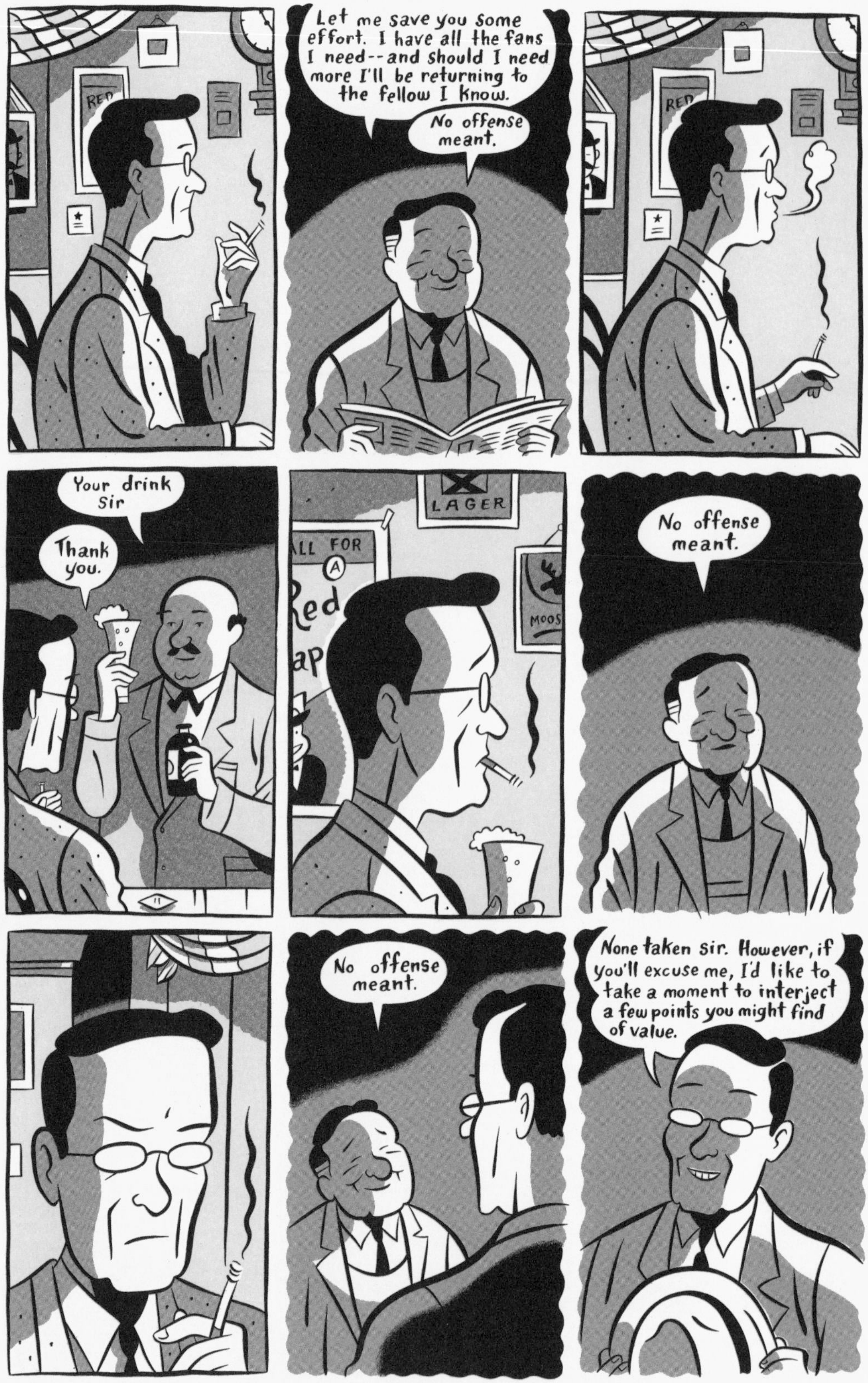

RED
Let me save you some effort. I have all the fans I need--and should I need more I'll be returning to the fellow I know.
No offense meant.
RED
Your drink sir
Thank you.
LAGER
ALL FOR
A
Red
ap
MOOS
No offense meant.
No offense meant.
None taken sir. However, if you'll excuse me, I'd like to take a moment to interject a few points you might find of value.

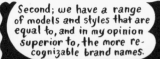

Number one--with a local manufacturer your access to quick re-stock and to parts and service is much improved.

Second; we have a range of models and styles that are equal to, and in my opinion superior to, the more recognizable brand names.

And finally--We want your business. We will offer a retailer discount that will be much more to your advantage than that of our competitors.

Well young man, when you put it like that... I guess I'd better place a starter order and see if you're as good as you claim.

RED

CAP

XXX STOUT

95 SIMCOE STREET

CON

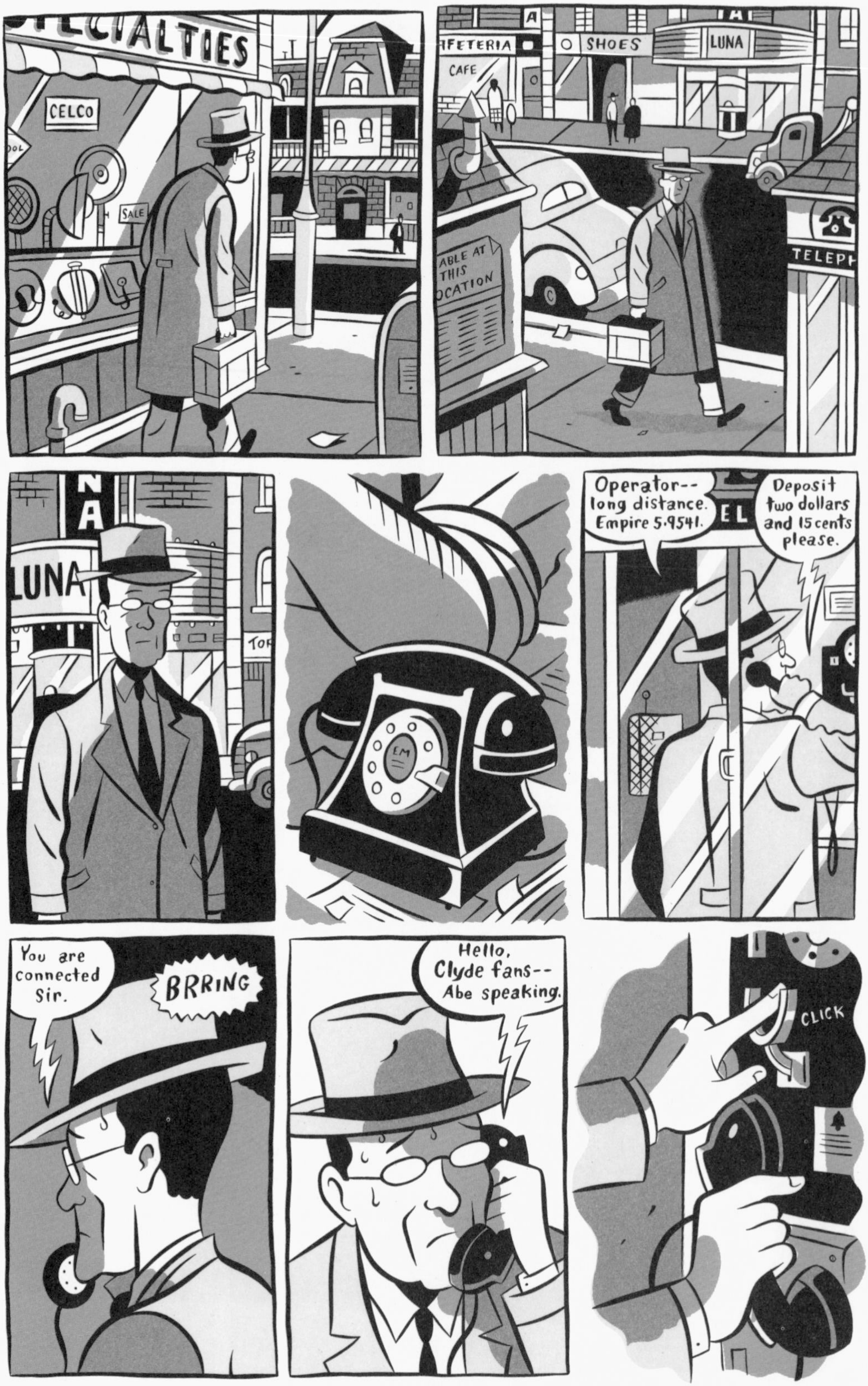
CELCO
SALE
SHOES
LUNA
CAFE
LUNA
Operator--
long distance.
Empire 5.9541.
Deposit
two dollars
and 15 cents
please.
You are
connected
Sir.
BRRING
Hello,
Clyde fans--
Abe speaking.
CLICK

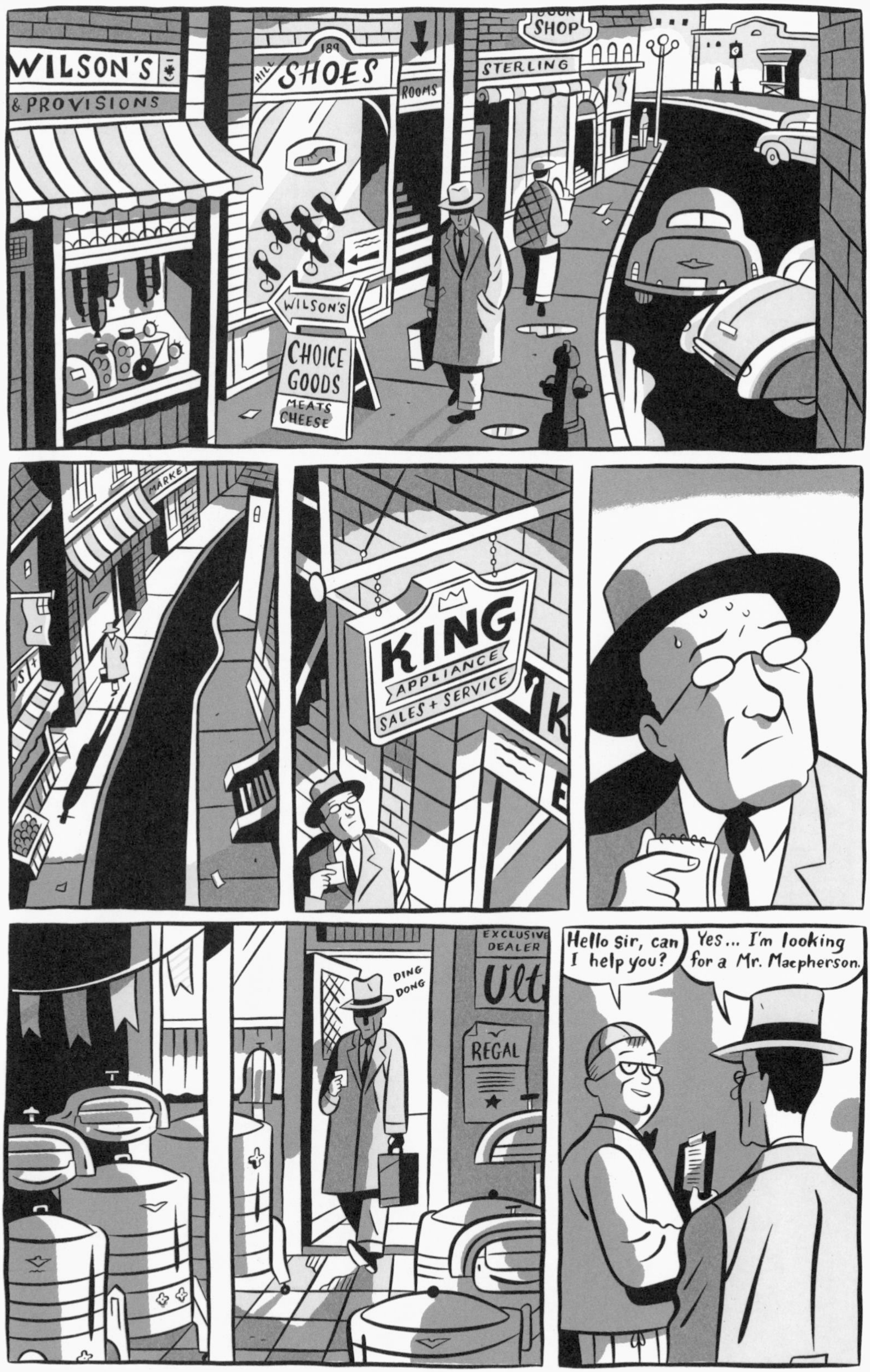
BOOK SHOP
WILSON'S
& PROVISIONS
189
HILL
SHOES
ROOMS
STERLING
WILSON'S
CHOICE GOODS
MEATS
CHEESE
MARKE
KING
APPLIANCE
SALES + SERVICE
EXCLUSIVE DEALER
Ult
DING DONG
REGAL
Hello sir, can I help you?
Yes... I'm looking for a Mr. Maepherson.

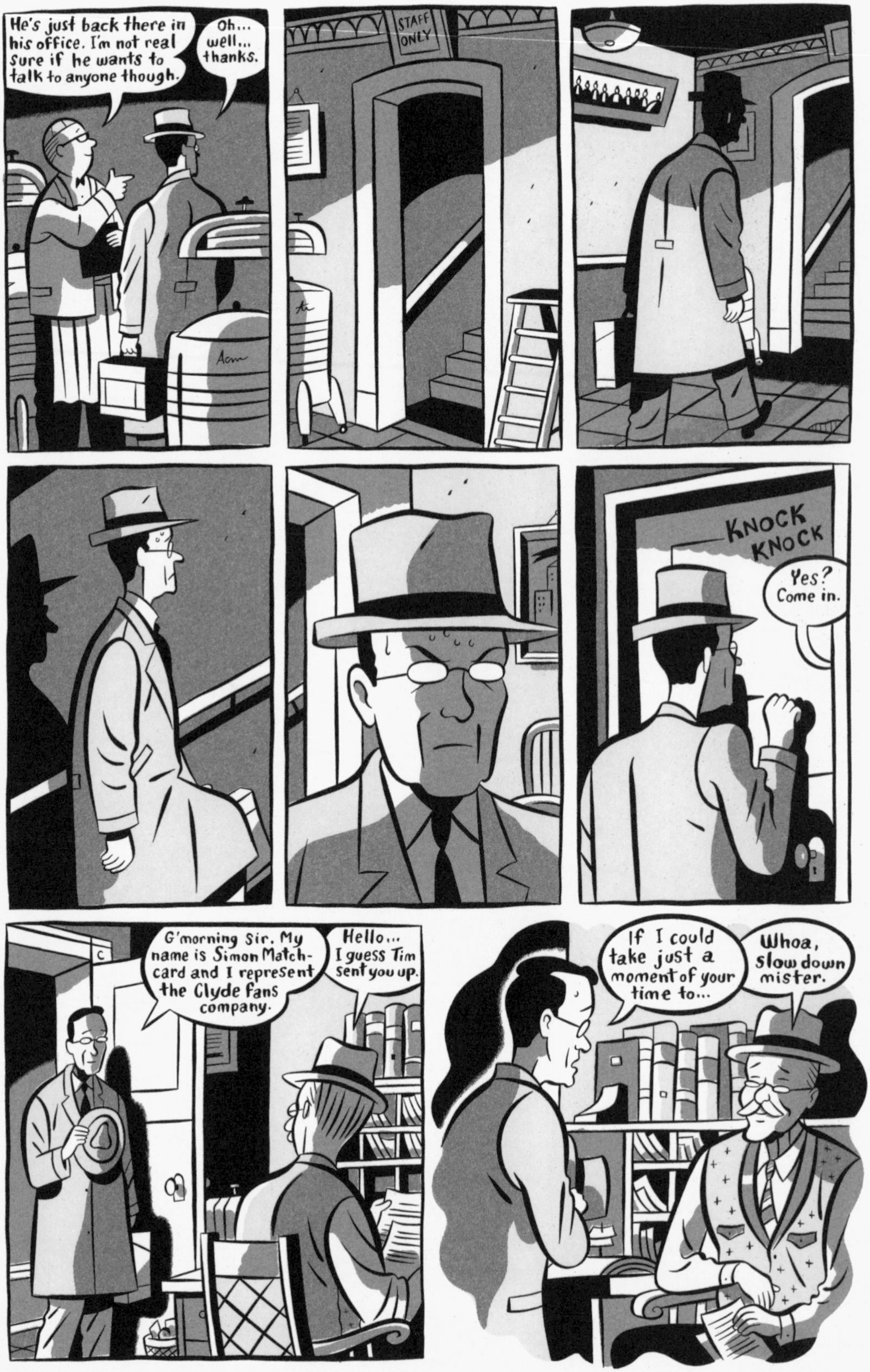
He's just back there in his office. I'm not real sure if he wants to talk to anyone though.
Oh... well... thanks.
STAFF ONLY
KNOCK KNOCK
Yes? Come in.
G'morning Sir. My name is Simon Matchcard and I represent the Clyde fans company.
Hello... I guess Tim sent you up.
If I could take just a moment of your time to...
Whoa, slow down mister.

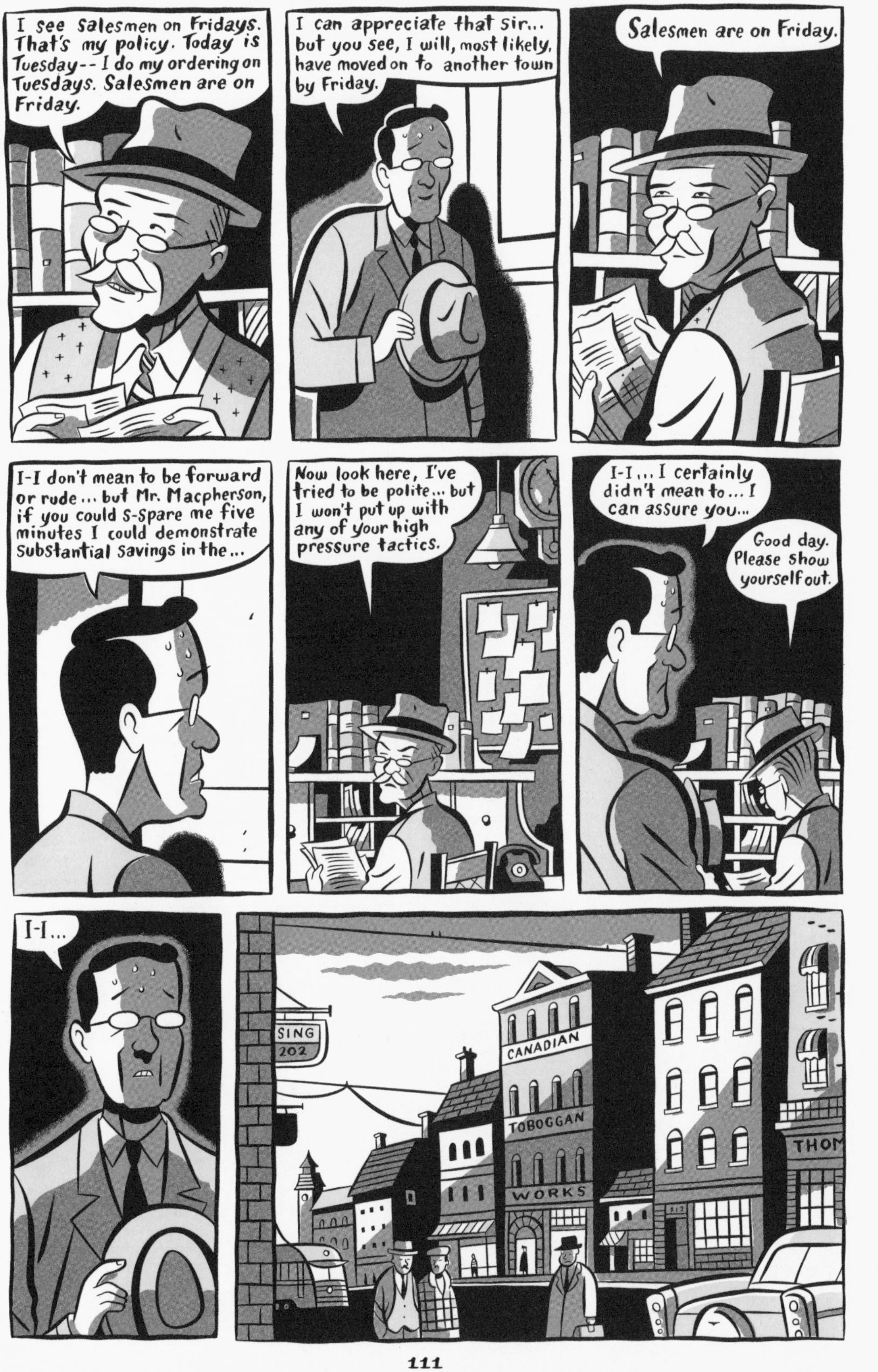
I see Salesmen on Fridays. That's my policy. Today is Tuesday-- I do my ordering on Tuesdays. Salesmen are on Friday.
I can appreciate that sir... but you see, I will, most likely, have moved on to another town by Friday.
Salesmen are on Friday.
I-I don't mean to be forward or rude... but Mr. Macpherson, if you could s-spare me five minutes I could demonstrate substantial savings in the...
Now look here, I've tried to be polite... but I won't put up with any of your high pressure tactics.
I-I... I certainly didn't mean to... I can assure you...
Good day. Please show yourself out.
I-I...
SING
202
CANADIAN
TOBOGGAN
WORKS
THOM

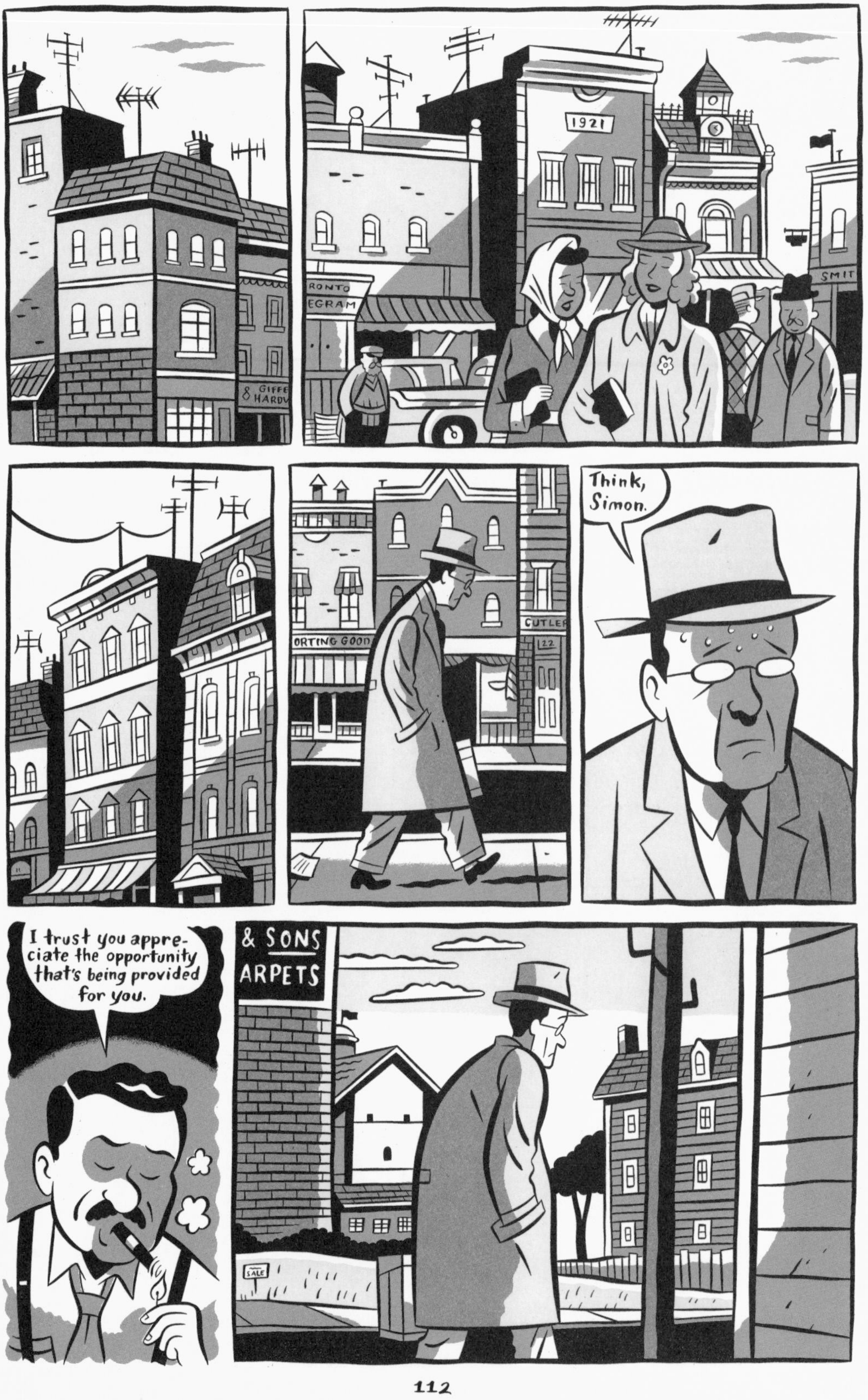
1921
RONTO
EGRAM
& GIFFE
HARDW
SMIT
ORTING GOOD
CUTLER
122
Think, Simon.
I trust you appreciate the opportunity that's being provided for you.
& SONS
ARPETS
SALE

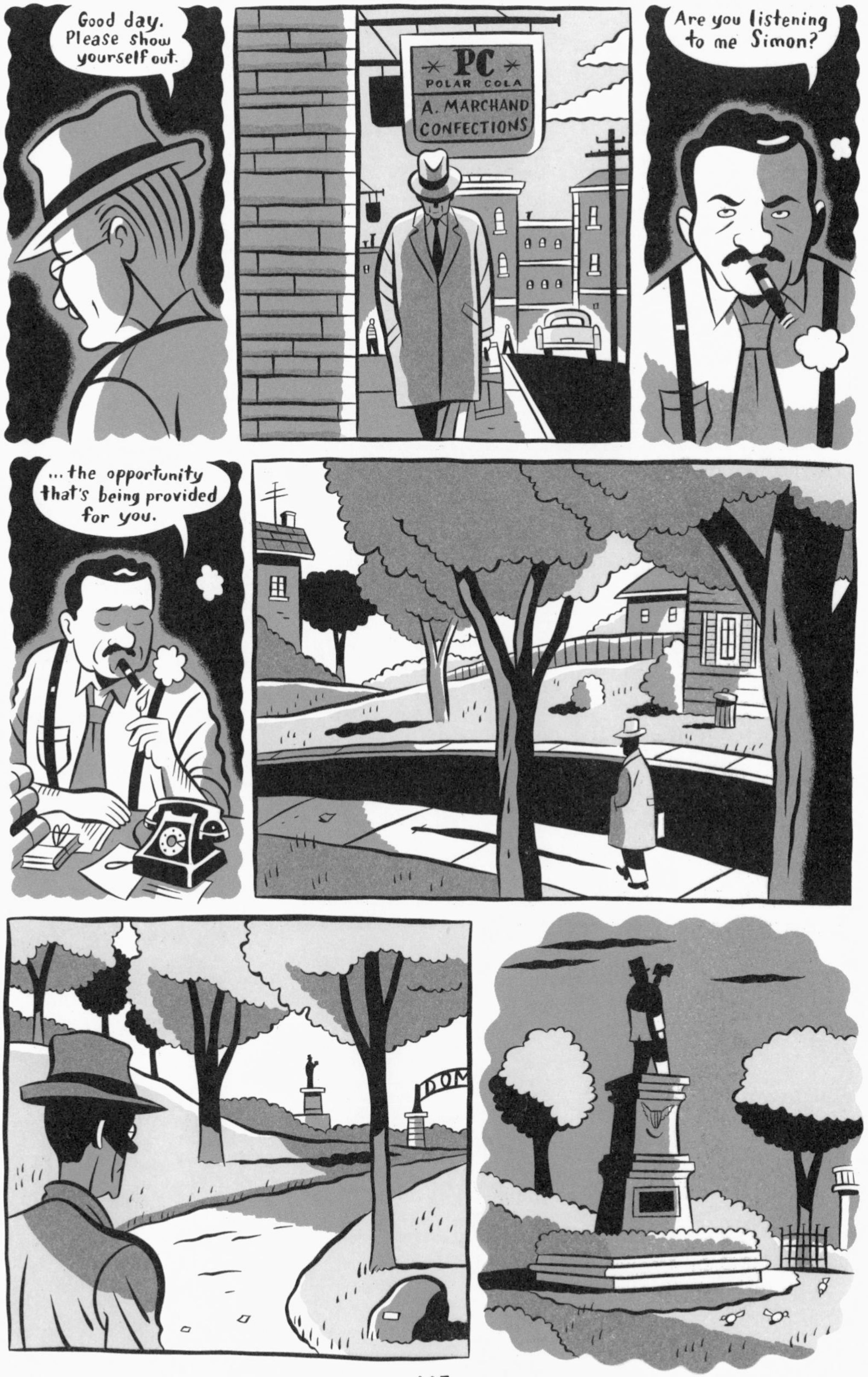
Good day. Please show yourself out.
PC
POLAR COLA
A. MARCHAND CONFECTIONS
Are you listening to me Simon?
...the opportunity that's being provided for you.
DOM

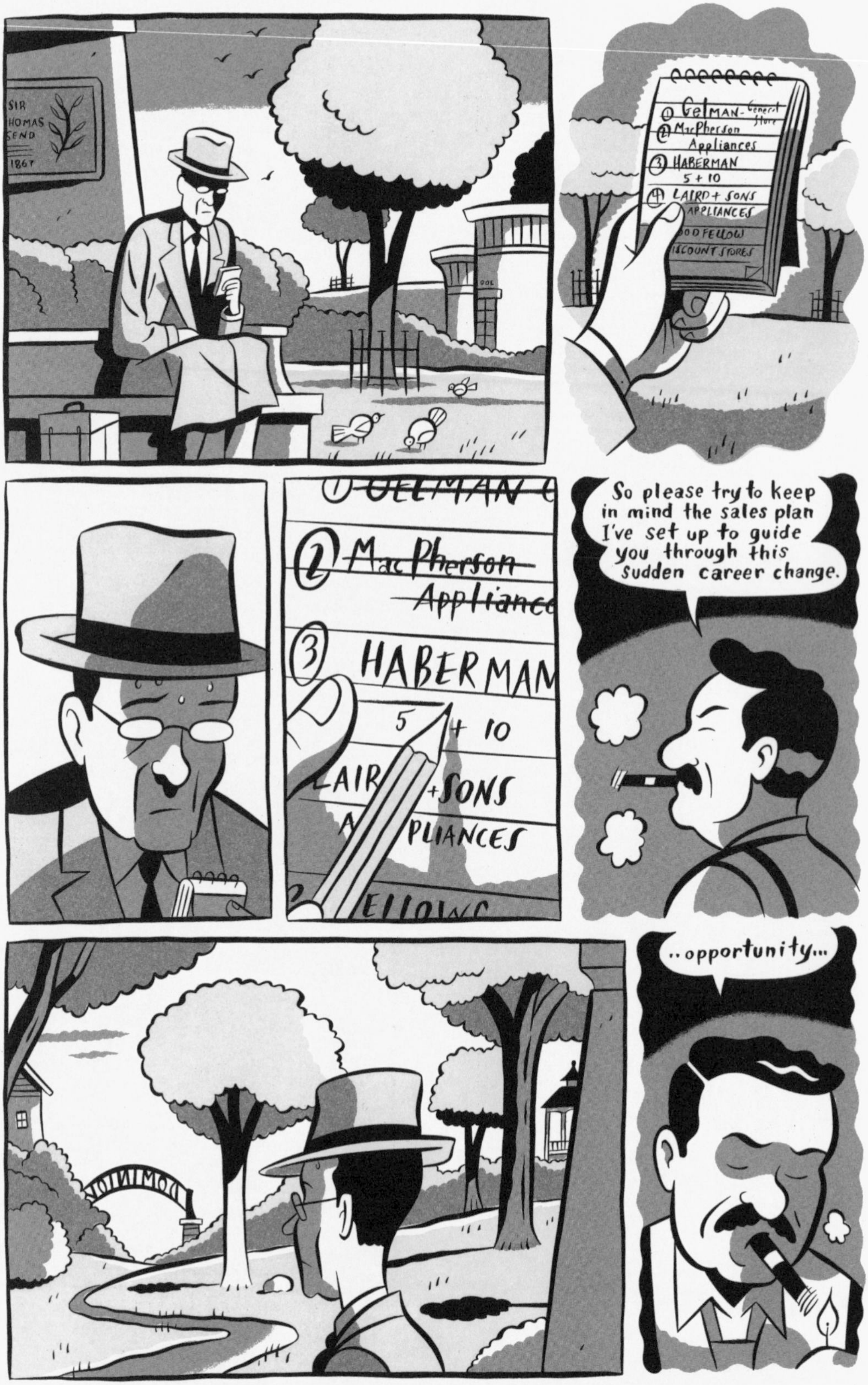
GELMAN - General Store
MacPherson Appliances
HABERMAN 5 + 10
LAIRD + SONS APPLIANCES
So please try to keep in mind the sales plan I've set up to guide you through this sudden career change.
..opportunity...

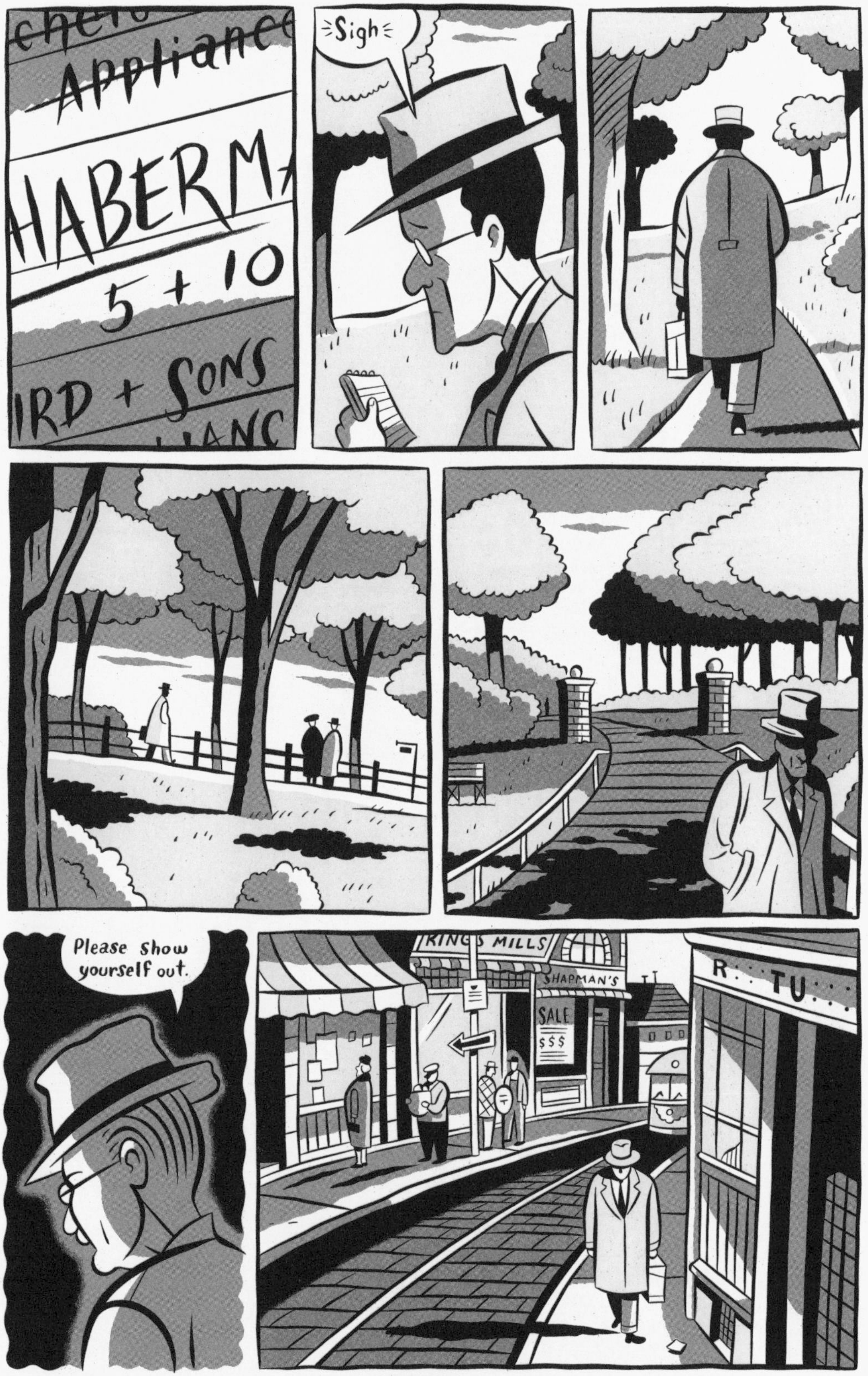
Appliance
HABERM
5 + 10
IRD + SONS
Sigh
Please show yourself out.
MILLS
SHAPMAN'S
SALE
$$$

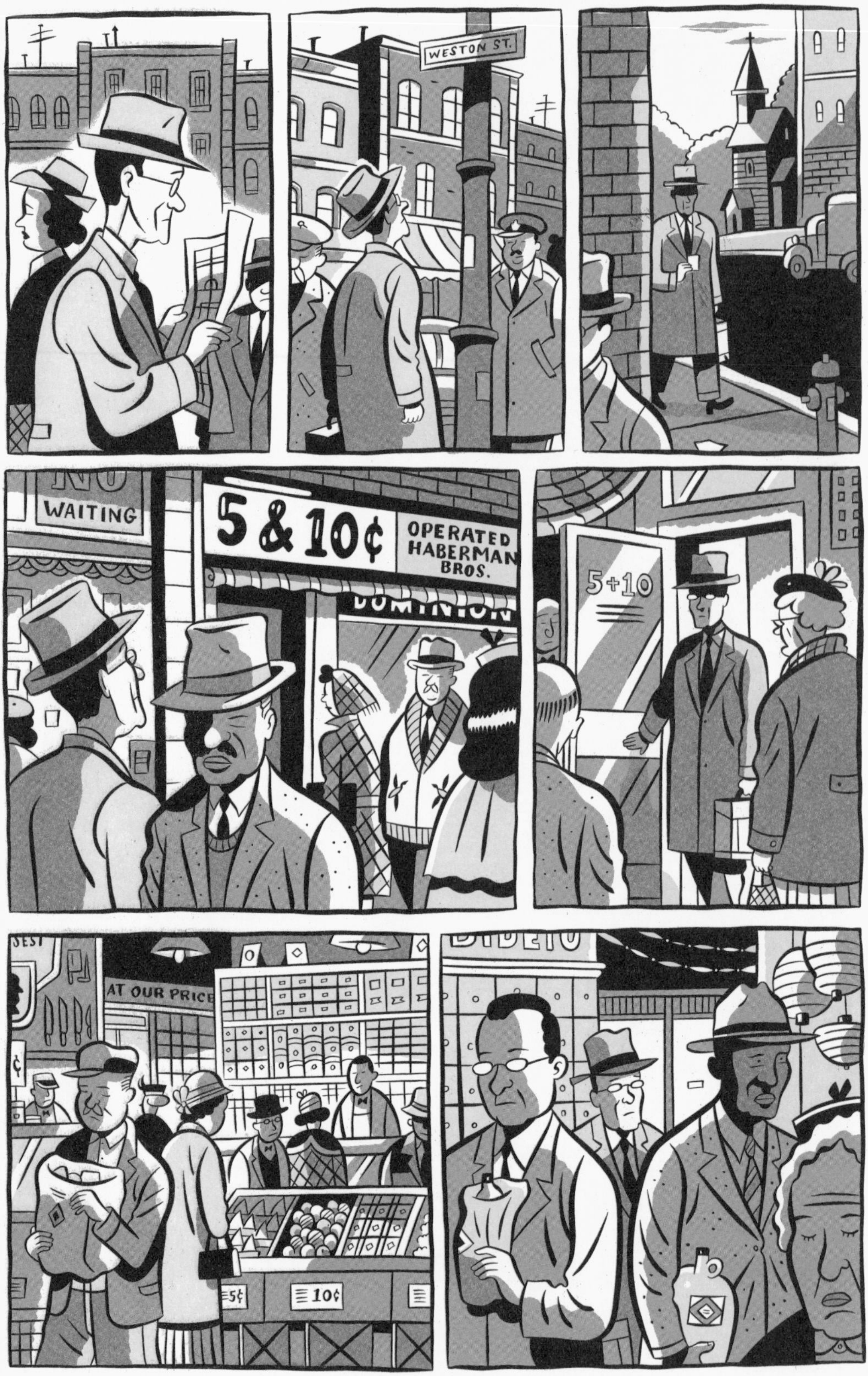
WESTON ST.
WAITING
5 & 10¢
OPERATED HABERMAN BROS.
5+10
5¢
10¢

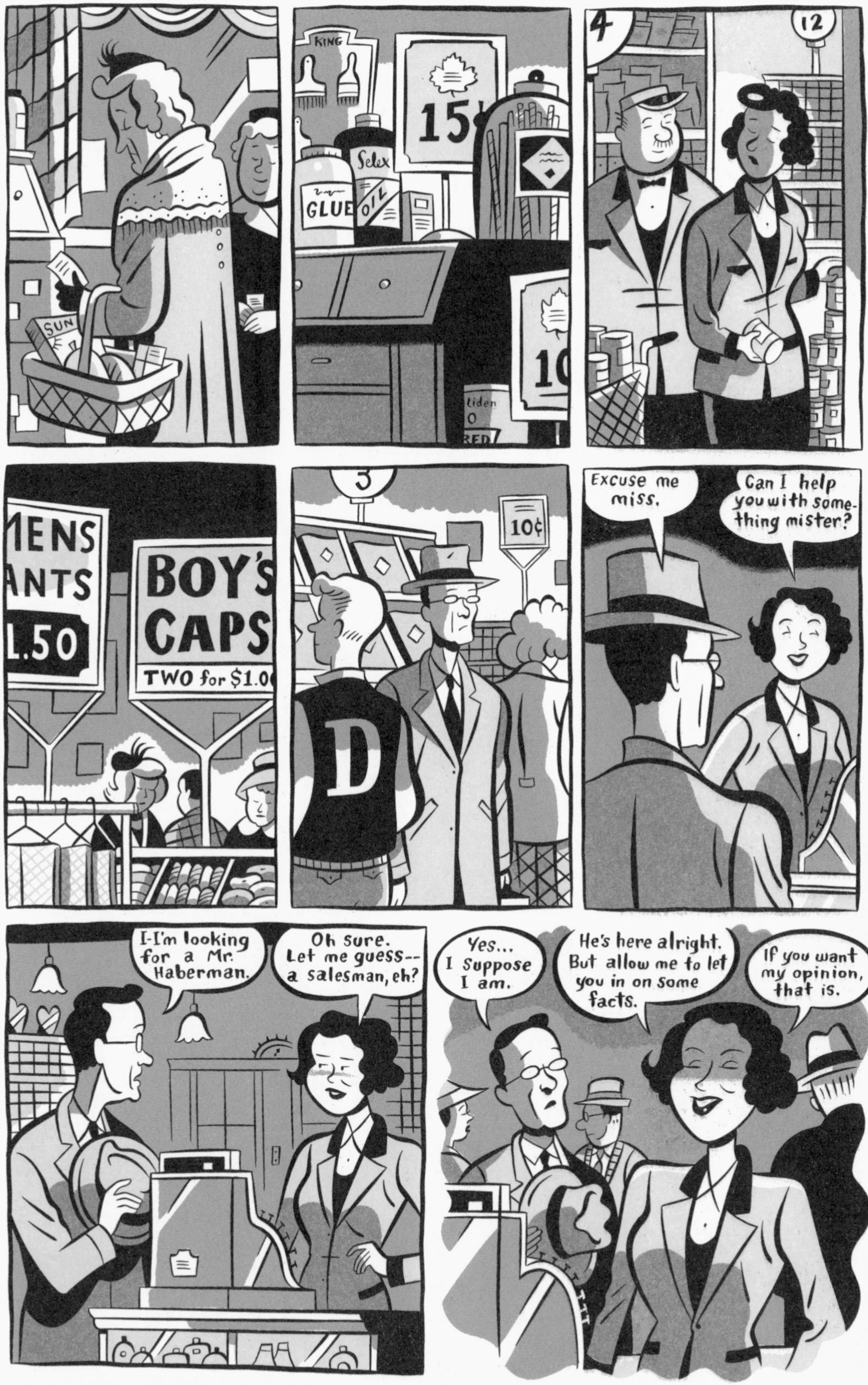

SUN
KING
15¢
Selex
GLUE
OIL
10
12
4
MENS
ANTS
1.50
BOY'S
CAPS
TWO for $1.0
3
10¢
D
Excuse me miss.
Can I help you with something mister?
I-I'm looking for a Mr. Haberman.
Oh sure. Let me guess-- a salesman, eh?
Yes... I suppose I am.
He's here alright. But allow me to let you in on some facts.
If you want my opinion, that is.

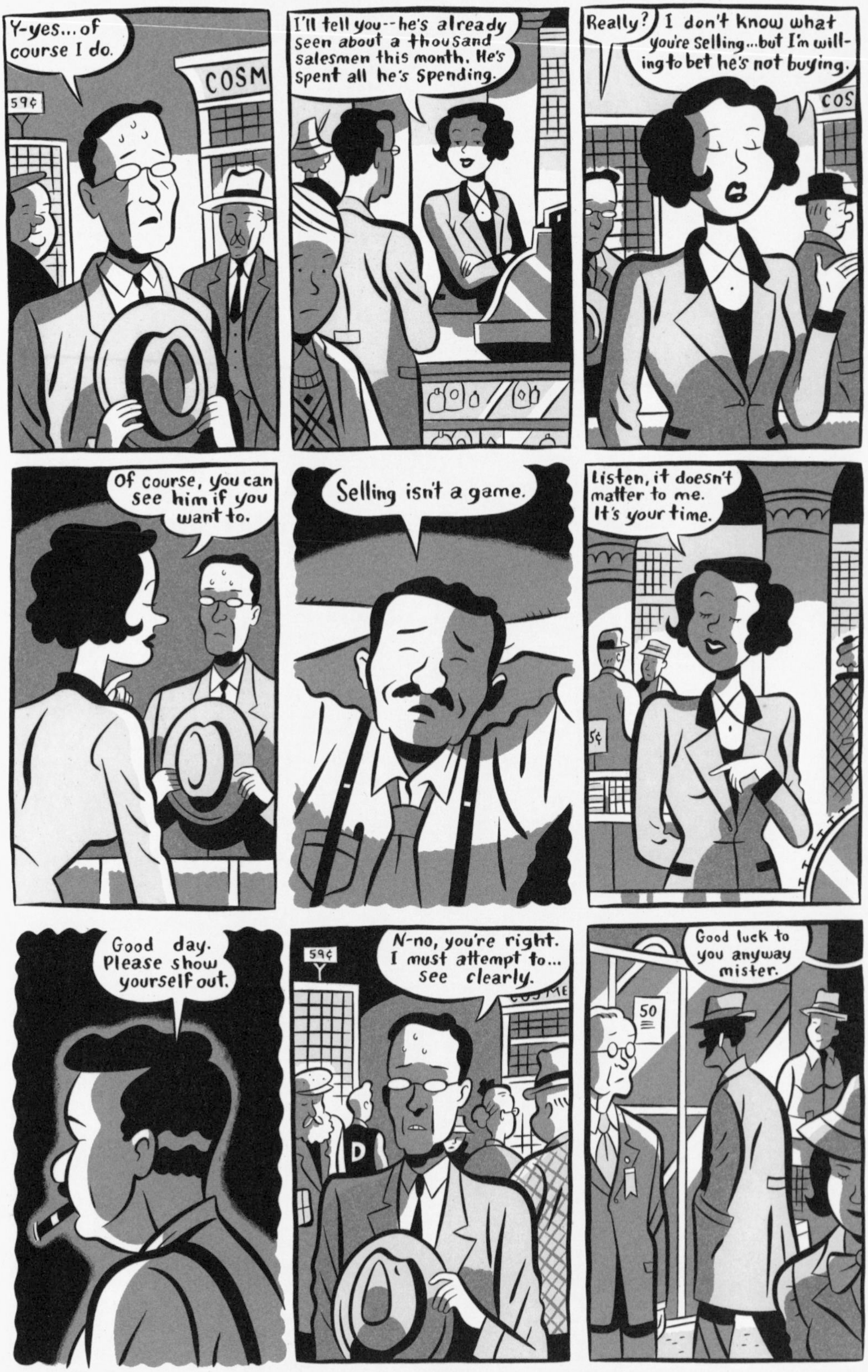
Y-yes... of course I do.
COSM
59¢
I'll tell you--he's already seen about a thousand salesmen this month. He's spent all he's spending.
Really?
I don't know what you're selling...but I'm willing to bet he's not buying.
COS
Of course, you can see him if you want to.
Selling isn't a game.
Listen, it doesn't matter to me. It's your time.
5¢
Good day. Please show yourself out.
59¢
N-no, you're right. I must attempt to... see clearly.
D
Good luck to you anyway mister.
50

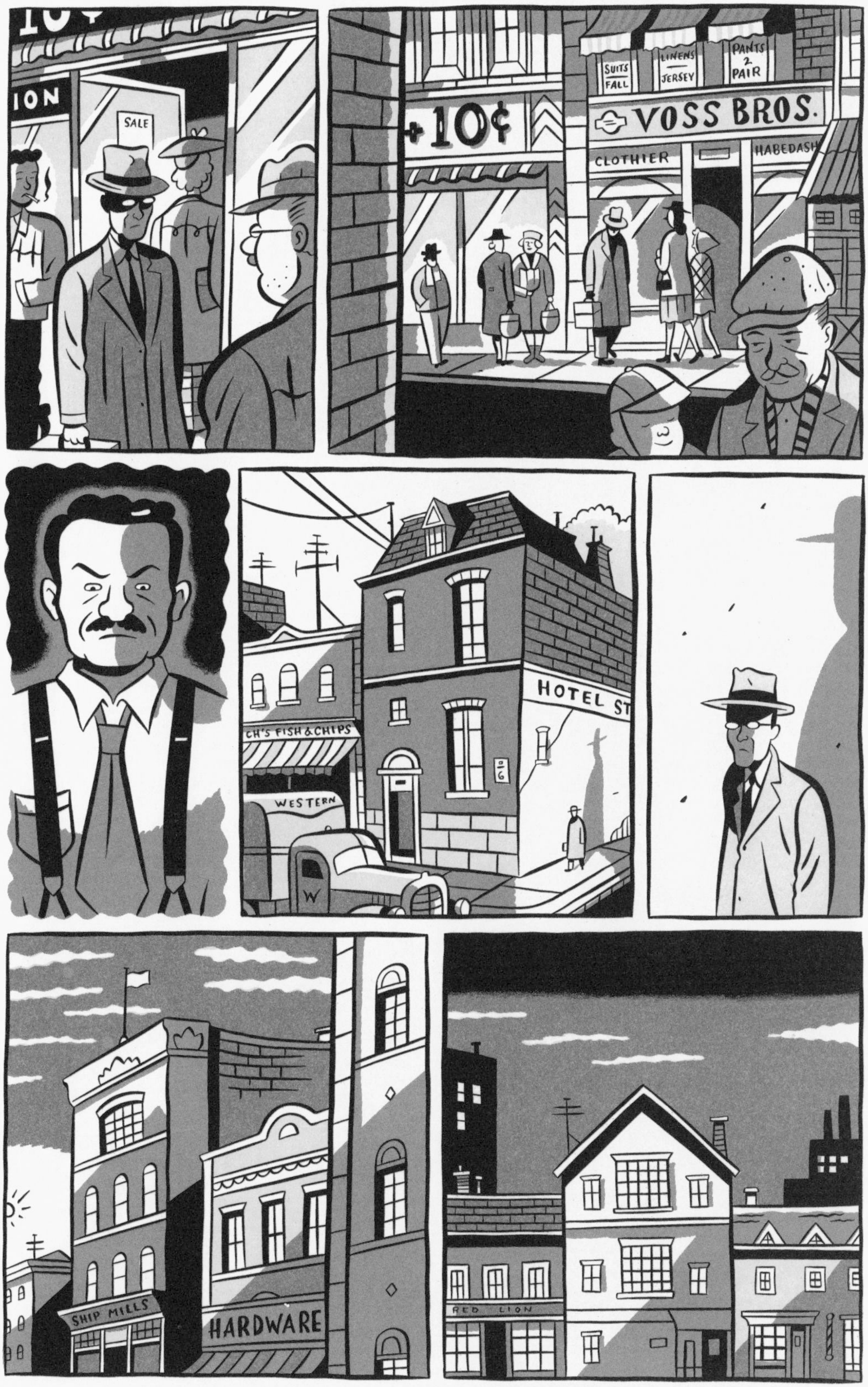
10¢
ION
SALE
SUITS FALL
LINENS JERSEY
PANTS 2 PAIR
10¢
VOSS BROS.
CLOTHIER
HABEDASH
HOTEL ST
CH'S FISH & CHIPS
WESTERN
SHIP MILLS
HARDWARE
RED LION

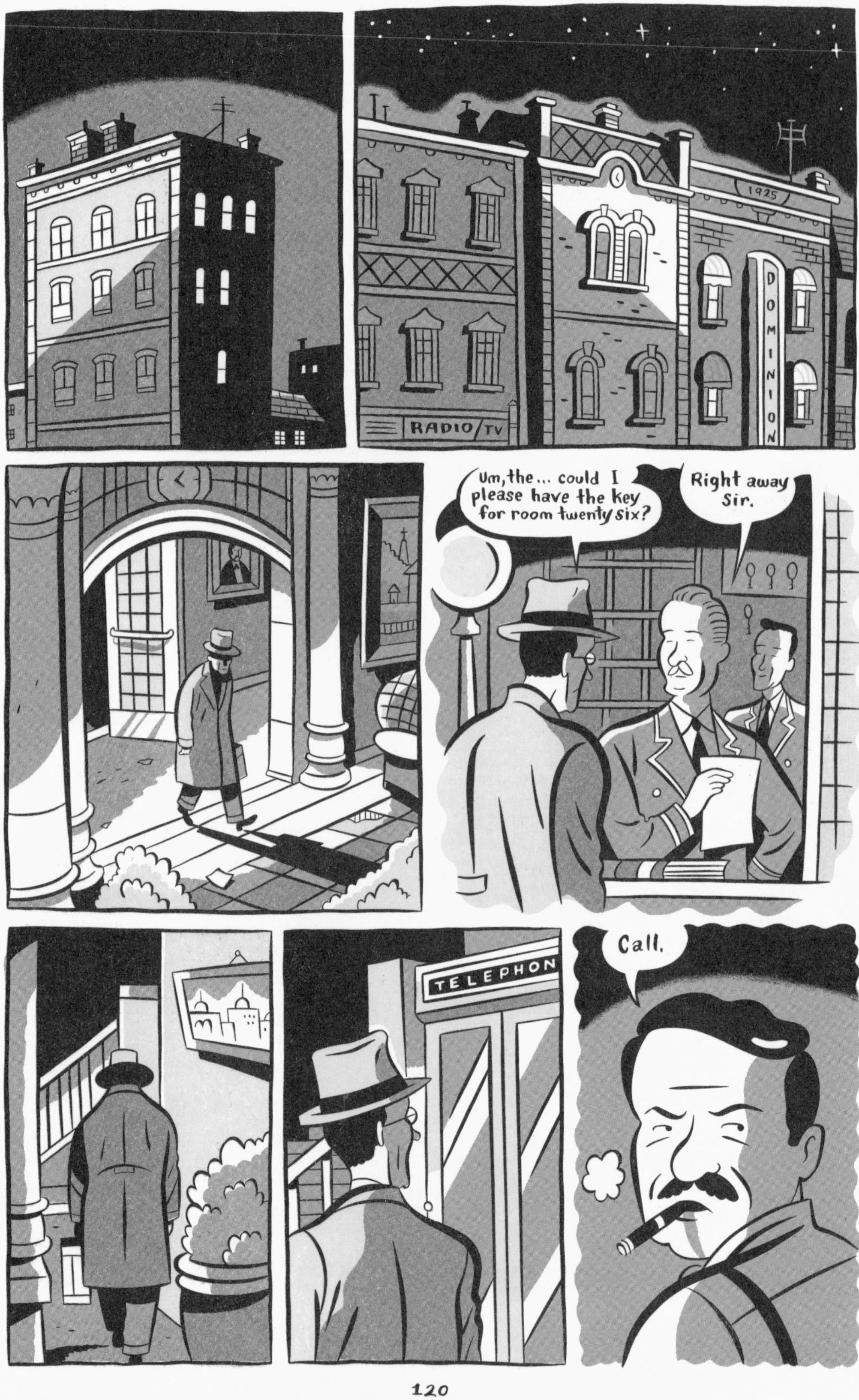
RADIO/TV
1925
DOMINION
Um, the... could I please have the key for room twenty six?
Right away Sir.
TELEPHON
Call.

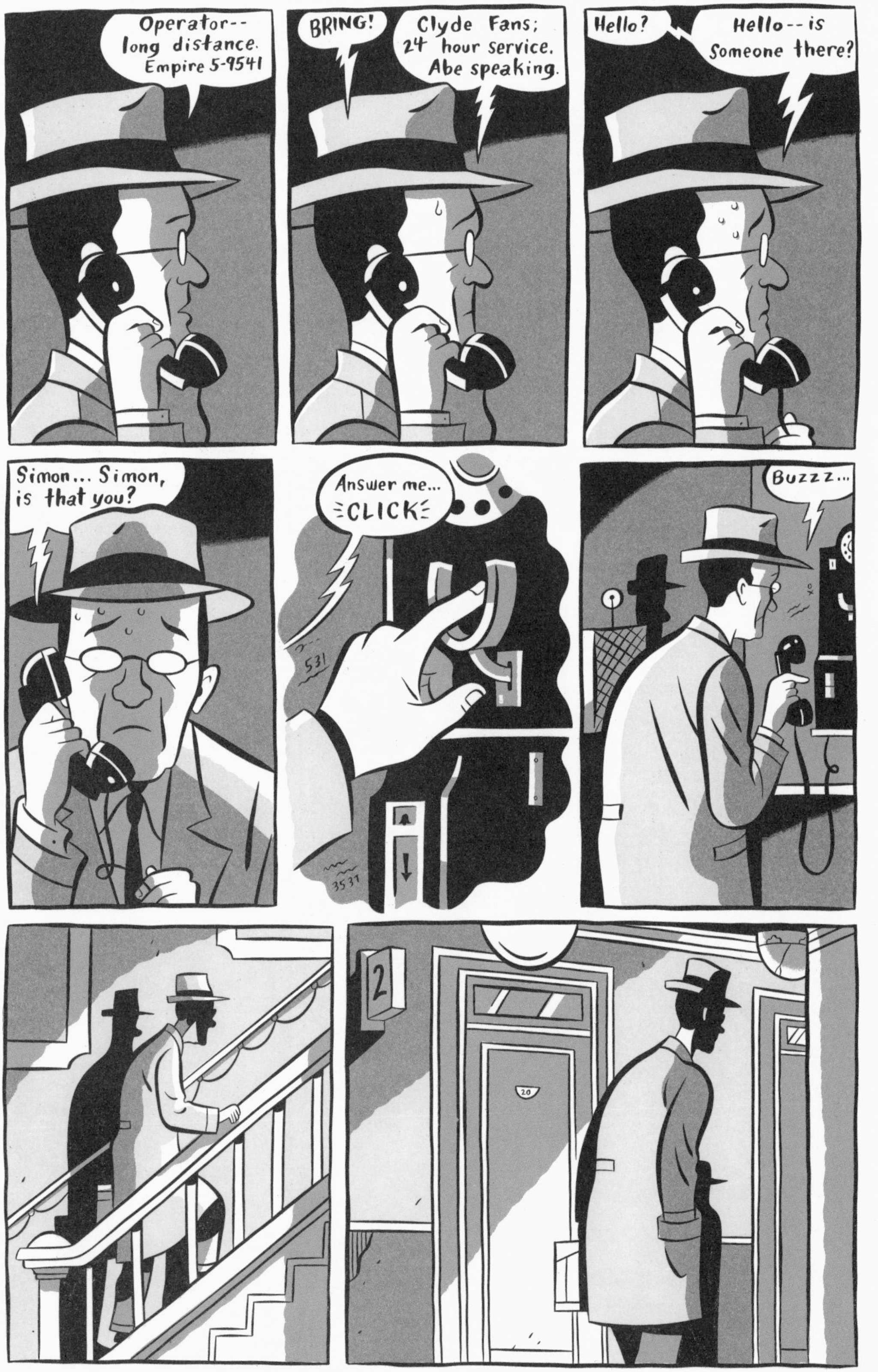
Operator--
long distance.
Empire 5-9541
BRING!
Clyde Fans;
24 hour service.
Abe speaking.
Hello?
Hello--is
Someone there?
Simon... Simon,
is that you?
Answer me...
CLICK
Buzzz...

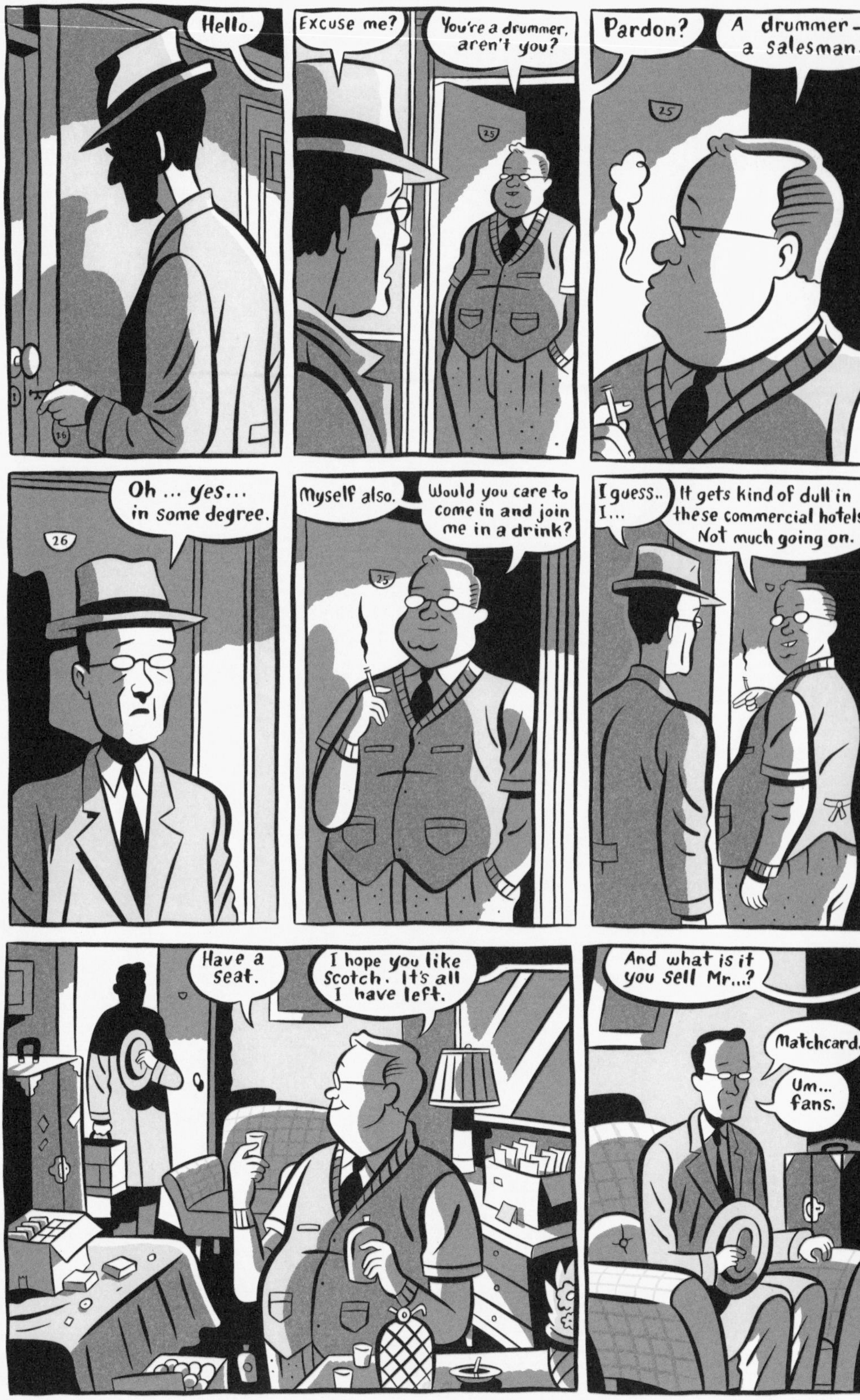
Hello.
Excuse me?
You're a drummer, aren't you?
Pardon?
A drummer - a salesman.
Oh ... yes... in some degree.
Myself also.
Would you care to come in and join me in a drink?
I guess.. I...
It gets kind of dull in these commercial hotels. Not much going on.
Have a seat.
I hope you like Scotch. It's all I have left.
And what is it you sell Mr...?
Matchcard.
Um... fans.

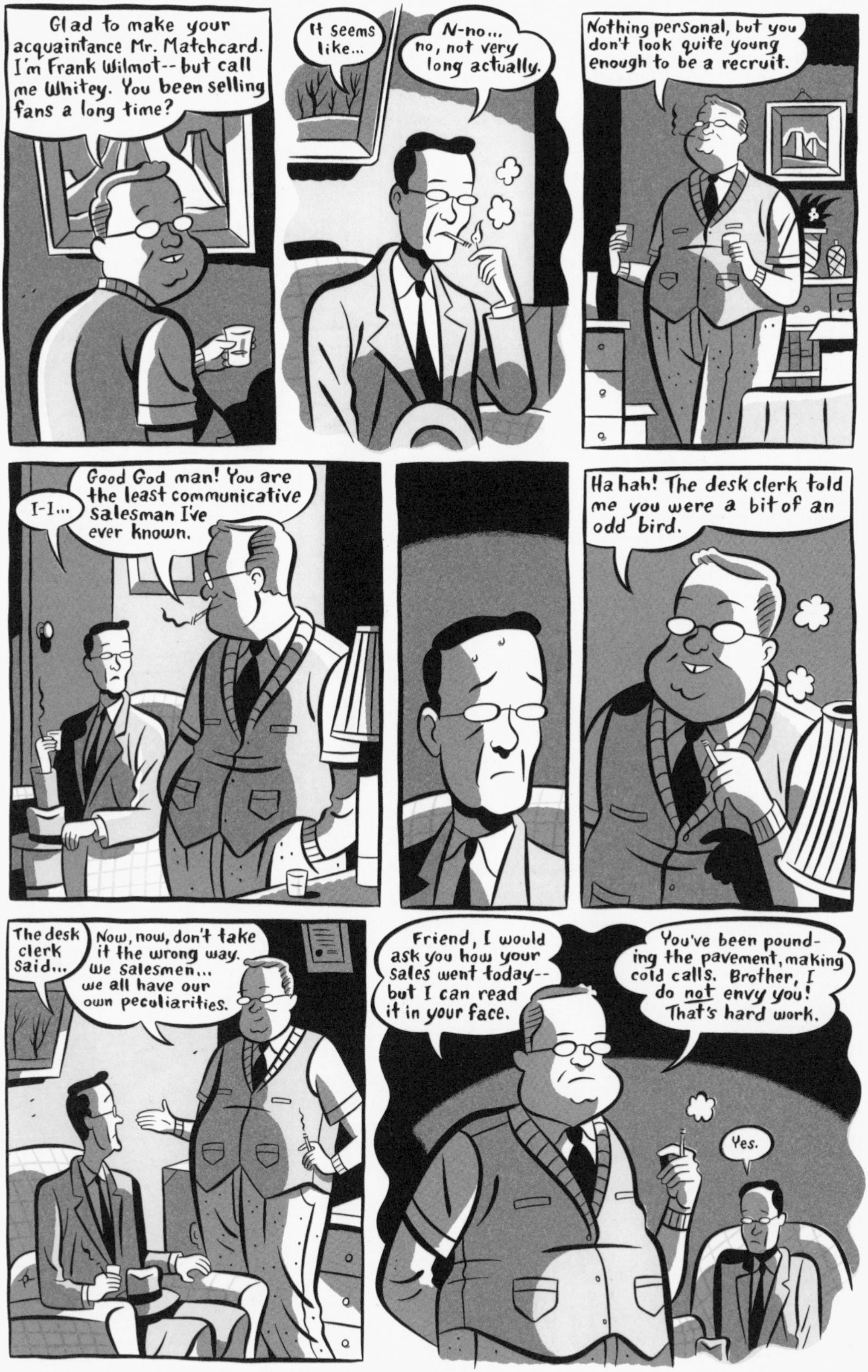

Glad to make your acquaintance Mr. Matchcard. I'm Frank Wilmot-- but call me Whitey. You been selling fans a long time?
It seems like...
N-no... no, not very long actually.
Nothing personal, but you don't look quite young enough to be a recruit.
I-I...
Good God man! You are the least communicative salesman I've ever known.
Ha hah! The desk clerk told me you were a bit of an odd bird.
The desk clerk said...
Now, now, don't take it the wrong way. We salesmen... we all have our own peculiarities.
Friend, I would ask you how your sales went today-- but I can read it in your face.
You've been pounding the pavement, making cold calls. Brother, I do not envy you! That's hard work.
Yes.

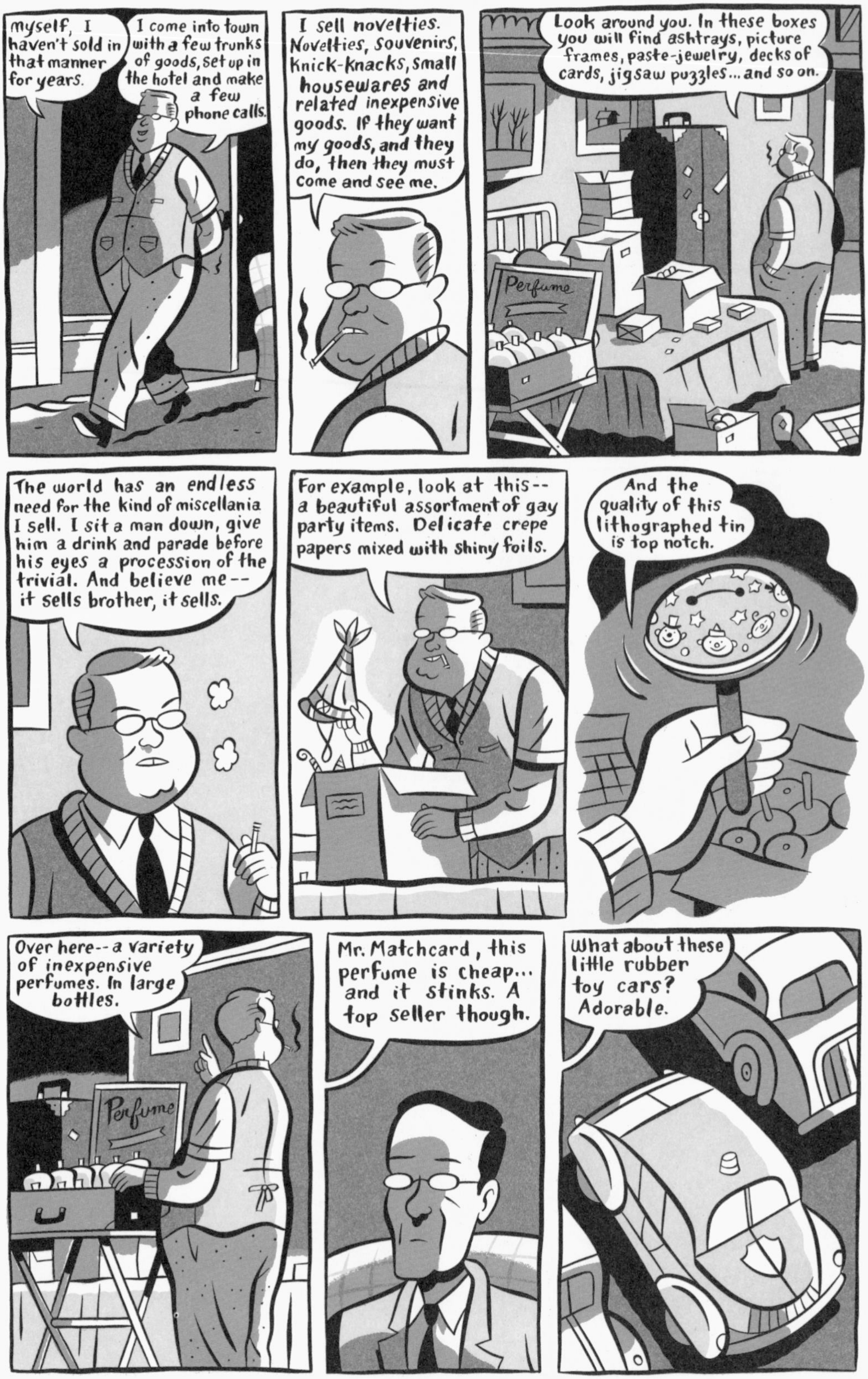
myself, I haven't sold in that manner for years.
I come into town with a few trunks of goods, set up in the hotel and make a few phone calls.
I sell novelties. Novelties, souvenirs, knick-knacks, small housewares and related inexpensive goods. If they want my goods, and they do, then they must come and see me.
Look around you. In these boxes you will find ashtrays, picture frames, paste-jewelry, decks of cards, jigsaw puzzles... and so on.
Perfume
The world has an endless need for the kind of miscellania I sell. I sit a man down, give him a drink and parade before his eyes a procession of the trivial. And believe me-- it sells brother, it sells.
For example, look at this-- a beautiful assortment of gay party items. Delicate crepe papers mixed with shiny foils.
And the quality of this lithographed tin is top notch.
Over here-- a variety of inexpensive perfumes. In large bottles.
Perfume
Mr. Matchcard, this perfume is cheap... and it stinks. A top seller though.
What about these little rubber toy cars? Adorable.

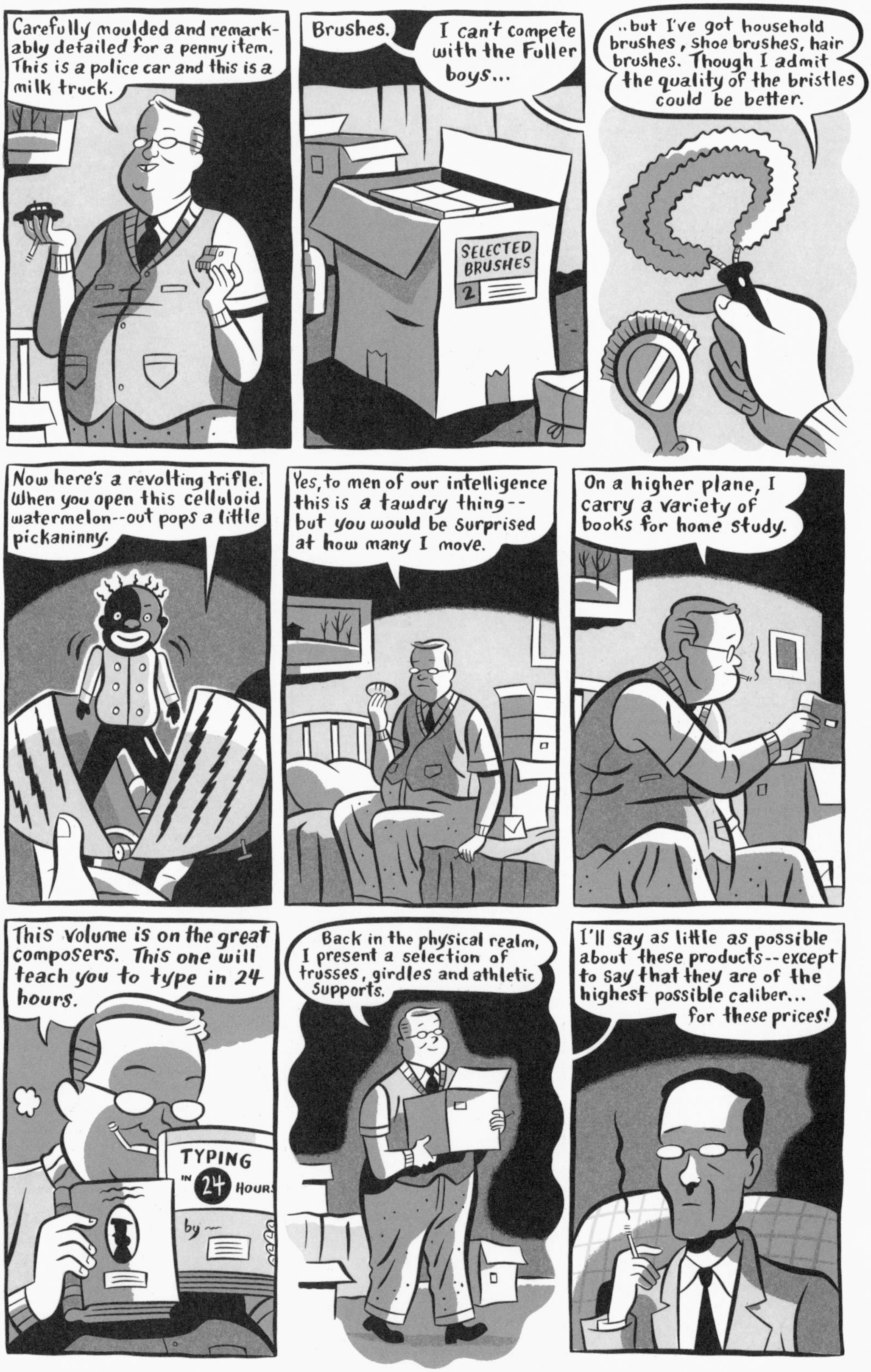
Carefully moulded and remarkably detailed for a penny item. This is a police car and this is a milk truck.
Brushes.
I can't compete with the Fuller boys...
..but I've got household brushes, shoe brushes, hair brushes. Though I admit the quality of the bristles could be better.
SELECTED BRUSHES
2
Now here's a revolting trifle. When you open this celluloid watermelon--out pops a little pickaninny.
Yes, to men of our intelligence this is a tawdry thing--but you would be surprised at how many I move.
On a higher plane, I carry a variety of books for home study.
This volume is on the great composers. This one will teach you to type in 24 hours.
TYPING IN 24 HOURS
by ~
Back in the physical realm, I present a selection of trusses, girdles and athletic supports.
I'll say as little as possible about these products--except to say that they are of the highest possible caliber... for these prices!

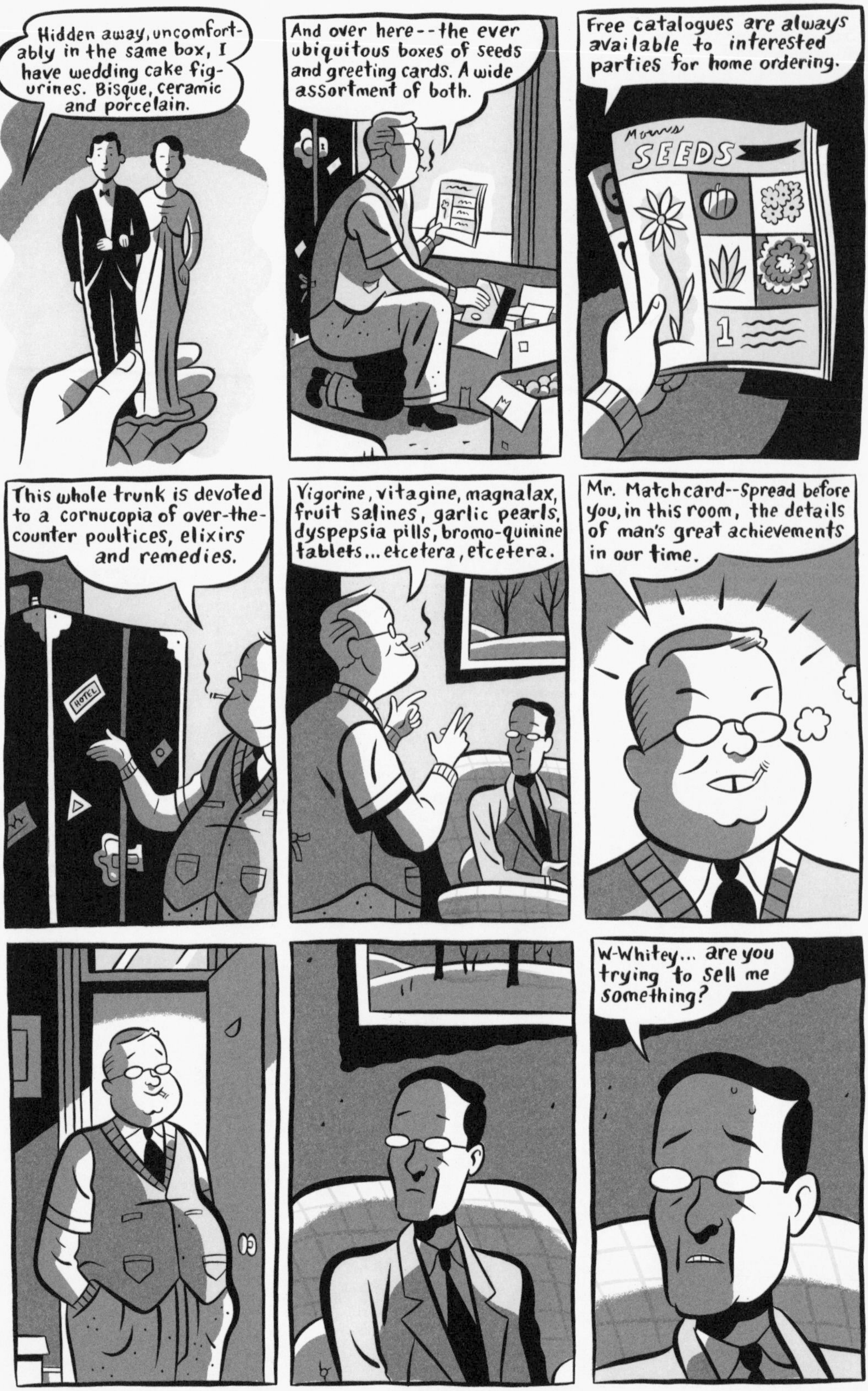
Hidden away, uncomfortably in the same box, I have wedding cake figurines. Bisque, ceramic and porcelain.
And over here--the ever ubiquitous boxes of seeds and greeting cards. A wide assortment of both.
Free catalogues are always available to interested parties for home ordering.
SEEDS
This whole trunk is devoted to a cornucopia of over-the-counter poultices, elixirs and remedies.
HOTEL
Vigorine, vitagine, magnalax, fruit salines, garlic pearls, dyspepsia pills, bromo-quinine tablets... etcetera, etcetera.
Mr. Matchcard--Spread before you, in this room, the details of man's great achievements in our time.
W-Whitey... are you trying to sell me something?

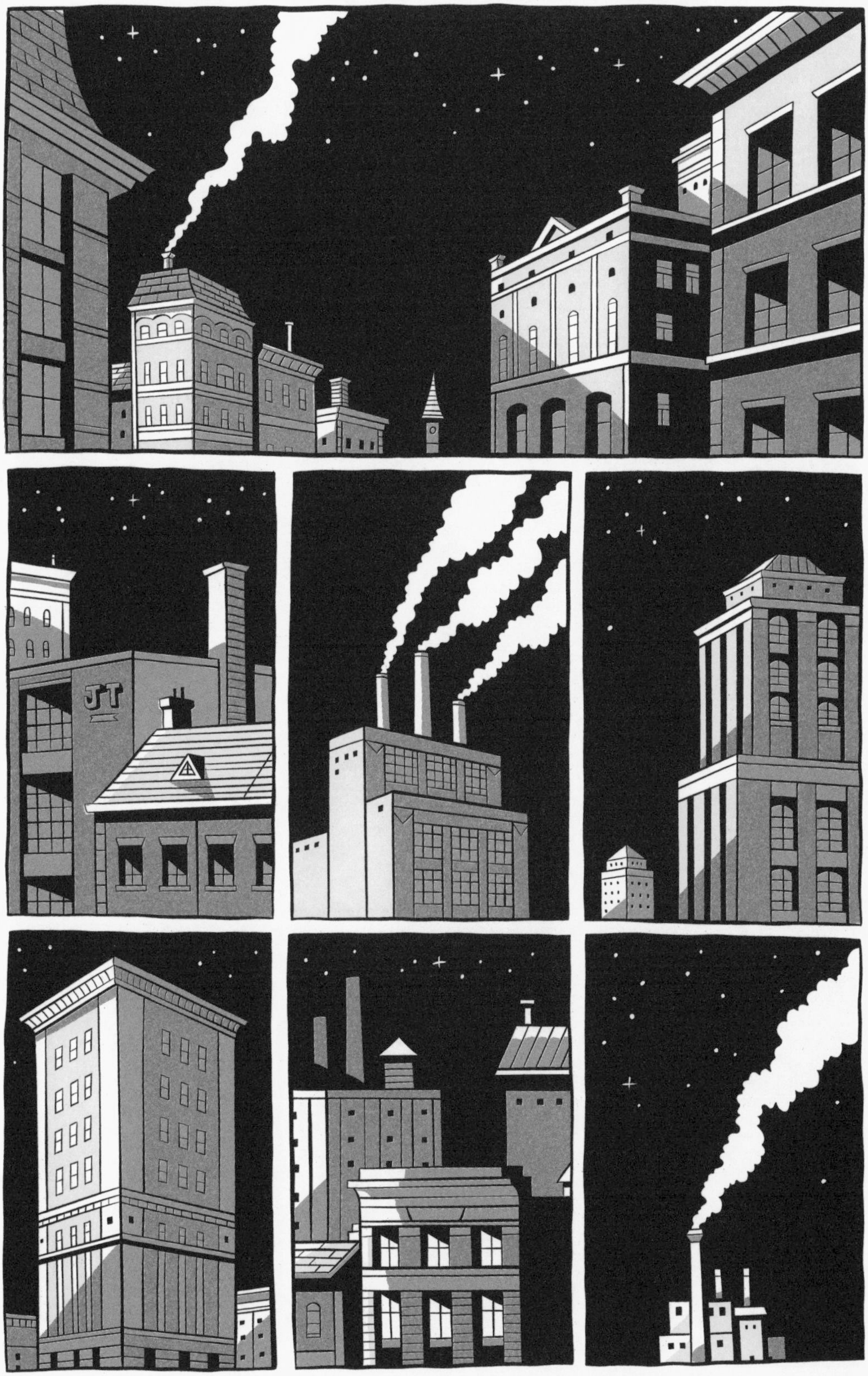
JT

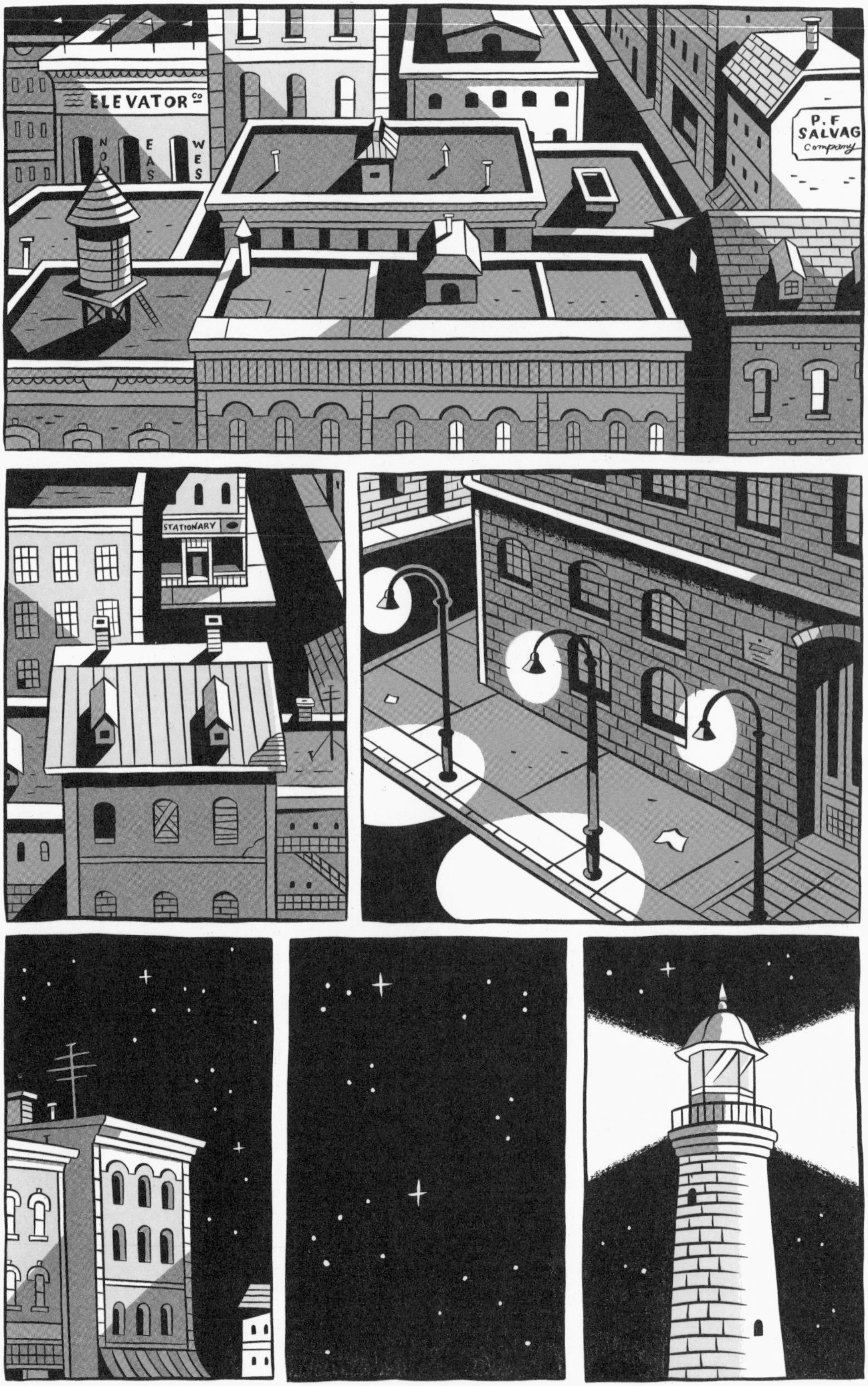
ELEVATOR Co
P. F
SALVAG
Company
STATIONARY

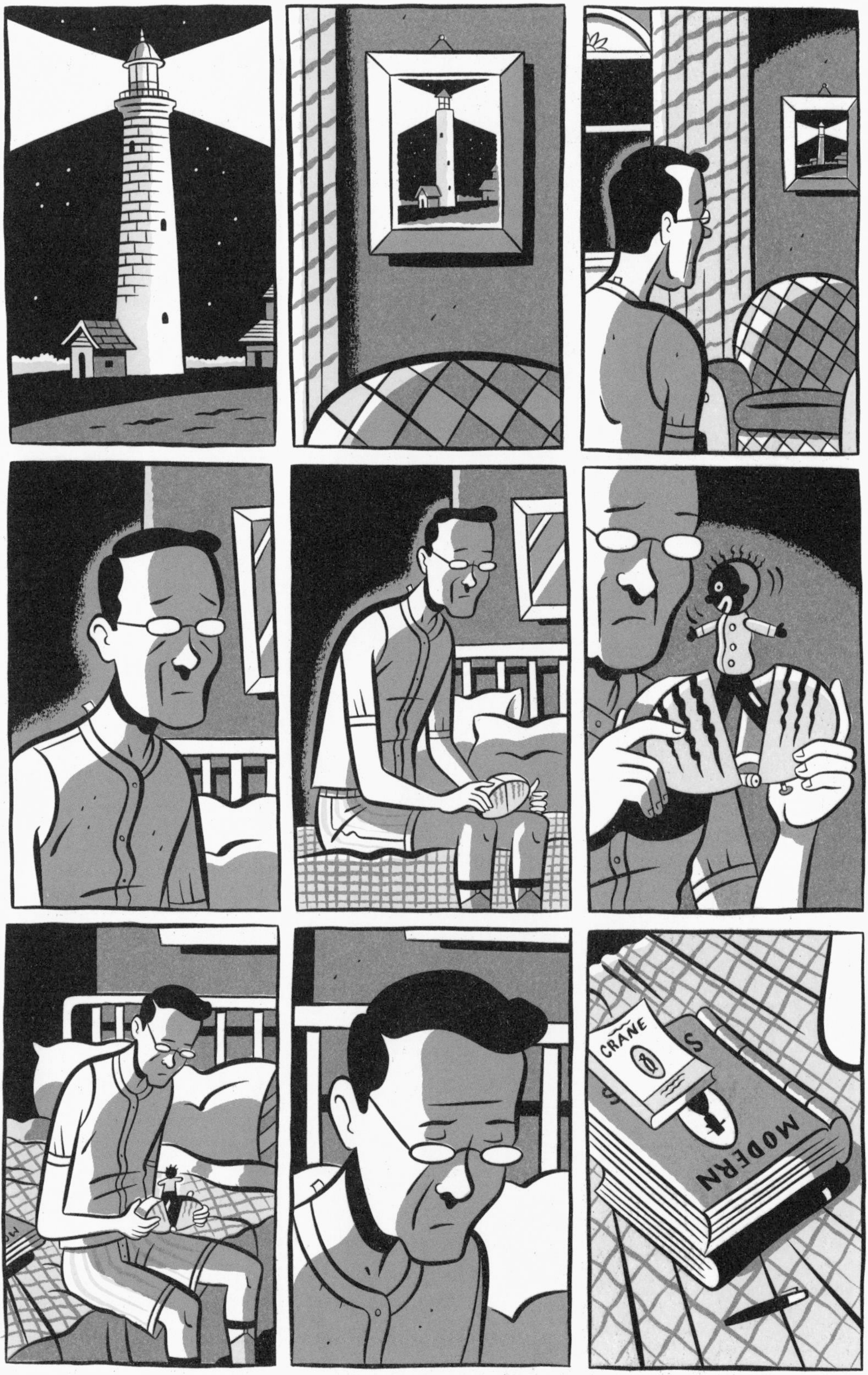
CRANE
MODERN

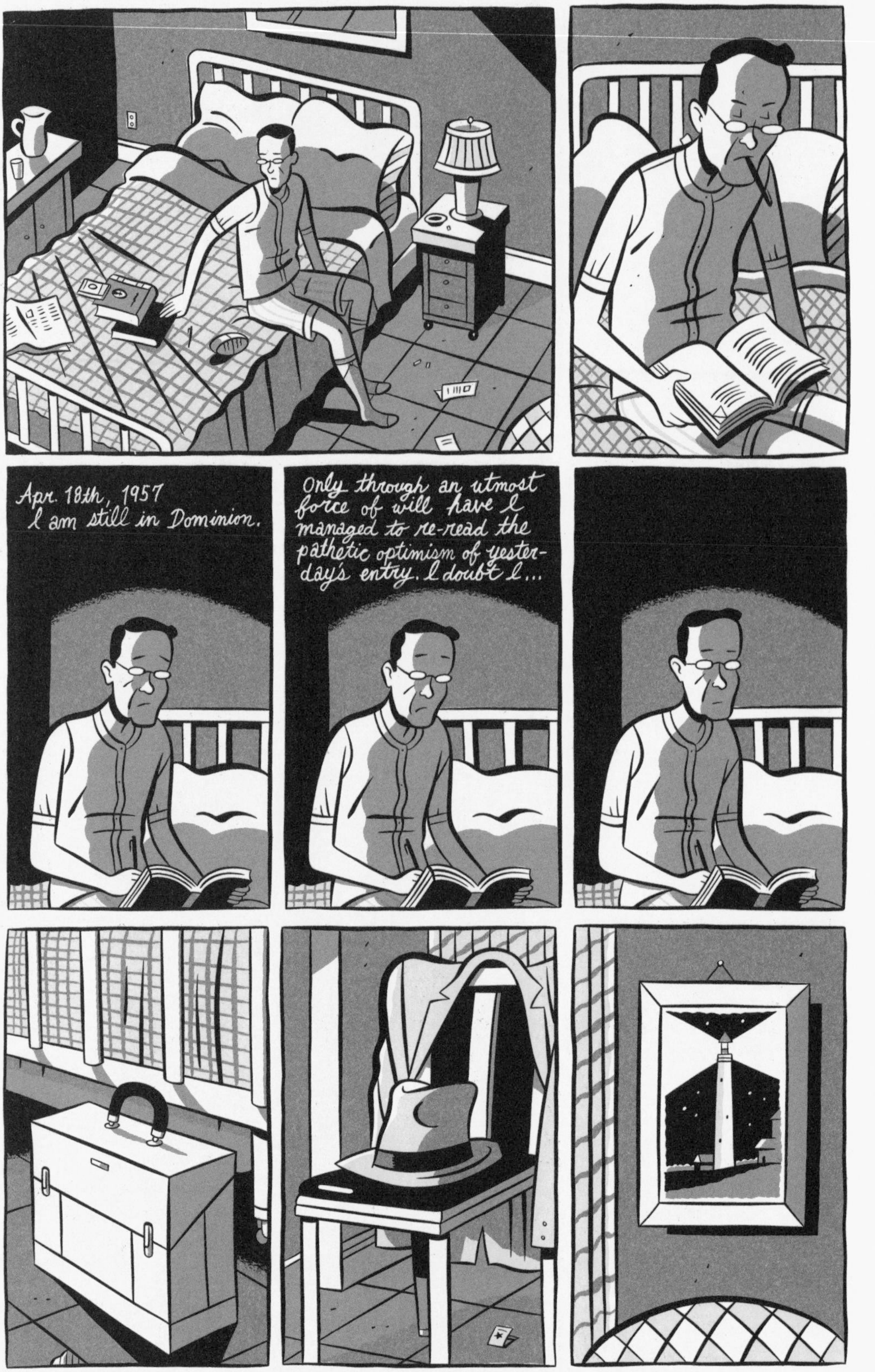
Apr. 18th, 1957
I am still in Dominion.
Only through an utmost force of will have I managed to re-read the pathetic optimism of yesterday's entry. I doubt I...

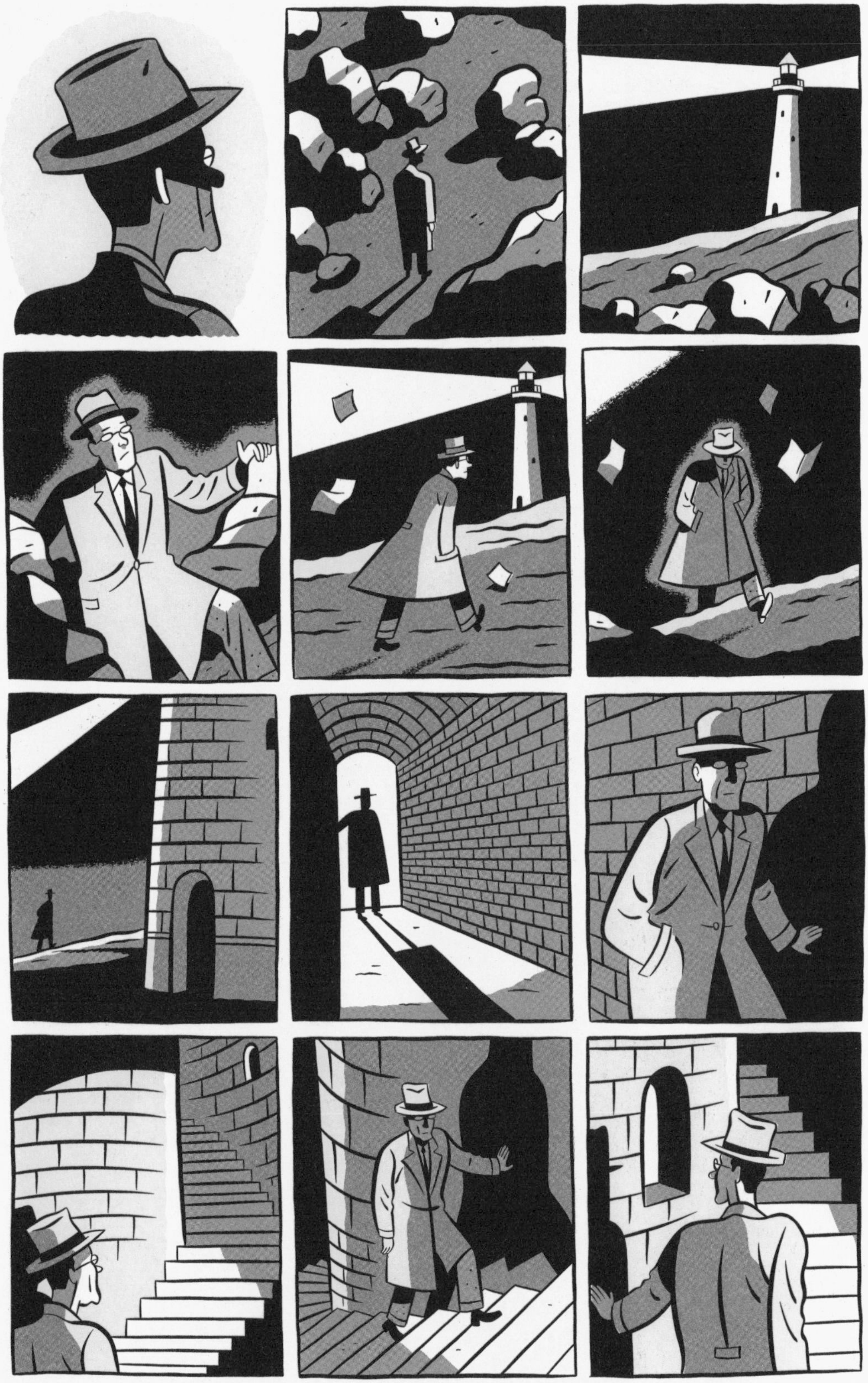

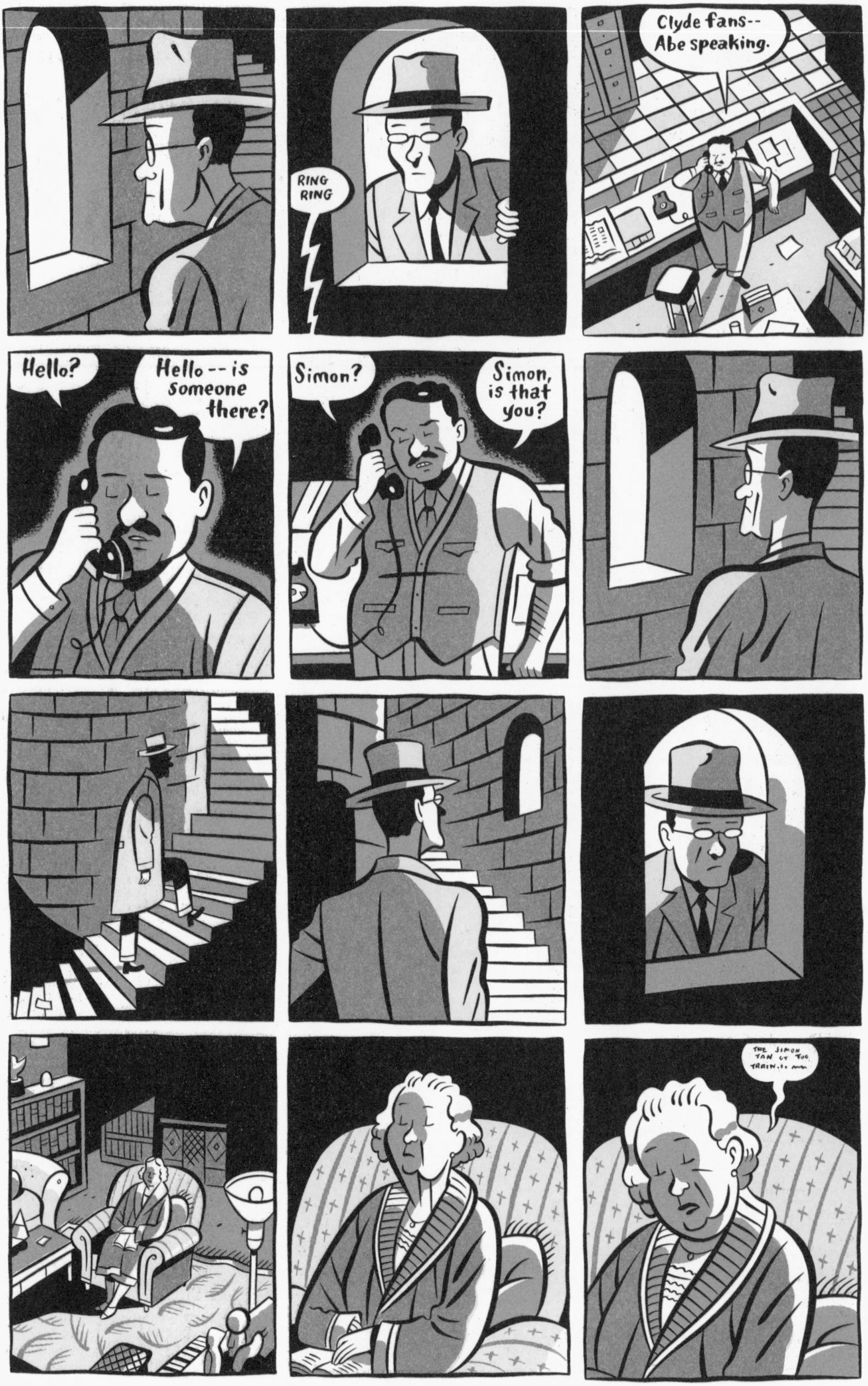

Clyde fans--
Abe speaking.
RING RING
Hello?
Hello -- is someone there?
Simon?
Simon, is that you?
THE SIMON TAN OT TOG TRAIN..

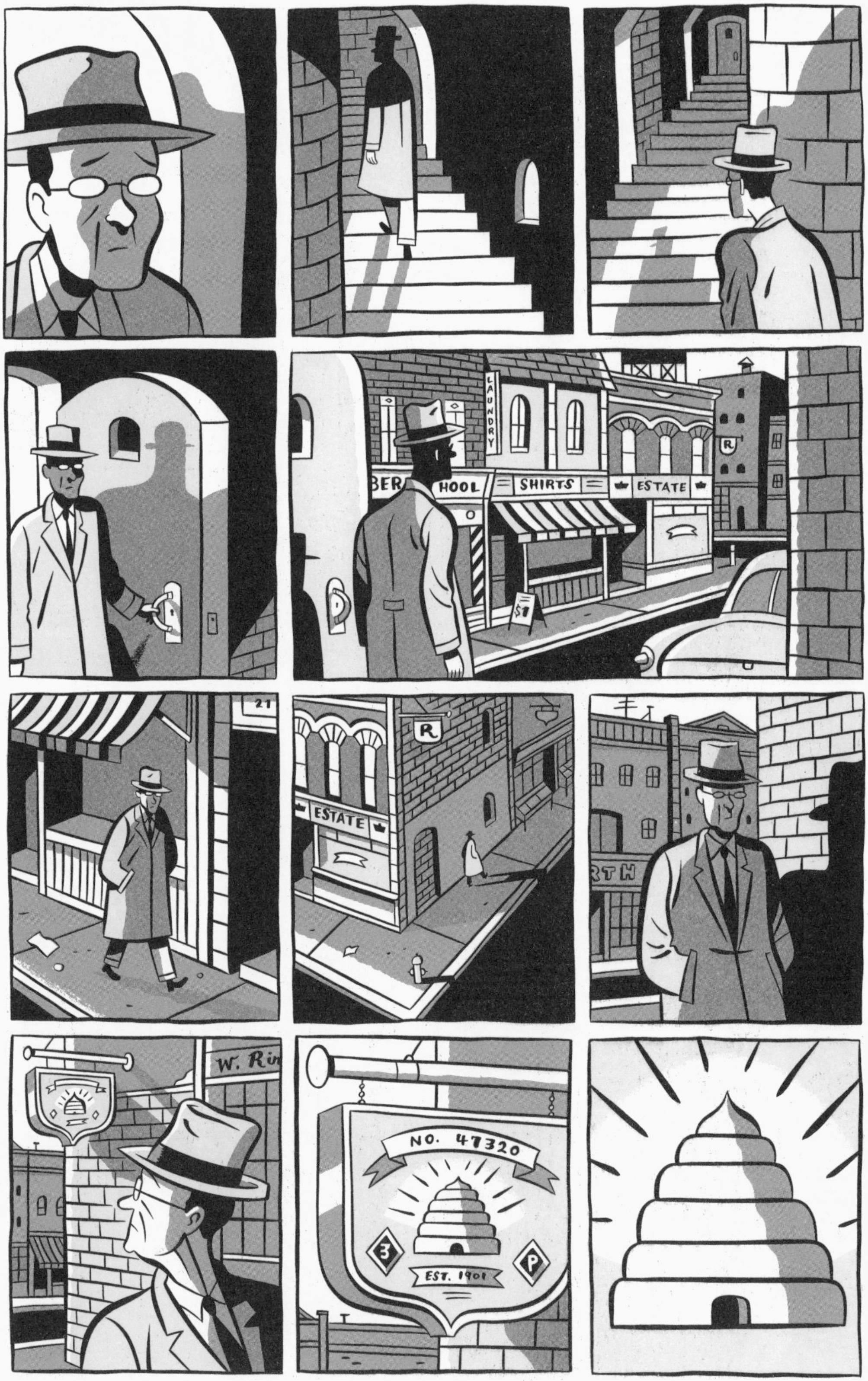
LAUNDRY
BER
HOOL
SHIRTS
ESTATE
$1
21
ESTATE
RTH
W. Ri
NO. 47320
3
P
EST. 1901

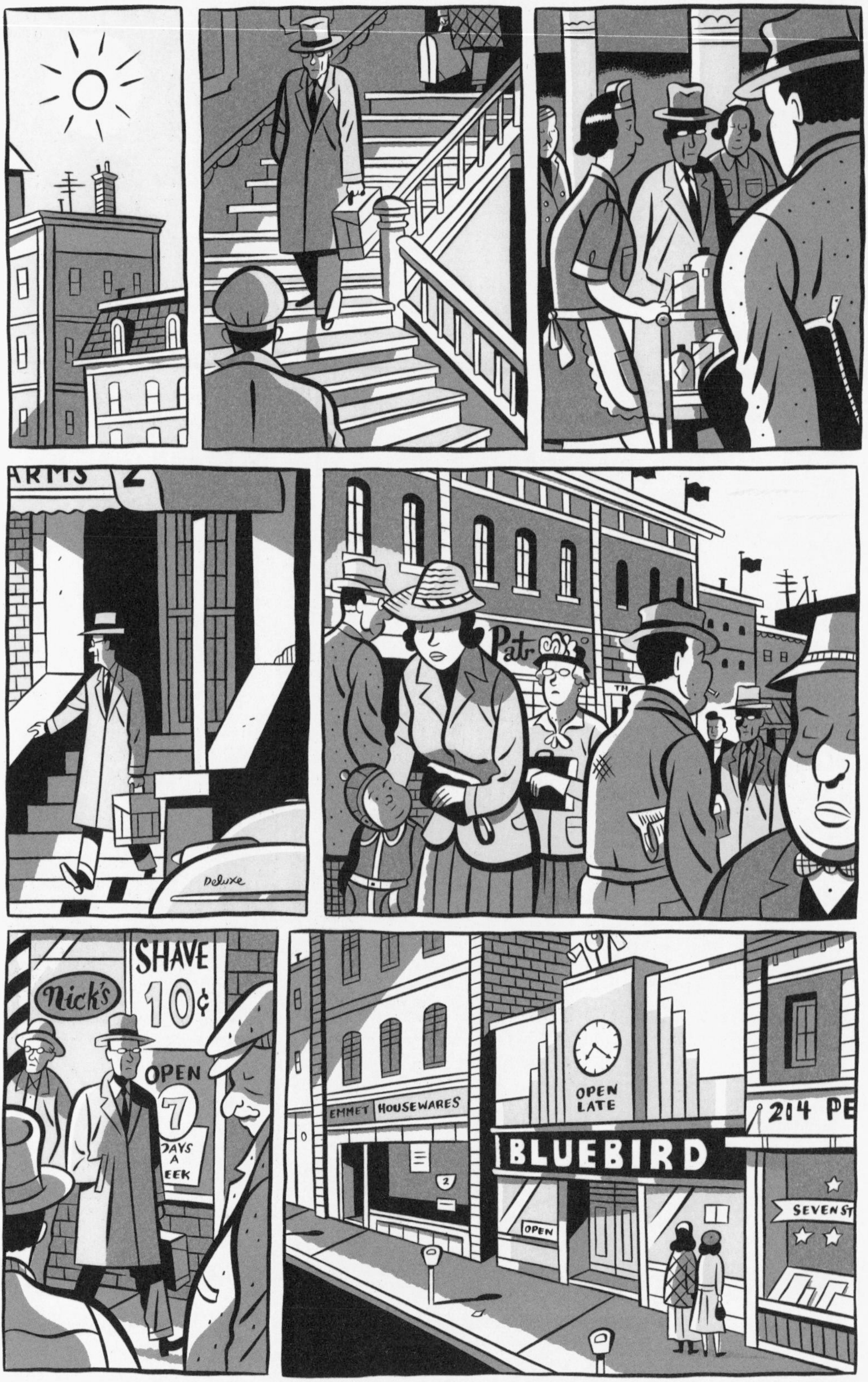
ARMS
2
Deluxe
Pat
TH
Nick's
SHAVE
10¢
OPEN
7
DAYS
A
EEK
EMMET
HOUSEWARES
2
OPEN
LATE
BLUEBIRD
OPEN
214 PE
SEVEN ST

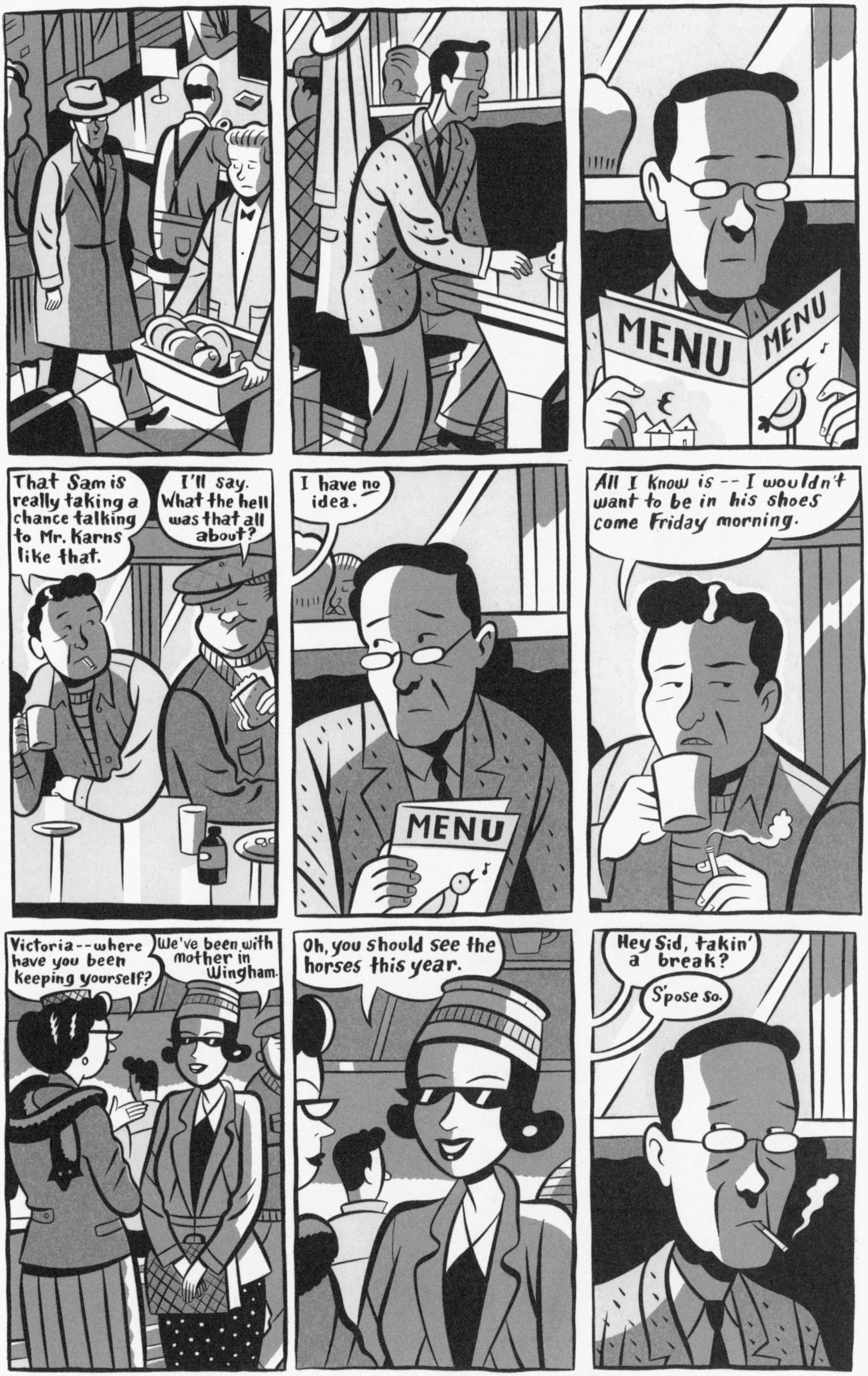
MENU
MENU
That Sam is really taking a chance talking to Mr. Karns like that.
I'll say. What the hell was that all about?
I have no idea.
MENU
All I know is -- I wouldn't want to be in his shoes come Friday morning.
Victoria--where have you been keeping yourself?
We've been with mother in Wingham.
Oh, you should see the horses this year.
Hey Sid, takin' a break?
S'pose so.

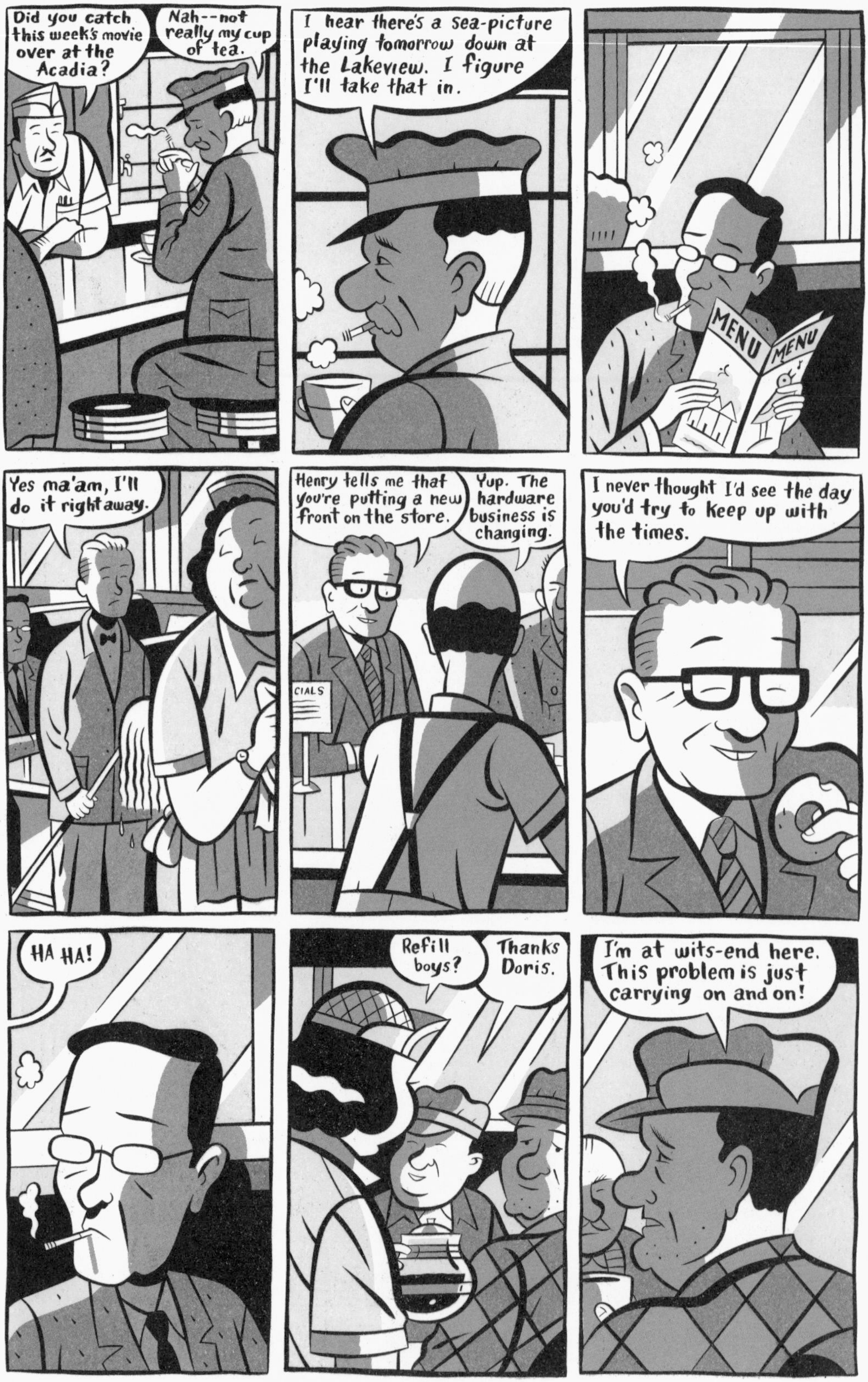
Did you catch this week's movie over at the Acadia?
Nah--not really my cup of tea.
I hear there's a sea-picture playing tomorrow down at the Lakeview. I figure I'll take that in.
MENU
MENU
Yes ma'am, I'll do it right away.
Henry tells me that you're putting a new front on the store.
Yup. The hardware business is changing.
CIALS
I never thought I'd see the day you'd try to keep up with the times.
HA HA!
Refill boys?
Thanks Doris.
I'm at wits-end here. This problem is just carrying on and on!

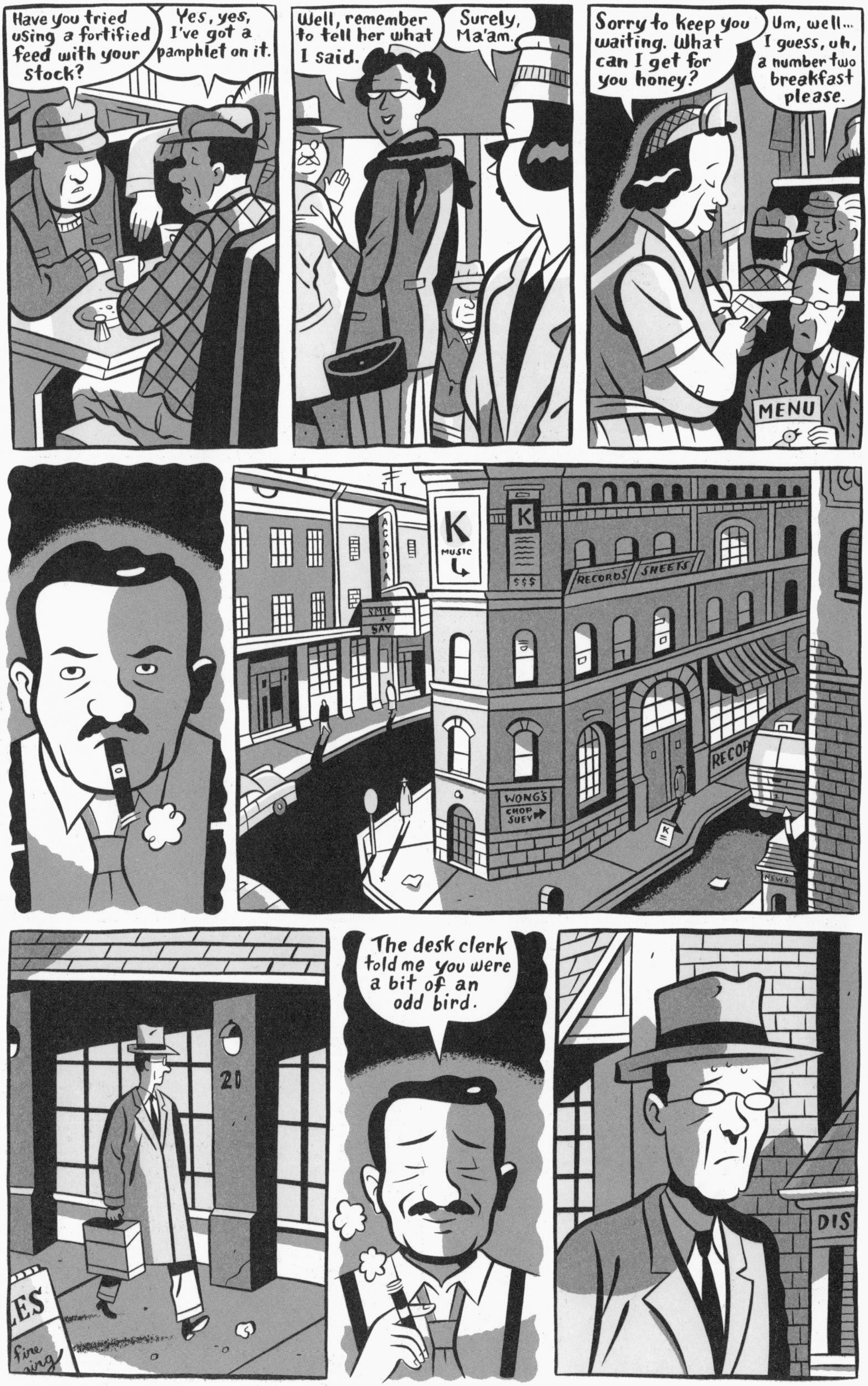
Have you tried using a fortified feed with your stock?
Yes, yes, I've got a pamphlet on it.
Well, remember to tell her what I said.
Surely, Ma'am.
Sorry to keep you waiting. What can I get for you honey?
Um, well... I guess, uh, a number two breakfast please.
MENU
K
MUSIC
K
$$$
ACADIA
SMILE + SAY
RECORDS
SHEETS
WONG'S CHOP SUEY
RECOR
NEWS
21
ES
The desk clerk told me you were a bit of an odd bird.
DIS

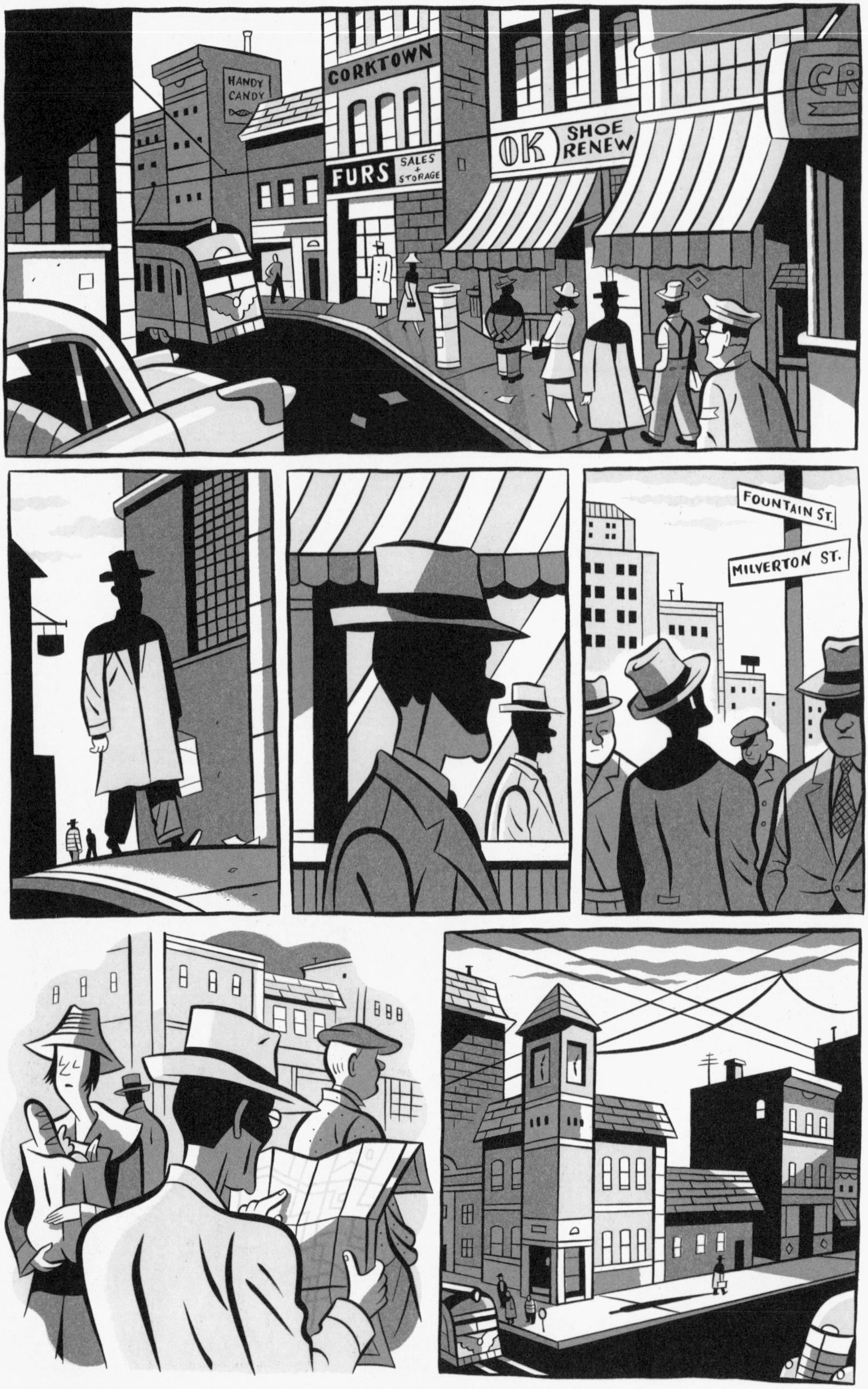
HANDY CANDY
CORKTOWN
FURS
SALES + STORAGE
OK
SHOE RENEW
FOUNTAIN ST.
MILVERTON ST.

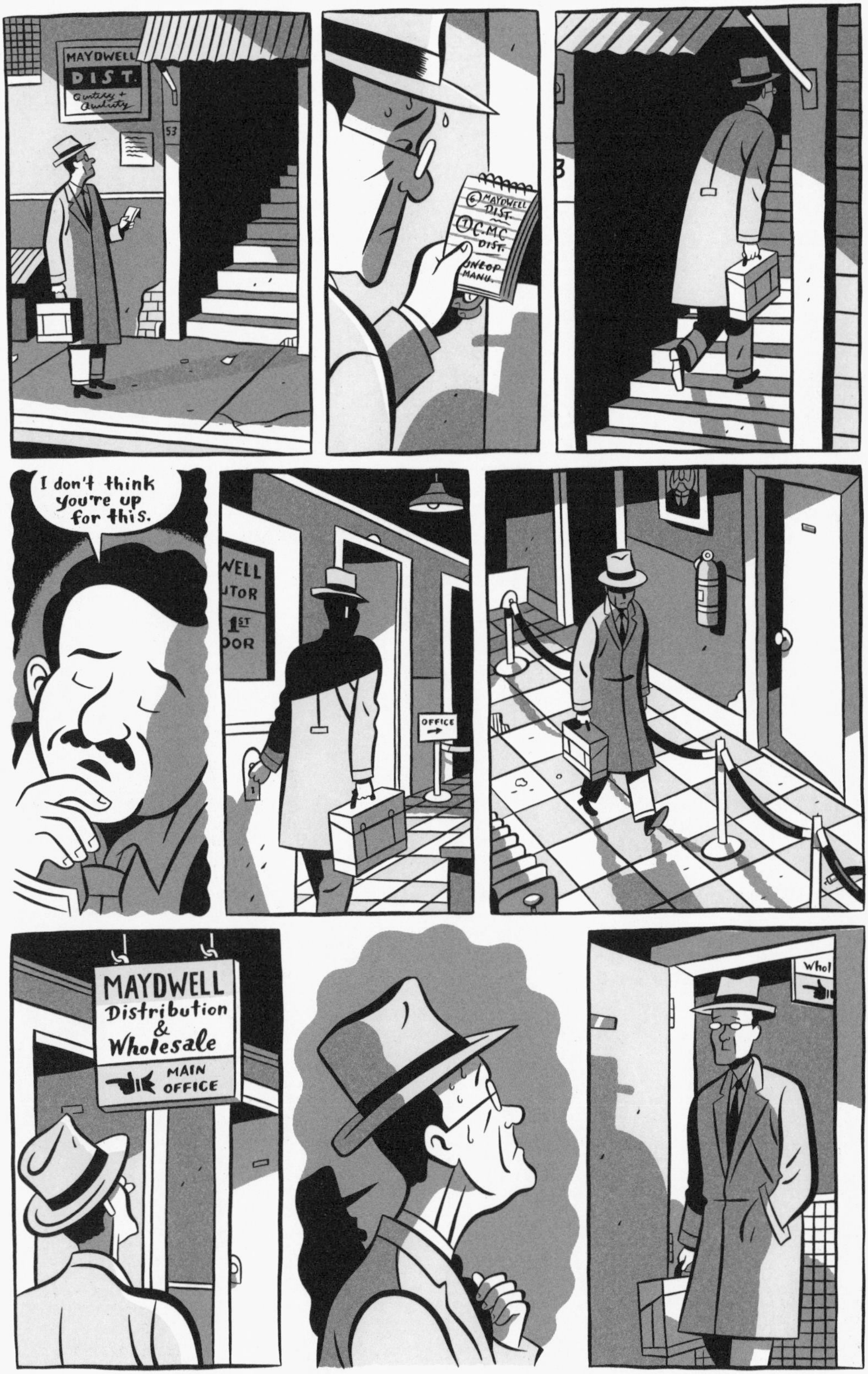
MAYDWELL
DIST.
53
MAYDWELL DIST.
C.M.C DIST.
I don't think you're up for this.
OFFICE
MAYDWELL
Distribution & Wholesale
MAIN OFFICE
Whol

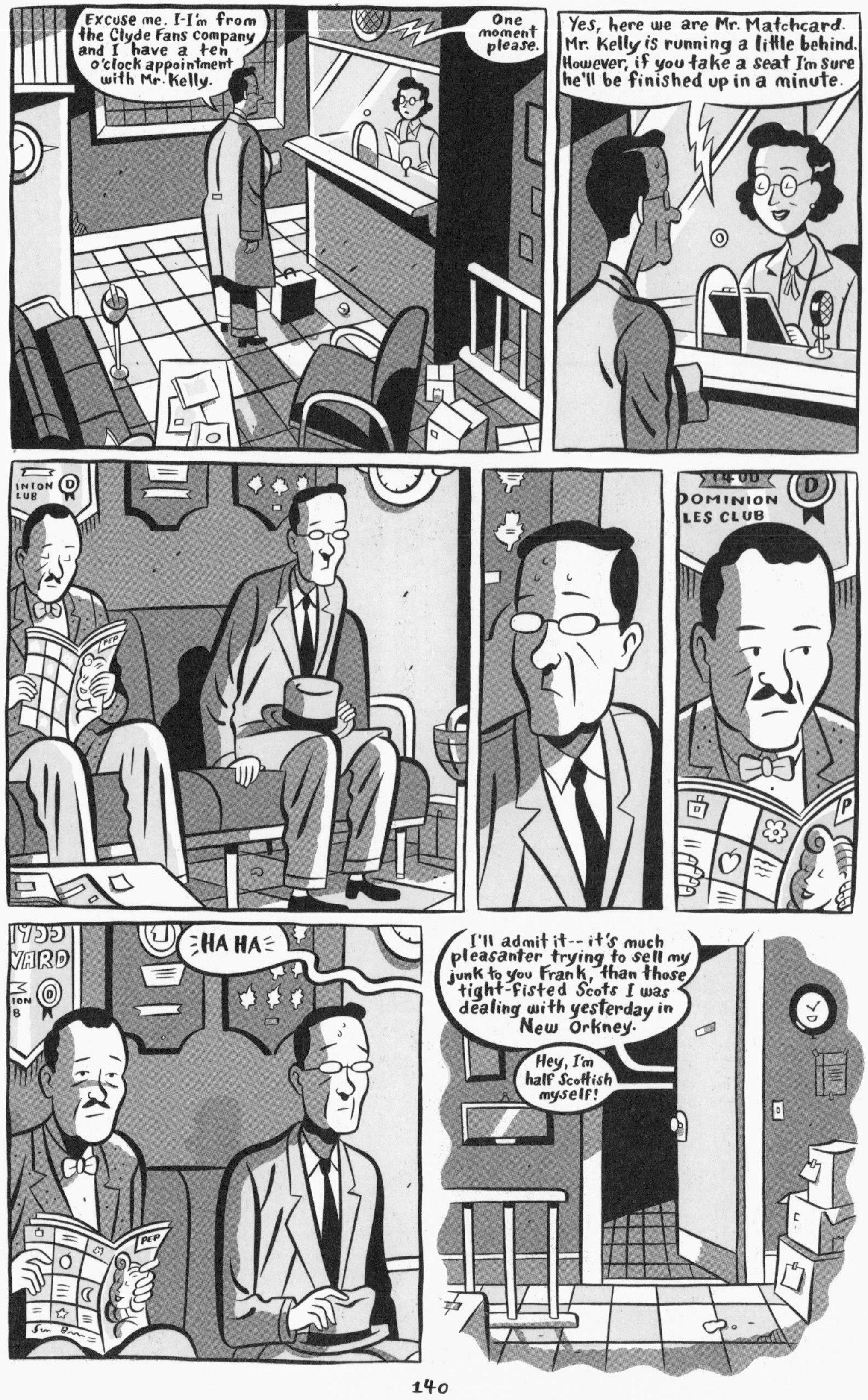
Excuse me. I-I'm from the Clyde Fans company and I have a ten o'clock appointment with Mr. Kelly.
One moment please.
Yes, here we are Mr. Matchcard. Mr. Kelly is running a little behind. However, if you take a seat I'm sure he'll be finished up in a minute.
DOMINION
HA HA
I'll admit it-- it's much pleasanter trying to sell my junk to you Frank, than those tight-fisted Scots I was dealing with yesterday in New Orkney.
Hey, I'm half Scottish myself!

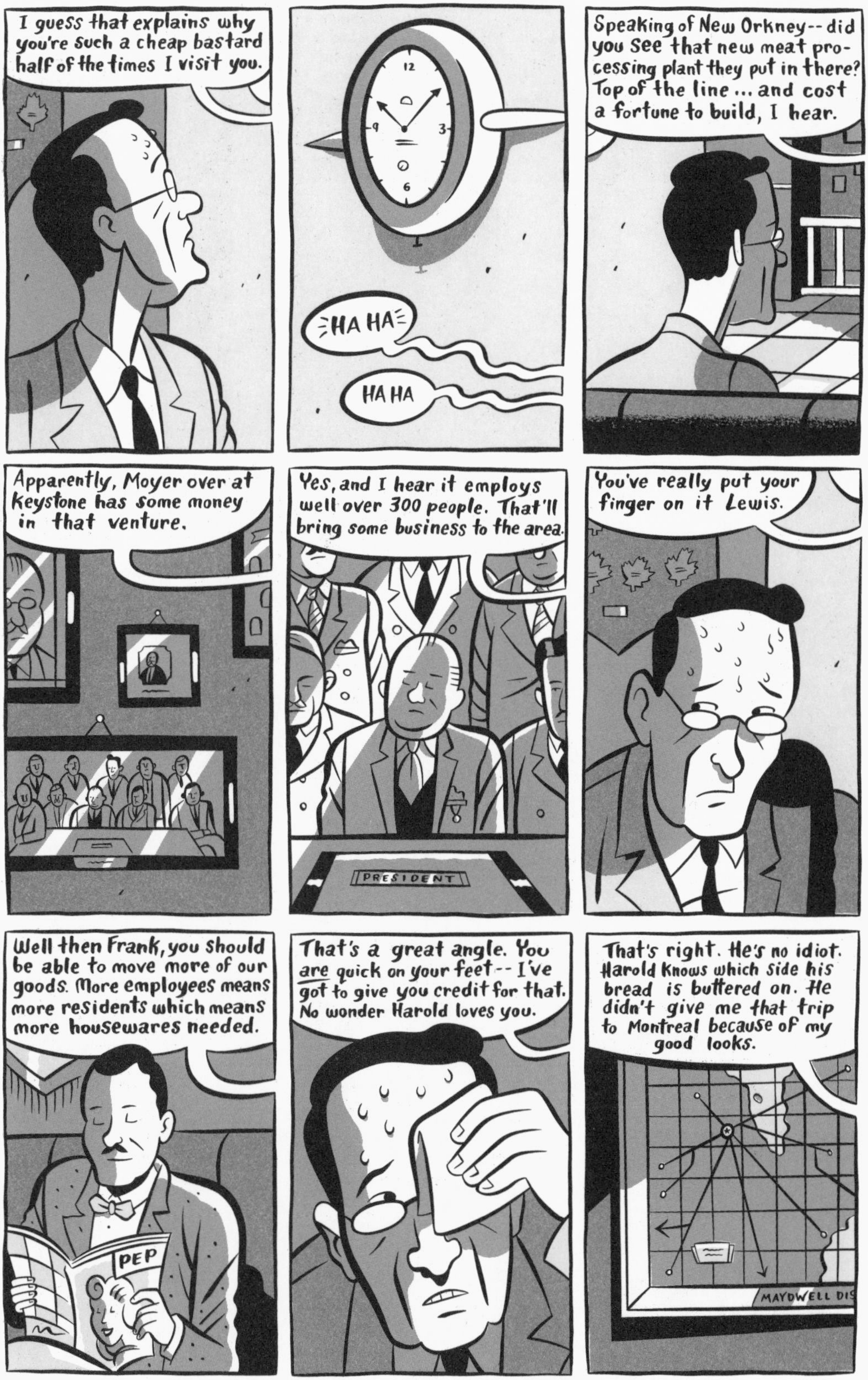
I guess that explains why you're such a cheap bastard half of the times I visit you.
HA HA
HA HA
Speaking of New Orkney -- did you see that new meat processing plant they put in there? Top of the line ... and cost a fortune to build, I hear.
Apparently, Moyer over at Keystone has some money in that venture.
Yes, and I hear it employs well over 300 people. That'll bring some business to the area.
PRESIDENT
You've really put your finger on it Lewis.
Well then Frank, you should be able to move more of our goods. More employees means more residents which means more housewares needed.
PEP
That's a great angle. You are quick on your feet -- I've got to give you credit for that. No wonder Harold loves you.
That's right. He's no idiot. Harold knows which side his bread is buttered on. He didn't give me that trip to Montreal because of my good looks.
MAYDWELL DIS

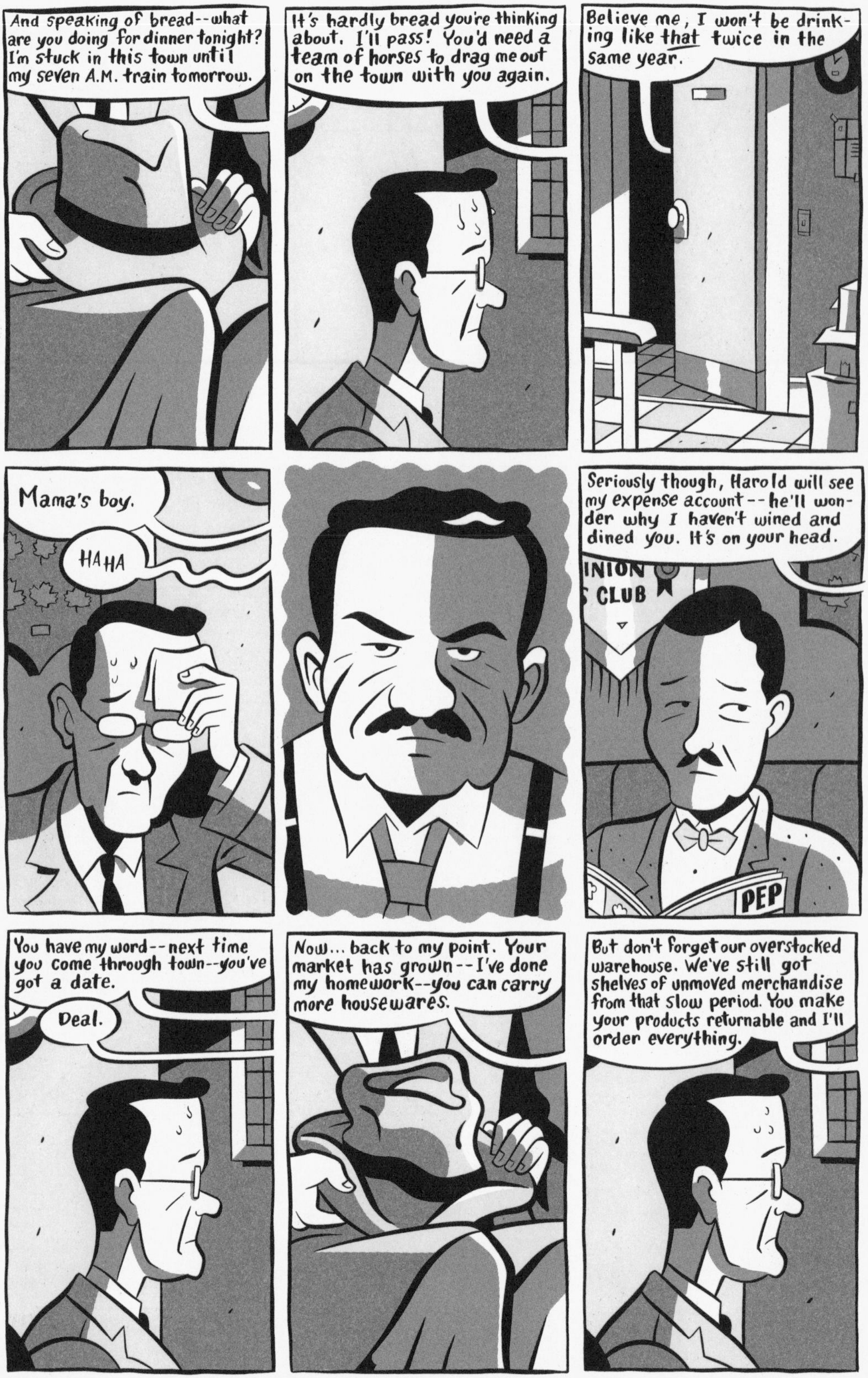
And speaking of bread--what are you doing for dinner tonight? I'm stuck in this town until my seven A.M. train tomorrow.
It's hardly bread you're thinking about. I'll pass! You'd need a team of horses to drag me out on the town with you again.
Believe me, I won't be drinking like that twice in the same year.
Mama's boy.
HAHA
Seriously though, Harold will see my expense account--he'll wonder why I haven't wined and dined you. It's on your head.
INION
CLUB
PEP
You have my word--next time you come through town--you've got a date.
Deal.
Now... back to my point. Your market has grown--I've done my homework--you can carry more housewares.
But don't forget our overstocked warehouse. We've still got shelves of unmoved merchandise from that slow period. You make your products returnable and I'll order everything.

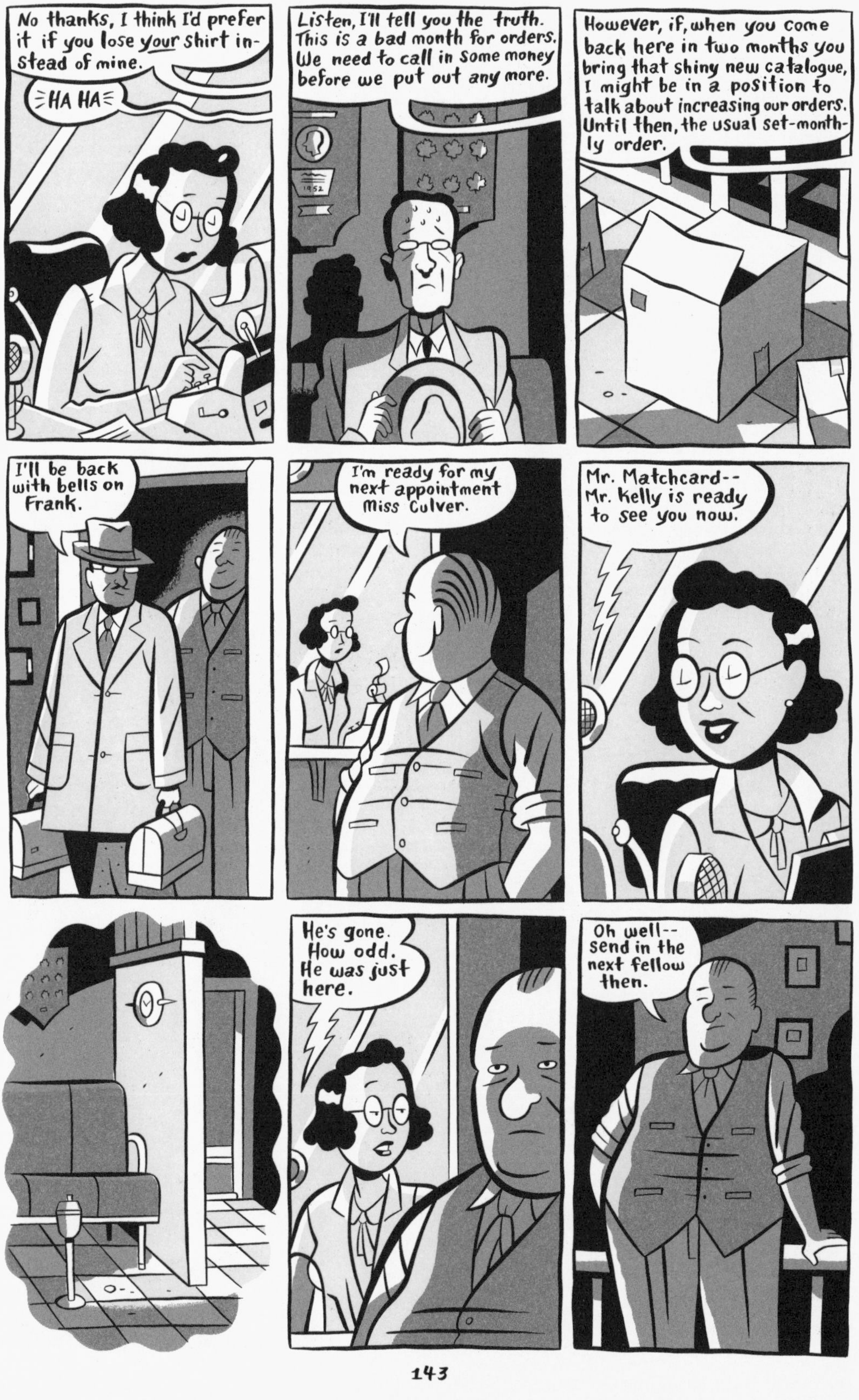
No thanks, I think I'd prefer it if you lose your shirt instead of mine.
HA HA
Listen, I'll tell you the truth. This is a bad month for orders. We need to call in some money before we put out any more.
However, if, when you come back here in two months you bring that shiny new catalogue, I might be in a position to talk about increasing our orders. Until then, the usual set-monthly order.
I'll be back with bells on Frank.
I'm ready for my next appointment Miss Culver.
Mr. Matchcard-- Mr. Kelly is ready to see you now.
He's gone. How odd. He was just here.
Oh well-- send in the next fellow then.

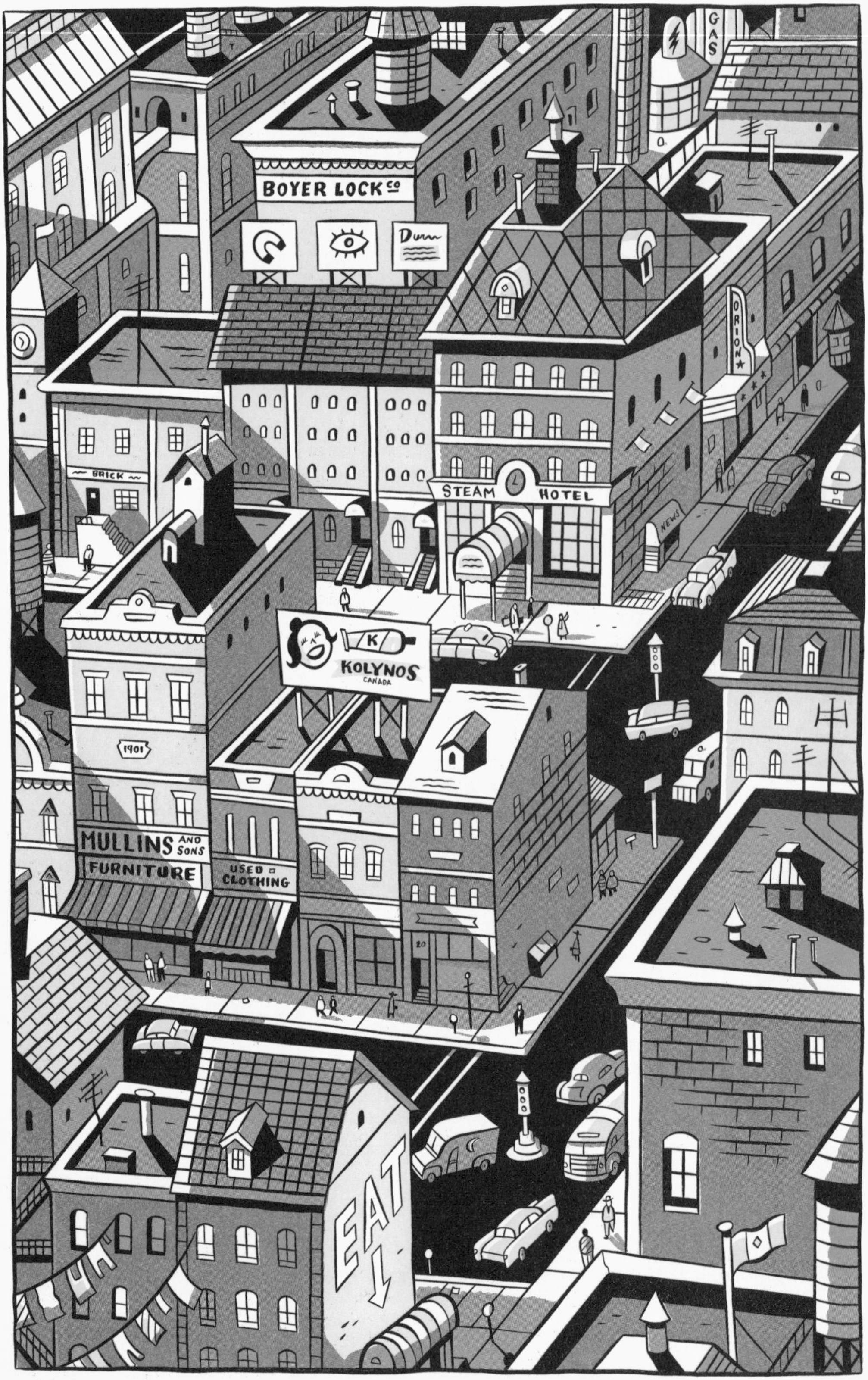
GAS
BOYER LOCK Co
ORION
STEAM HOTEL
BRICK
NEWS
KOLYNOS
CANADA
1901
MULLINS AND SONS
FURNITURE
USED CLOTHING
20
EAT

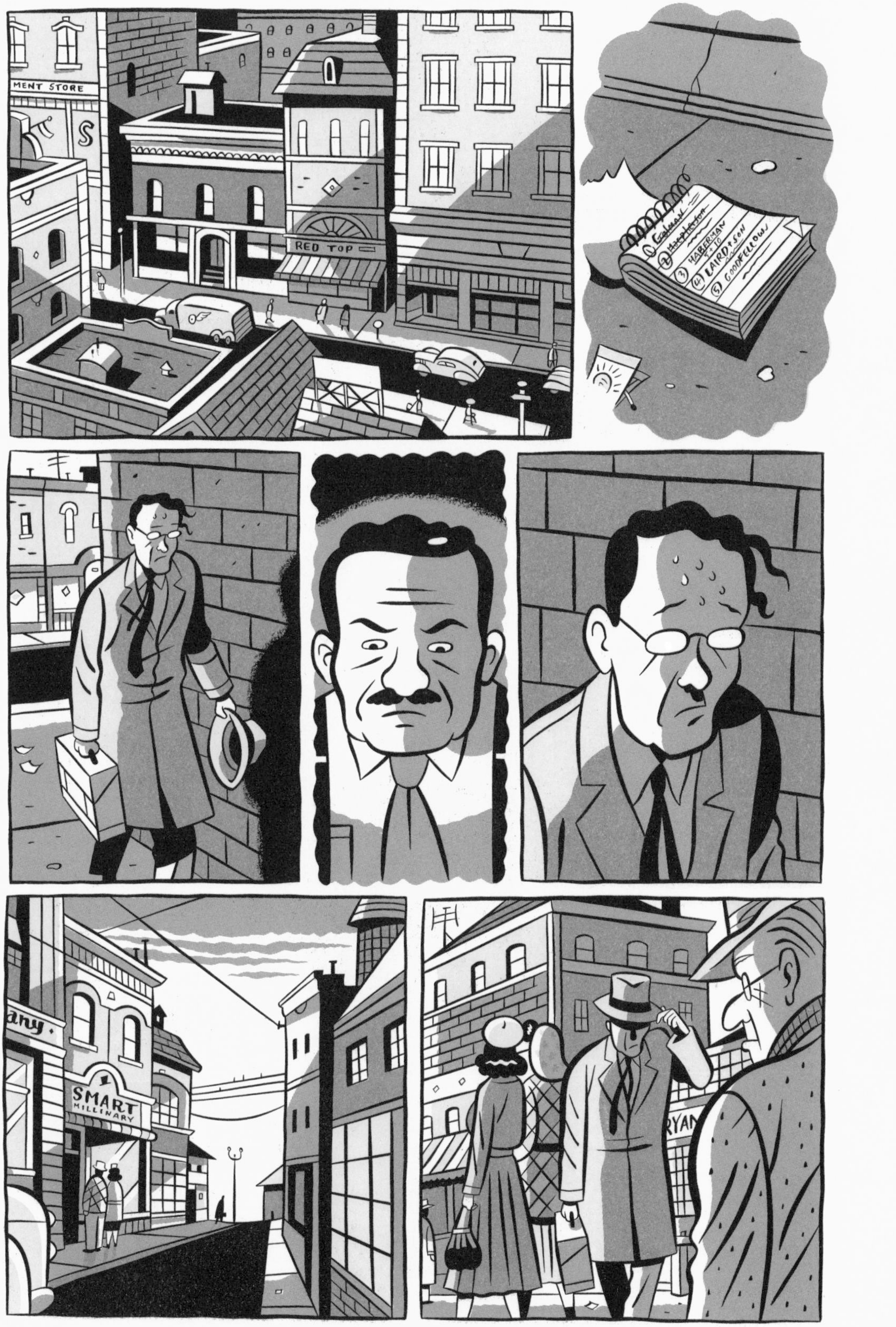
MENT STORE
RED TOP
HABERMAN
5 + 10
LAIRD + SON
GOODFELLOWS
SMART
MILLINERY

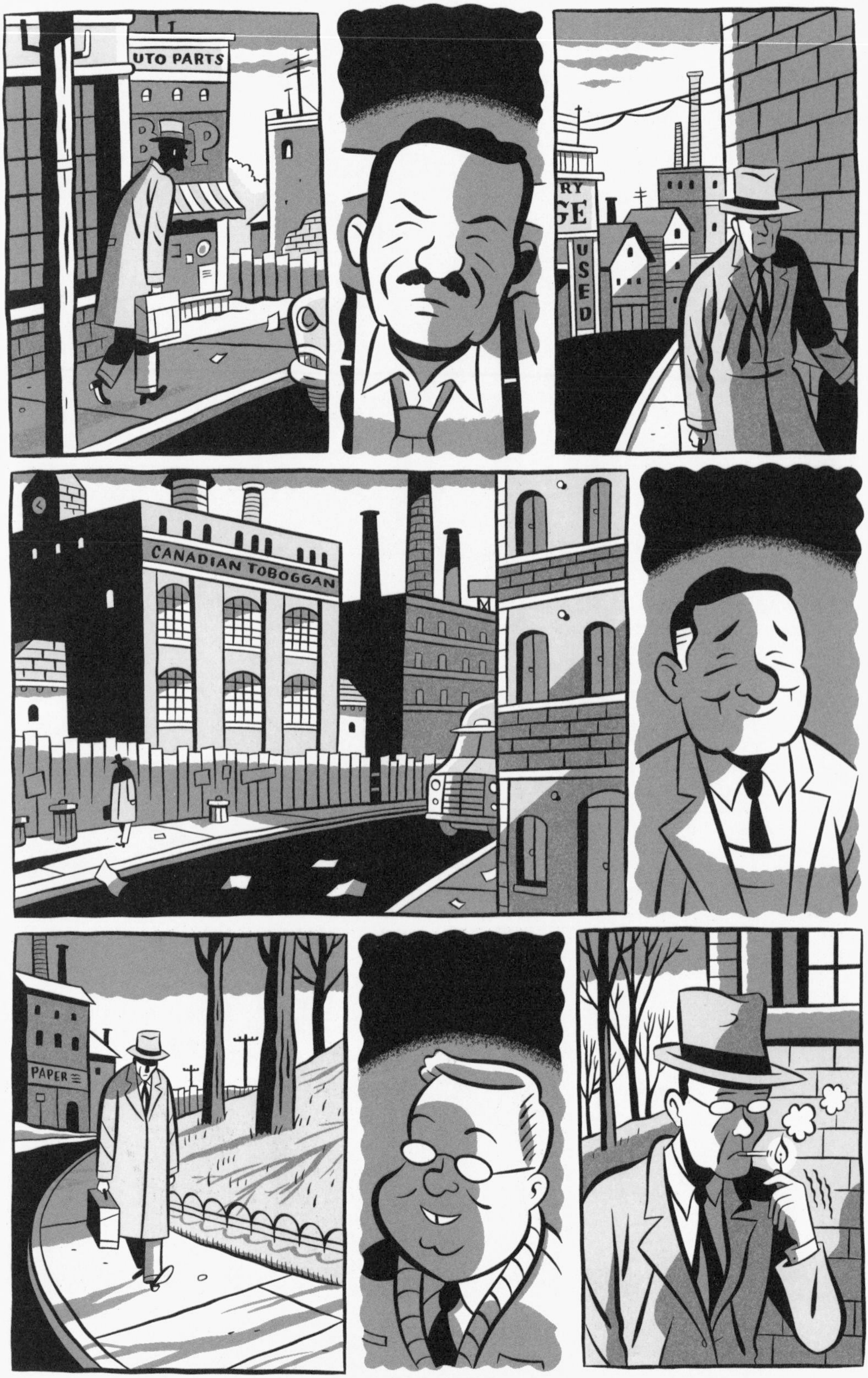
UTO PARTS
USED
CANADIAN TOBOGGAN
PAPER

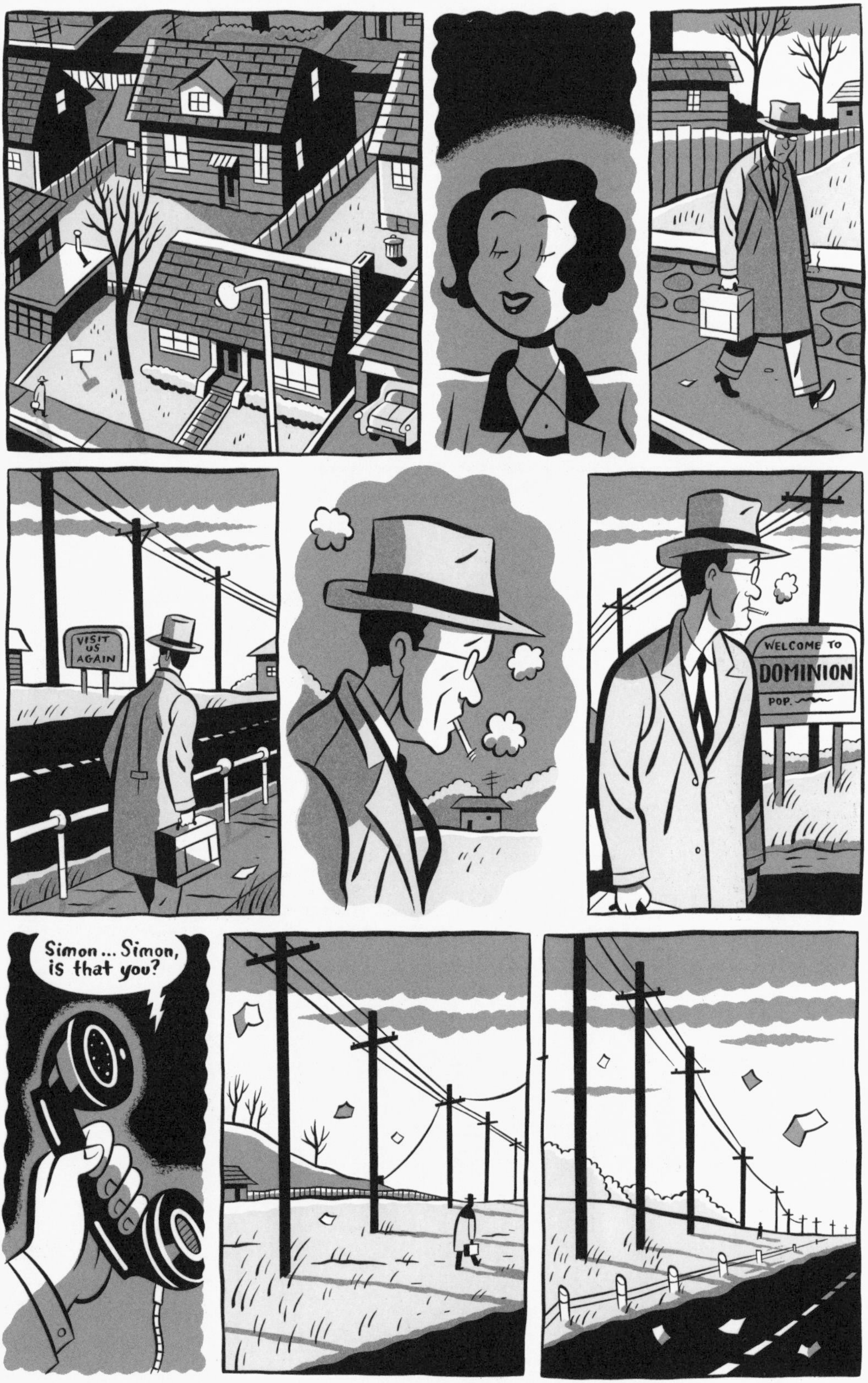
VISIT US AGAIN
WELCOME TO
DOMINION
POP.
Simon ... Simon, is that you?

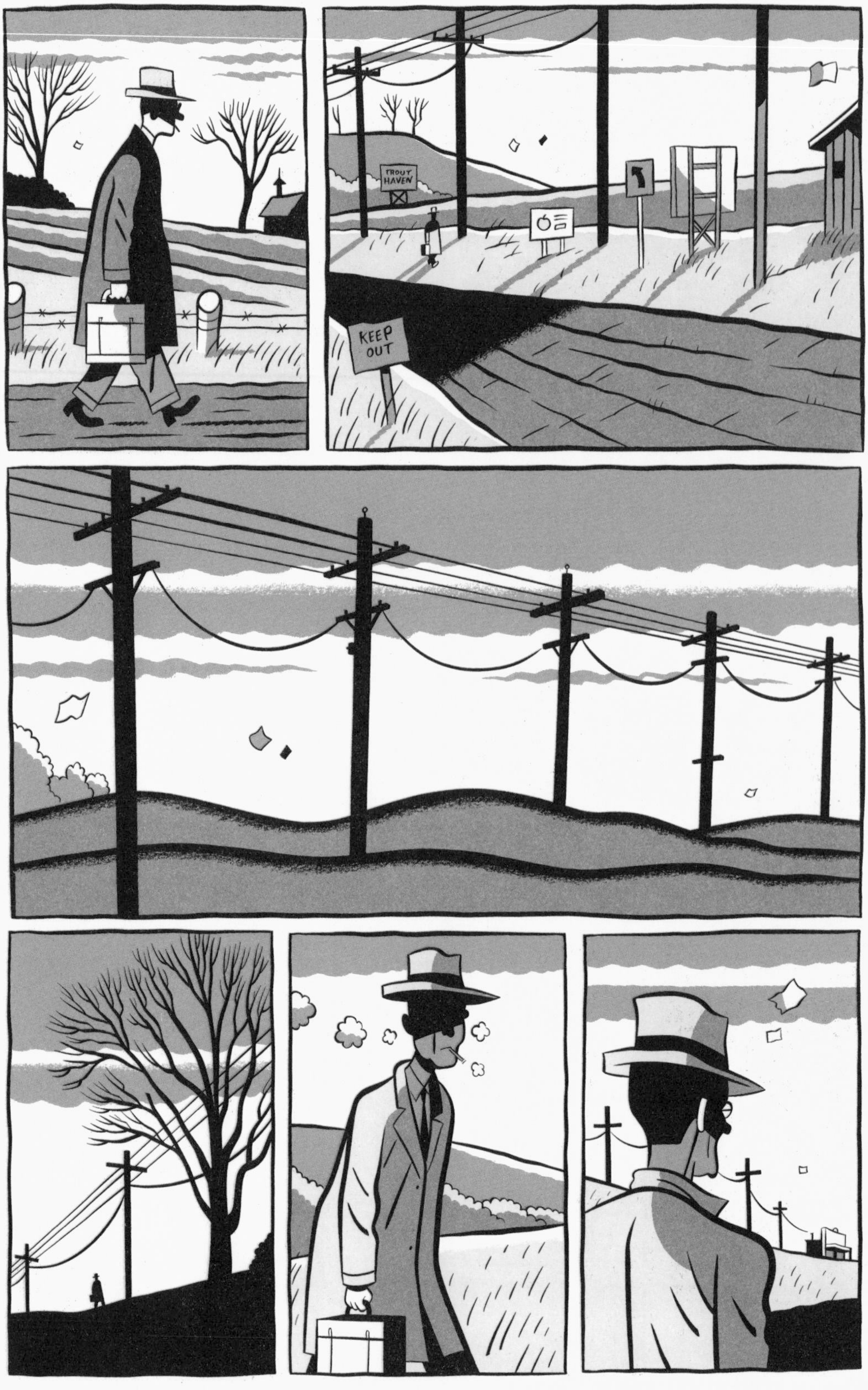
TROUT HAVEN
KEEP OUT

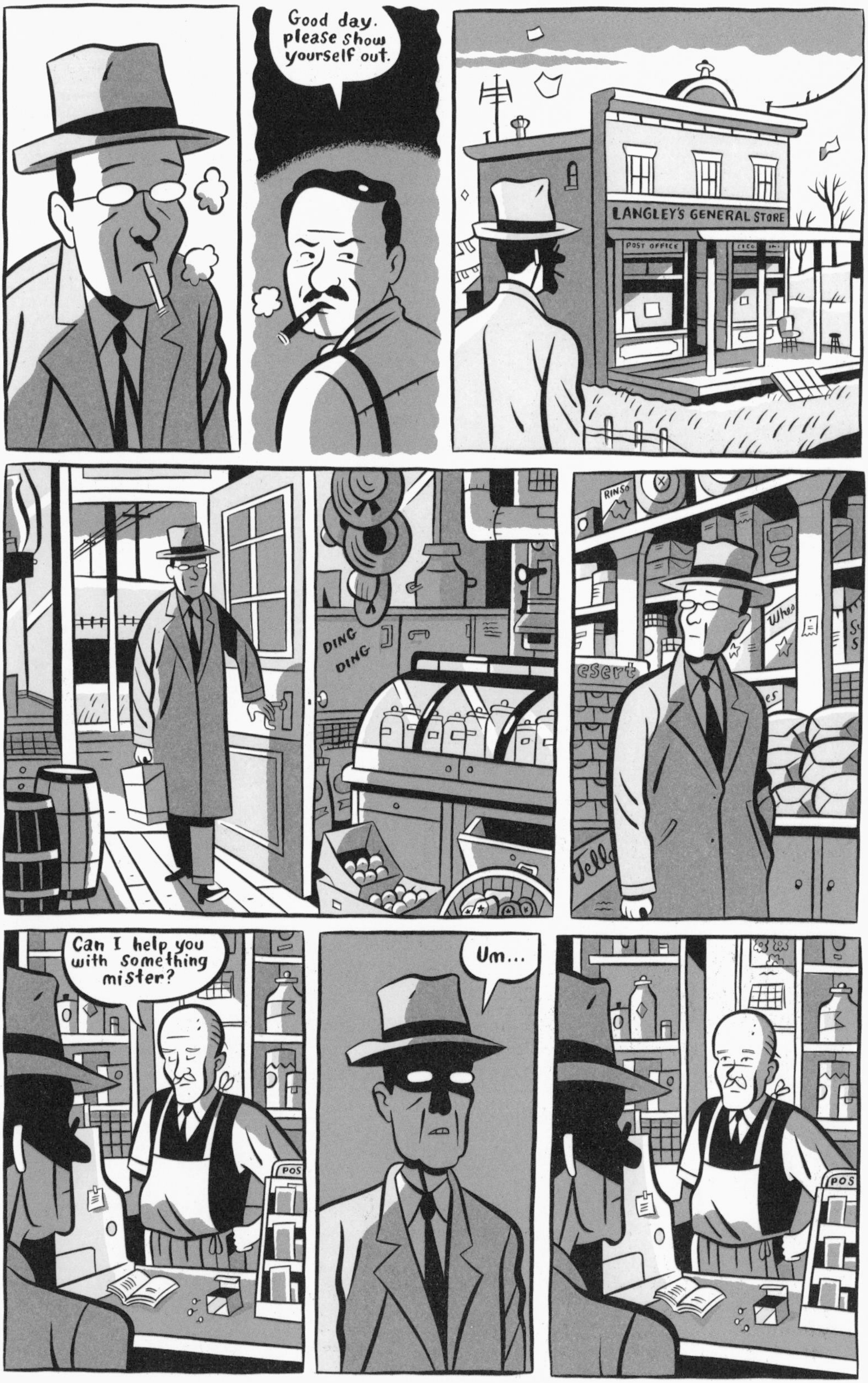
Good day. please show yourself out.
LANGLEY'S GENERAL STORE
POST OFFICE
DING DING
RINSO
Can I help you with something mister?
Um...
POS

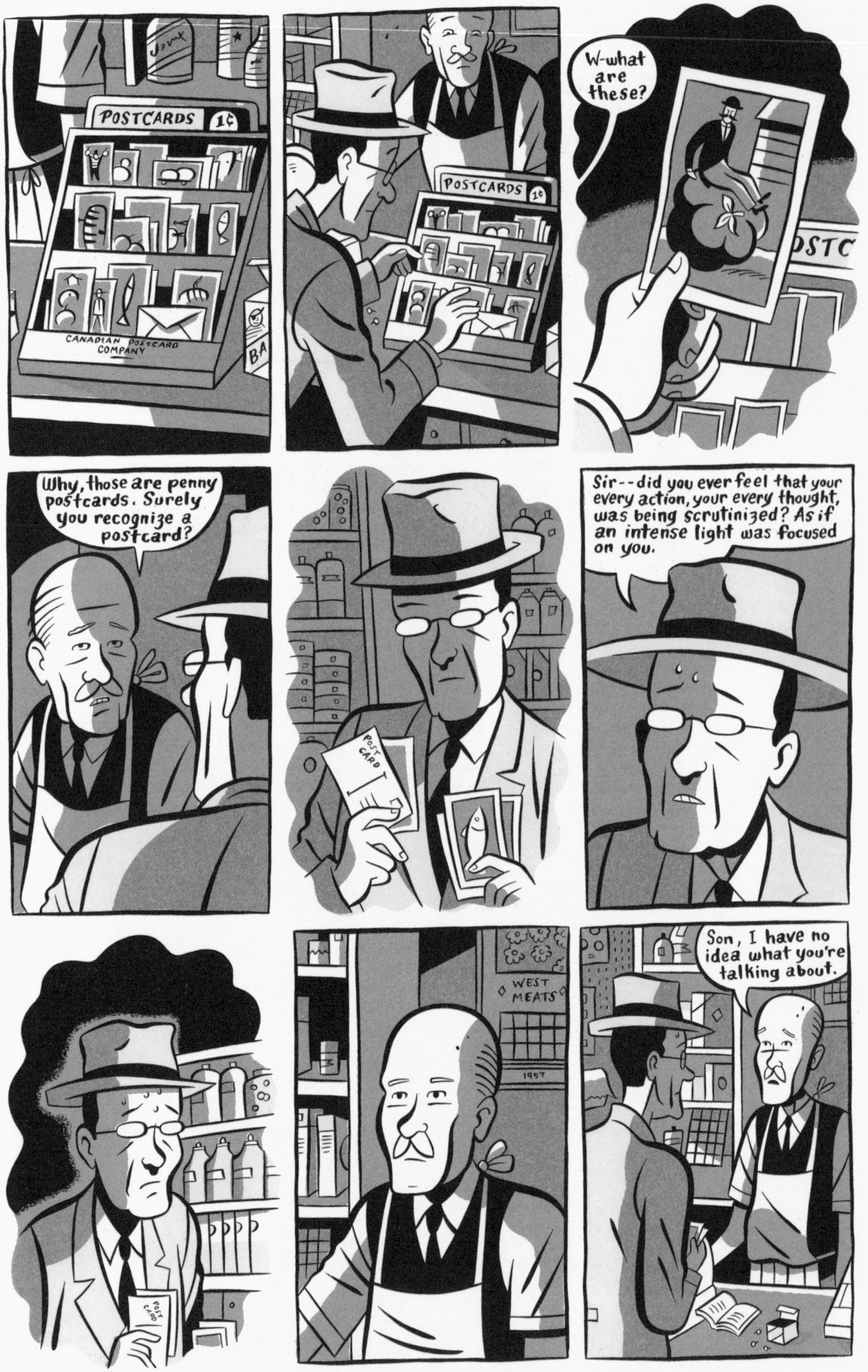
POSTCARDS 1¢
CANADIAN POSTCARD COMPANY
POSTCARDS 1¢
W-what are these?
Why, those are penny postcards. Surely you recognize a postcard?
POST CARD
Sir--did you ever feel that your every action, your every thought, was being scrutinized? As if an intense light was focused on you.
POST CARD
WEST MEATS
1957
Son, I have no idea what you're talking about.

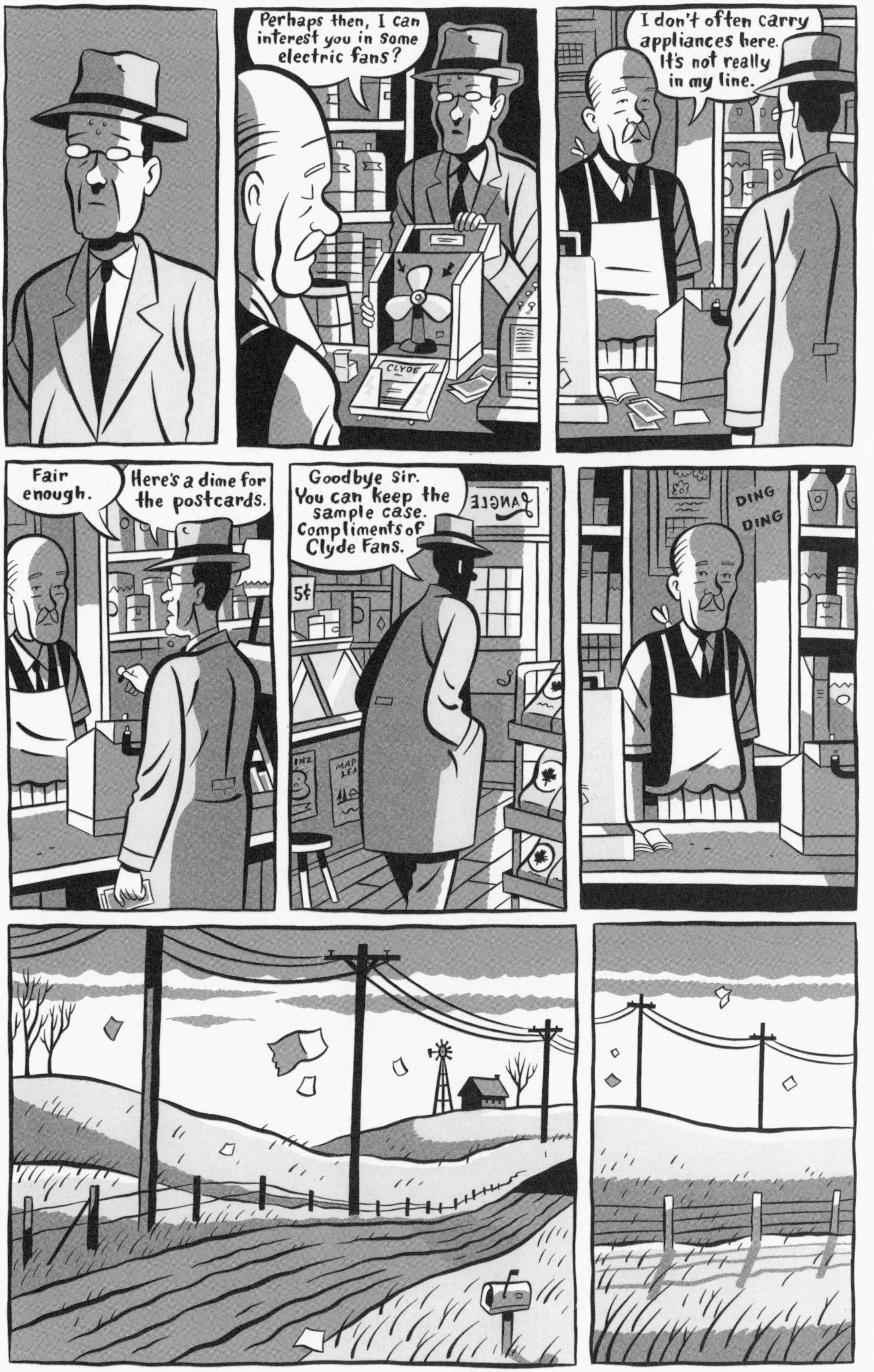
Perhaps then, I can interest you in some electric fans?
CLYDE
I don't often carry appliances here. It's not really in my line.
Fair enough.
Here's a dime for the postcards.
Goodbye sir. You can keep the sample case. Compliments of Clyde Fans.
5¢
DING DING

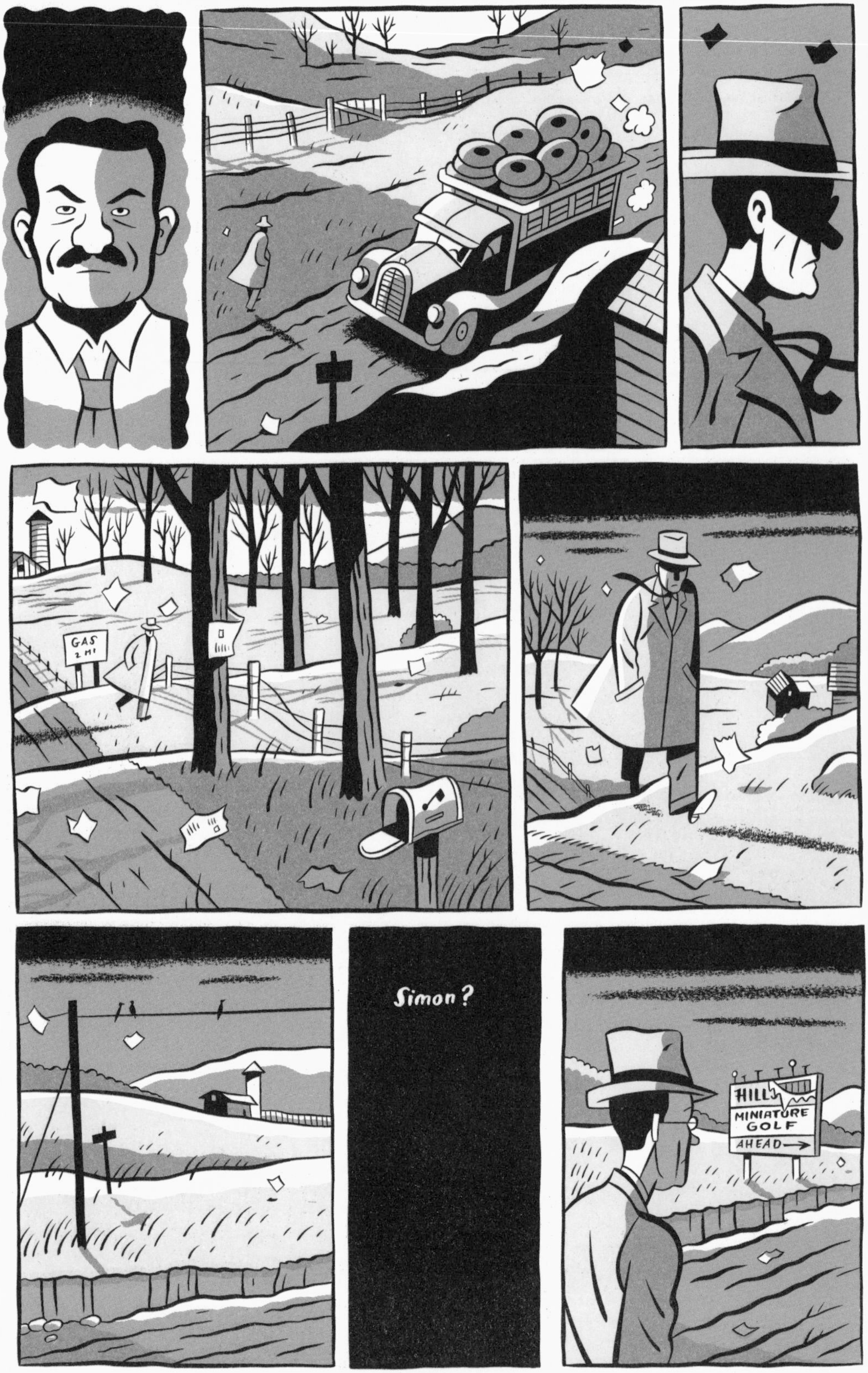
GAS
2 MI
Simon?
HILL
MINIATURE
GOLF
AHEAD

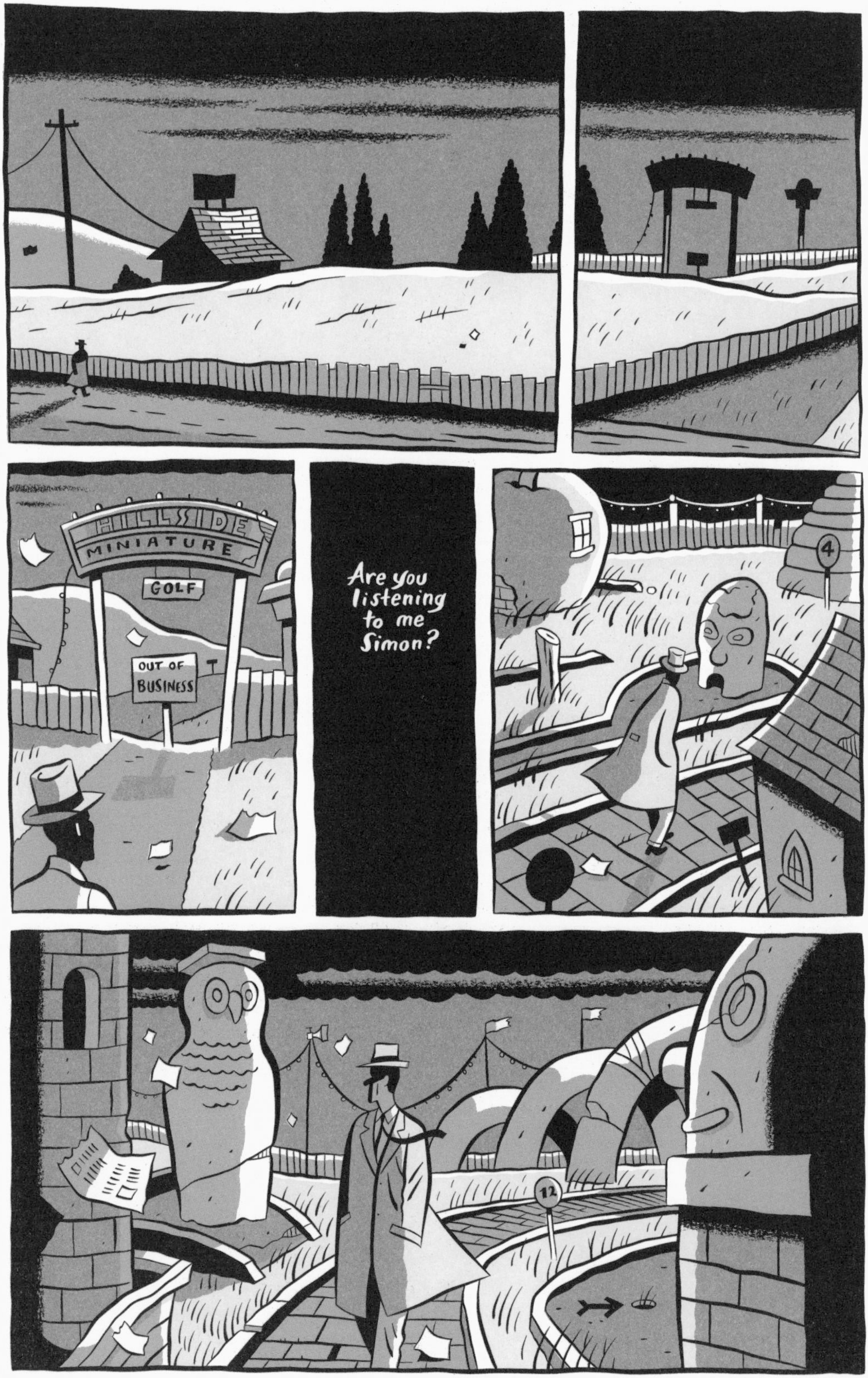
HILLSIDE
MINIATURE
GOLF
OUT OF BUSINESS
Are you listening to me Simon?
4
12

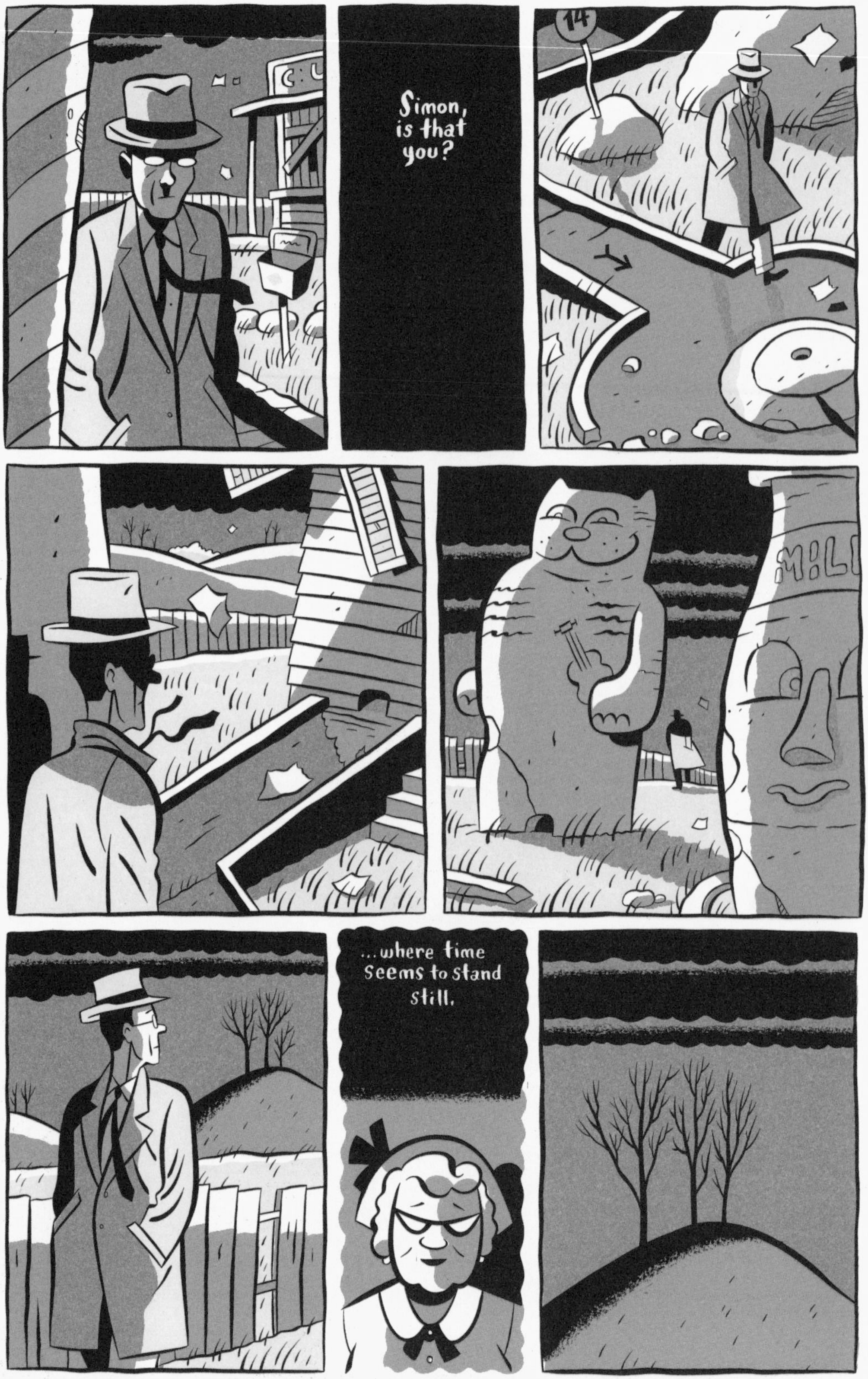
Simon, is that you?
14
...where time seems to stand still.

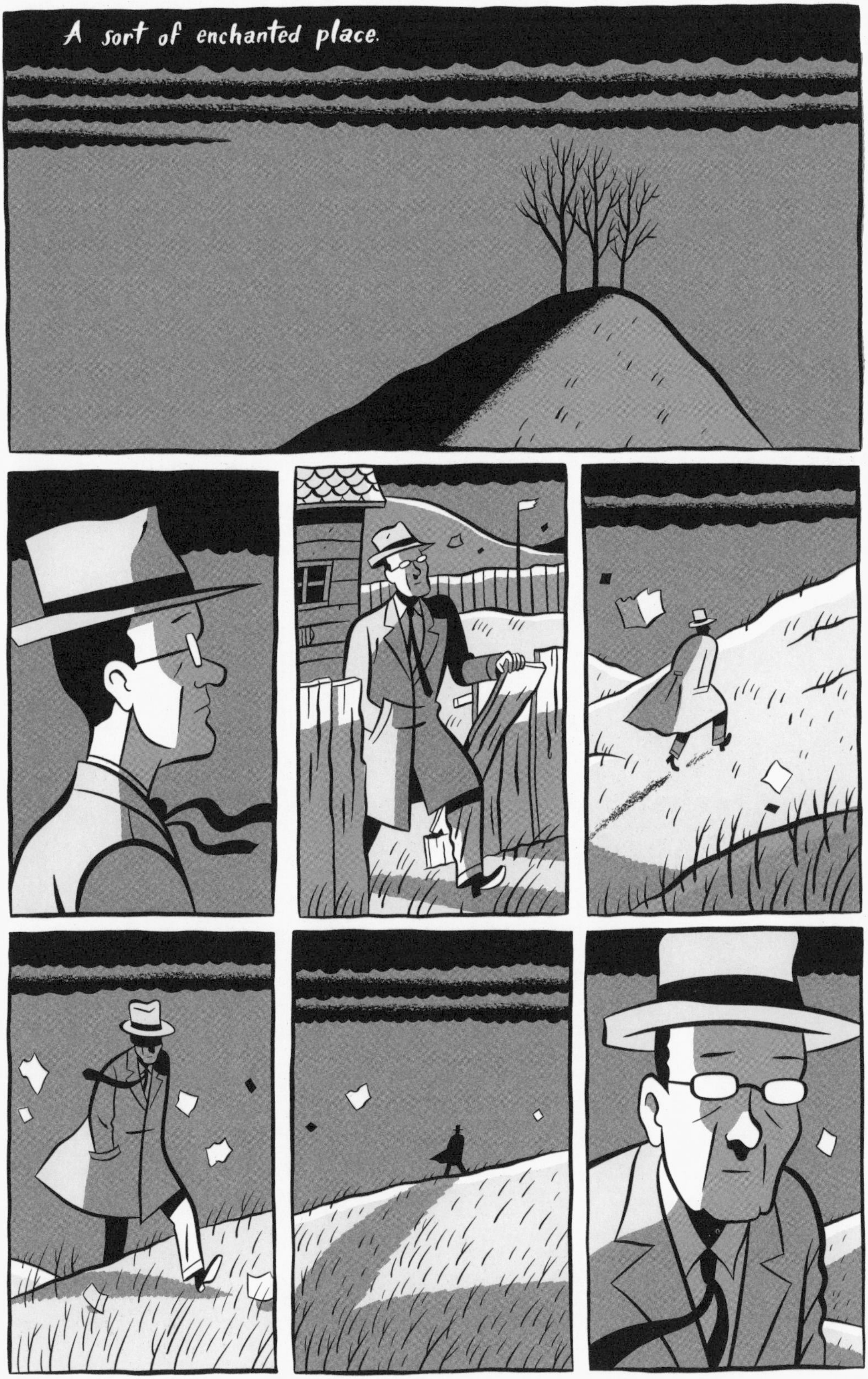
A sort of enchanted place.

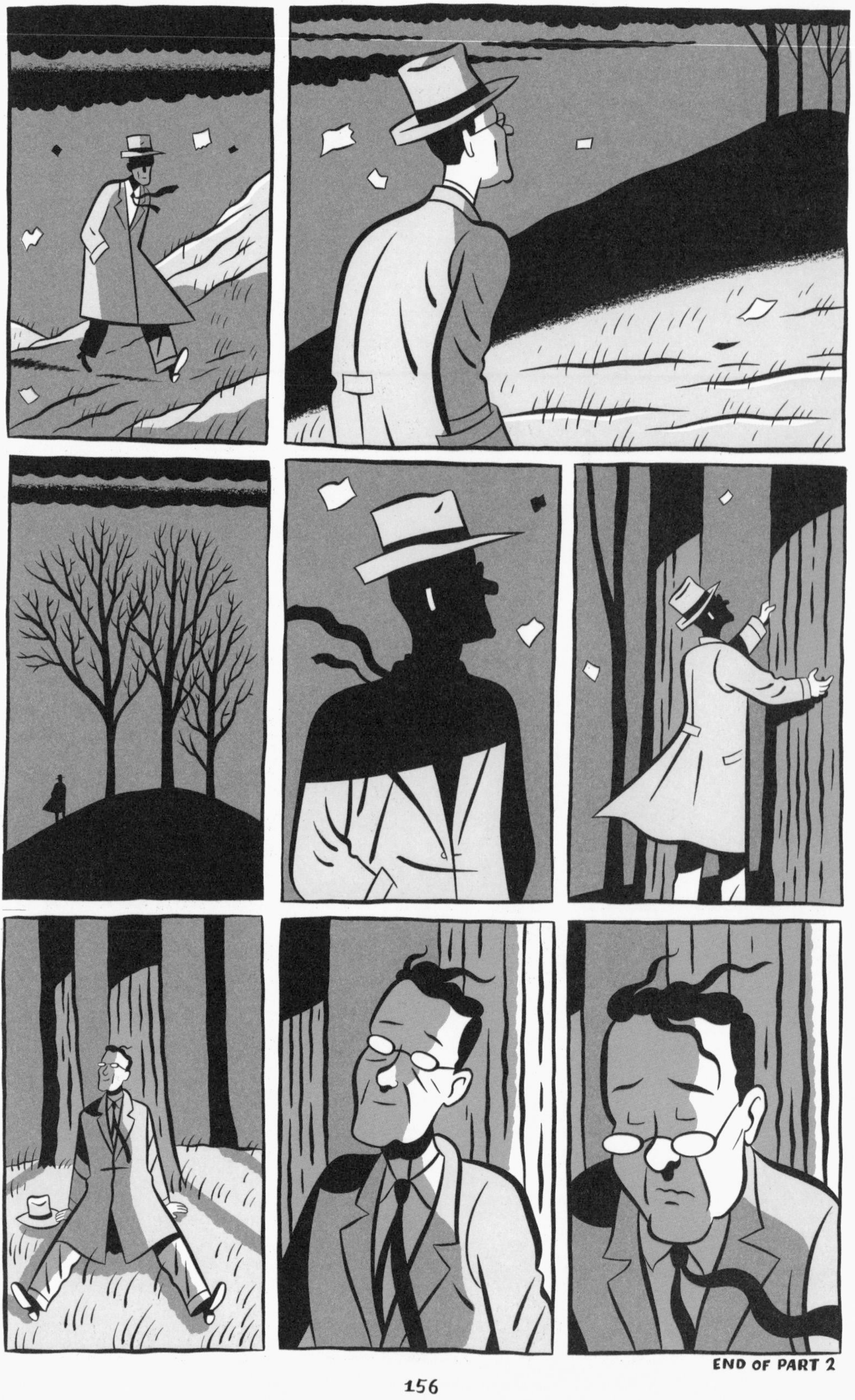

END OF PART 2